FORGOTTEN GENERALS

FORGOTTEN GENERALS

'ASSIGNED FROM ABOVE AND CONFIRMED FROM BELOW'

Dorian Bond

For David Ward MA. An inspirational teacher of history.

First published 2025

Amberley Publishing
The Hill, Stroud
Gloucestershire, GL5 4EP

www.amberley-books.com

Copyright © Dorian Bond, 2025

The right of Dorian Bond to be identified as the Author of this work has been asserted in accordance with the Copyright, Designs and Patents Act 1988.

ISBN 978 1 3981 1785 3 (hardback)
ISBN 978 1 3981 1786 0 (ebook)

All rights reserved. No part of this book may be reprinted or reproduced or utilised in any form or by any electronic, mechanical or other means, now known or hereafter invented, including photocopying and recording, or in any information storage or retrieval system, without the permission in writing from the Publishers.

British Library Cataloguing in Publication Data.
A catalogue record for this book is available from the British Library.

1 2 3 4 5 6 7 8 9 10

Typesetting by SJmagic DESIGN SERVICES, India.
Printed in the UK.

Appointed GPSR EU Representative:
Easy Access System Europe Oü, 16879218
Address: Mustamäe tee 50, 10621,
Tallinn, Estonia
Contact Details: gpsr.requests@easproject.com,
+358 40 500 3575

CONTENTS

Preface 7
Introduction 8

1 Publius Cornelius Scipio 'Africanus' 12
2 Belisarius 39
3 Bohemond of Taranto, Prince of Antioch 65
4 Albrecht Wenzel Eusebius von Wallenstein 89
5 Doge Francesco Morosini 112
6 Prince Eugene of Savoy-Carignano 137
7 King Charles XII of Sweden 165
8 Maurice of Saxony 183
9 Alexander Vasilyevich Suvorov 208
10 Field Marshal Viscount Gough 240

Epilogue 277
Index 279

PREFACE

Field Marshals, or Marshals as they are called in some countries, are a rare breed. At the time of writing there are only three living non-royal Field Marshals in the British Army. There are more Royal Dukes than Field Marshals. The great Duke of Wellington, 44 years old at the time of his promotion after the Battle of Vitoria, was the youngest non-royal officer to earn the rank of Field Marshal and the only one of that rank to become Prime Minister.

I was lucky enough to meet one of this rare breed some years ago when I was placed next to Field Marshal Lord Harding at a dinner at the Savile Club in London. Harding was one of the last surviving senior generals of the Second World War, having served with General O'Connor in the Western Desert, before, under General Montgomery, commanding the 7th Armoured Division at El Alamein. He then was Chief of Staff with the 15th Army Group under General Alexander in Italy in 1944, finally commanding the XIII Army Corps as the war ended. In the ensuing years he held many senior positions before being created Field Marshal in 1953. He was a true soldier, a worthy Field Marshal, a man who had earned his supreme rank.

I asked him which commanders he most admired in history. Without missing a beat, the elderly Field Marshal leaned forward, looked me in the eye and said one word: 'Nelson.'

Dorian Bond
Marlborough, 2025

INTRODUCTION

'If Socrates and Charles XII of Sweden were present in any company and Socrates said, "Follow me, and hear a lecture on philosophy" and Charles, laying has hand on his sword, were to say, "Follow me and dethrone the Czar," a man would be ashamed to follow Socrates. Sir, the impression is universal, yet it is strange.'

Doctor Johnson knew about the allure of good generals. They have the ability to lead men to high endeavours. Napoleon rated Alexander the Great, Hannibal, Julius Caesar, Gustavus Adolphus, Turenne, Prince Eugene of Savoy and Frederick the Great as the seven greatest commanders in history. He probably rated himself pretty highly, too, but modesty forbids. Hannibal told Scipio that he rated Pyrrhus as the greatest, apart from himself, of course.

This book is not about who was the best, it is meant to be more about those who have been somewhat overlooked. Any student of history can make their own list. Even looking at the military commanders of the Second World War such as Montgomery, Patton, Rommel, Guderian or Zhukov, it is hard to make a final judgement. Where does Eisenhower stand, for example, if you are to include a political element into the qualities you look for in a commander? And I've not mentioned Stillwell or McArthur. They are certainly not forgotten, but sometimes O'Connor is.

What follows is a diverse assembly of generals, a Roman, a Byzantine, a Norman, a Bohemian, a Venetian, an Italian, a

Swede, a Saxon, a Russian, and an Anglo-Irishman. They are certainly diverse in terms of their eras and in how they looked and the clothes they wore, but they all had a number of qualities in common. They must all have been fine horsemen considering the hundreds of miles they rode during their lives, they were physically brave, decisive, ruthless in carrying through their objectives, honourable in victory and brave in defeat. But above all, they all had the opportunity to test themselves in the cauldron of war during numerous battles with their enemies. Not all generals have had this opportunity, which reminds us of Napoleon's remark about wanting lucky generals.

When the dust of battle has settled, the thunder of the guns ceased, the smoke and smell of gunpowder drifted on the wind, the cries of wounded men faded away over the twisted bodies of the fallen thousands, victors and vanquished equal in death, all the historian can do is look back and try to understand what motivated these commanders and the men that followed them into the maelstrom.

They say that some battalions, on that hot 1 July morning in 1916 on the Somme, leaned forward and shielded their faces as though walking into a rainstorm when in fact they were advancing into machine gun fire. Charles XII of Sweden, when going into action for the first time, asked what the strange noise was. When told it was enemy musket fire, he replied, 'I shall make that my music.'

To command thousands of men formed up in battle order, most visible to the naked eye, must be a humbling experience. To direct operations in situations where mistakes cannot be made but where risks have to be taken and every second counts must test any man to the limit. It is not always easy to find the real men behind the gaudy fabrications of their portraits. The worlds in which they existed gone, each one different and far from our own. After all, to really know an individual you need to be familiar with the timbre of their voice, their habits, their strengths and weaknesses, their idiosyncrasies.

The world has changed much, but in our concept of a hero, and the meaning that we attach to the word glory, we remain the same, though even in this we seem to find as much bravery in passive acts of protest as in warfare. The soldier, if brave and successful, is still a hero, though war is looked on nowadays with more suspicion.

In days long gone, the favourite pursuit of royalty and the aristocracy, and the one that they felt was closely interlinked with their caste, their honour and their pride, was war. To be tried in battle was the ultimate test of physical courage, strategic judgement, intelligence, loyalty and patriotism. Even their leisure pursuits of tournaments or fencing or hunting were training for the real tests that lay ahead. Team sports, so popular from the Victorian era onwards, are part of the same ethos, teaching players that each one was dependent on another, one for all and all for one. To be a fine horseman, or a sportsman with a good eye for the ball, or to have an 'eye' for country or distances, were considered qualities required of men and admired by women. So the past was a different playing field, no longer played upon, many of its pursuits and practices destroyed by the iron machines that came into being just over a hundred years ago.

Amid unimaginable carnage and bloodshed of the European wars waged between 1914 and 1945, two generations, notions of honour, courage and heroism were ground into hopelessness and history. The second generation of technology produced the knights of the sky who would eventually rain cataclysms upon innocent civilians cowering in their houses. Today we have another invention, drones, piloted by those far from the battlefield, inflicting an impersonal death on the soldiers or civilians below them.

At least in ancient times, to kill an opponent you had to look him in the eye before administering the coup de grace. As gunpowder improved the efficiency of killing, the worst experience of fighting men was witnessing the aftermath of cannon ball or musket ball as mangled bodies, slippery with still warm blood lay exposed, like carcases of butchered animals. Thus it was across the fields of Zama, Lutzen, Malplaquet, Waterloo, El Alamein and hundreds of other nameless places. As the pale winter sun set over Lutzen, the Swedish soldiery had great difficulty finding the naked body of their fallen King, Gustavus Adolphus, lying amongst so many others in death, before they could begin to honour him.

Always remember that the generals in these pages were playing high-stakes games and had the nerve and courage to make brave decisions and follow them through, whatever the consequences. They say that to understand a man, you have to walk a mile in his shoes, or boots, in this case. Few of us have stood in the boots of great generals, or even ridden a hundred miles at their side. So all we can do is learn their stories and marvel at their achievements.

I

PUBLIUS CORNELIUS SCIPIO 'AFRICANUS' 236–183 BC

> We cannot separate the nobility of Scipio's moral conduct, throughout his career, from the transcendent clearness of his mental vision – they blended to form not only a great general but a great man.
>
> B.H. Liddell Hart

If you write about Scipio, you write about Hannibal. The two names are inextricably linked. They are both regarded as amongst the best military commanders in history. Hannibal is the more famous of the two, but it was Scipio who was the eventual winner; some portents here of Napoleon and Wellington, the eventual winner being less famous than the eventual loser.

An amusing story comes from the last time Scipio met Hannibal face to face at Ephesus following the defeat of Antiochus; whether it is true or allegorical is beside the point. Their only previous meeting had been on the eve of Zama more than a decade before.

Now the exiled Hannibal was nearing sixty years old and Scipio Africanus, as he was now known, was in his late forties. Both were legends in their own lifetimes in the true sense, experienced soldiers and politicians. They had both seen and suffered much, their past triumphs matched by the struggles they had both endured. Heroes are not born, they earn their reputations by force of character and luck, and the scars they carry with them bear witness to this. The Roman asked the Carthaginian who he considered the greatest commander in history. Hannibal named Alexander the Great, followed by Pyrrhus of Epirus. Scipio then enquired who was third and Hannibal, without hesitation, replied, 'Myself.'

Scipio pressed him: 'What would you say if you had vanquished me?'

'In that case,' replied Hannibal, 'I would say that I surpassed Alexander and Pyrrhus, and all other commanders in the world.'

Scipio was delighted with the answer; Hannibal had spoken with all the adroitness of a Carthaginian, combining unexpected flattery with his own arrogance. Hannibal had obliquely set him apart from ordinary generals as an incomparable commander.

Publius Cornelius Scipio was a Roman aristocrat born into the Cornelius family, one of the leading patrician clans who dominated the Roman Republic for decades. His father, also Publius Cornelius Scipio, was a consul, his grandfather was a consul, his great grandfather was a consul, his mother's father and his father-in-law were consuls and he, too, became a consul.

The Punic or Carthaginian Wars lasted a very long time. The First Punic War, primarily a naval confrontation, had continued for an astonishing twenty-three years The Second Punic War lasted pretty much a generation, seventeen years; enough time for the callow seventeen-year-old Scipio to grow from a well educated youth into an experienced man of thirty-five. The Third Punic War was a perfunctory three years in which time the oft-repeated demand of Cato, 'Carthago delenda est', was finally fulfilled by Scipio's grandson.

What is more, the theatre of this deadly struggle between these two great powers of the ancient world, the young Rome and the worldly Carthage, was spread across most of the western Mediterranean, a vast distance considering the only means of transport were either by oar or sail, on foot or on horseback. It was indeed a world war. Battles were fought right down the peninsula of Italy from the Alps to Calabria and into Sicily and Sardinia, all across central and southern Spain and over huge tracts of North Africa.

Hannibal's legendary crossing of the Alps took place early on in the war, in April 218 BC, his famous victory at Cannae in the middle, August 216 BC, and his final defeat in North Africa at the end, October 202 BC. The perception of these significant events is somewhat confusing: not one of them really decided this epic war, with both sides struggling for their very survival.

Scipio was raised in the political and military practices of the young republic. He was an educated young man of intellect and culture who could speak and read Greek in addition to his native Latin. His love of the Greek lifestyle and his unconventional way of wearing the Roman toga showed that. After all, Alexander the Great had died less than a hundred years before and Macedon was still a European power. Scipio also introduced the fashion for being clean shaven to high-class Romans in imitation of Alexander. This look lasted until the time of the Emperor Hadrian and would be revived by Constantine the Great. Scipio was also, from a young age, an effective orator, radiating self-confidence and an innate sense of justice.

Scipio's father, Publius Cornelius Scipio, was one of Rome's leaders, and as a recently elected consul he declared war on Carthage in 218 BC when the Carthaginian leader, Hannibal, attacked the treaty-protected and pro-Roman city of Saguntum, near modern-day Valencia. The younger Scipio, aged only seventeen, inevitably joined the Roman struggle against Carthage in that first year of the Second Punic War.

Three years earlier, Hannibal Barca had been appointed supreme leader of all Carthaginian forces in Hispania at the tender age of twenty-six. He was the son of the legendary Hamilcar Barca, who had campaigned in Sardinia and North Africa alongside Hanno the Great and had conquered most of Spain, or Hispania, following his arrival there in 237 BC. Though Hamilcar was drowned in a river crossing in 229 BC, the Carthaginian dominance continued under Hasdrubal the Fair, his son-in-law.

In 226 BC, having mastered most of southern and central Hispania, Hasdrubal signed a truce with Rome known as the Punic Faith, promising not to cross the River Ebro in the north-east of the vast territory; but Hannibal, having sworn a childhood oath to his father never to make peace with Rome, was not going to agree to this arrangement. Planning to eject the Romans from all Hispania, he decided to attack the formidable fortress of Saguntum, peopled by allies of Rome. To capture this stronghold was essential to his plan for dominance in the territory, and he realised that to leave the city under the control of the Romans would have been strategically unfeasible. Hannibal was also looking for plunder to pay his troops, many of whom were from North Africa. Saguntum was a rich city.

The siege lasted eight months, the Saguntines fighting desperately behind the formidable defences of the city. Hannibal himself was wounded, which extended the siege as the attackers waited for their leader to recover. Despite appeals to Rome for support, none was forthcoming and in 218 BC Hannibal finally offered the inhabitants the opportunity to leave in just the clothes they stood up in and without their weapons. The offer was declined, and the people began to destroy their possessions. This enraged Hannibal who proceeded to put all survivors to death. Thus the Second Punic War began.

The Romans, exasperated at Carthage's inability to keep to their peace agreements, in response to the attack on Saguntum dispatched one army to Sicily to attack Carthage itself while another was to sail to Hispania to claim those lands for Rome.

As soon as Hannibal had secured the important strategic base of Saguntum, he approached the Senate of Carthage to ensure their support. But many, including the moderate Hanno the Great, were not altogether happy with Hannibal's brutal tactics and this clash between the moderates who wanted to reach an accord with Rome and the hawks who wanted nothing but complete victory was a theme that continued throughout the war. Not for the last time in history was a general hindered by the contrary opinions of politicians. War is a simple business, but politics tend to be more complicated. The Carthaginian politicians did not even fully side with him when he was at the head of his army only a few kilometres from the gates of Rome at a moment of potential triumph.

Hannibal now marched to New Carthage, modern Cartagena, further down the coast from Saguntum and there made a dramatic speech declaring his ambitions to destroy Rome by marching through Iberia, over the Pyrenees, across the River Rhone, over the Alps and down into Cisalpine Gaul, where he would destroy the Roman armies. Hannibal was true to his word and, after praying to his pagan gods, began his epic march at the head of his army, replete with African elephants, in the late spring of 218 BC.

The reason why Hannibal went overland is simply because Rome controlled the seas of the western Mediterranean. He often took an inland route to avoid the danger of a Roman seaborne attack and even had to fight a battle against local Gallic tribes on the east bank of the river when traversing the mighty River Rhone delta. He overcame this problem by making a crossing further up the river with an advanced unit, who then moved south and attacked the enemy from the rear while making the crossing with the main army. The elephants were placed on giant rafts covered in soil to make them think they were on dry land.

In the meantime the Roman fleet carrying the army led by Publius Cornelius Scipio, Scipio's father, had sailed from Pisa bound for Hispania to confront Hannibal, and had landed at Massalia for supplies at the mouth of the Rhone. Surprised at the news that Hannibal had left Hispania already and was nearby, he disembarked his army in an attempt to intercept him, but Hannibal managed to escape, though there was a fierce clash between the advance cavalry units.

The Carthaginians reached the foothills of the Alps by the end of the summer and managed with the help of local guides to cross them, despite hostile attacks by local tribes. In fifteen days, they descended precipitous paths into Cisalpine Gaul in late autumn. The Romans, already in their winter quarters, were taken by surprise as Hannibal's army of 20,000 infantry, 6,000 cavalry plus thirty-seven elephants emerged onto the plain of the Po.

Meanwhile, Publius Scipio, having entrusted the command of the army to his brother, Gnaeus Cornelius Scipio the Bald, and sent him on to Hispania to carry out the originally planned mission, returned to Italy to take command of the Roman troops in Cisalpine Gaul. Once there, he advanced at once to meet the enemy. In his army rode his seventeen-year-old son.

In a cavalry engagement near the Ticinus, a tributary of the Po River, the two armies came face to face for the first time and fierce fighting ensued. At one point Publius Cornelius was cornered by the enemy and the young Scipio immediately charged into the melee and saved his wounded father's life. This was Scipio's first experience of combat and clearly, he more than did his duty. Following this the Romans retreated to the southern bank of the river to the colony of Placentium where the wounded, including Publius Cornelius, were tended to.

Now the Romans had another problem, when Celtic mercenaries mutinied, killing some of the Romans camped near them and defecting to the Carthaginians. But two days later, as Hannibal and his army approached ready for battle, Publius Cornelius realised the danger, broke camp at dawn and marched west to the Tribbia River, another tributary of the Po, and crossed it onto more suitable ground to defend. He dug trenches and built a palisade on a piece of high ground and camped while waiting for his fellow consul, Tiberius Sempronius Longus, to arrive with his army. He had already sailed from Sicily and captured Malta when he was recalled to support Publius Cornelius in the north. It was an epic journey by sea and land from the west coast of Sicily, then up the length of Italy to Ariminum on the Adriatic coast where the army regrouped before marching west across the width of Italy to Placentium. The journey took forty days.

Within hours of his arrival, Sempronius Longus, realising Publius Cornelius was still convalescing, decided to attack. He sent out a foraging cavalry party which soon engaged with the enemy, and the Romans came off best. This made Longus over-confident. Publius Cornelius's view was that it would be better to winter where they were, to train more and, furthermore, give time to the Celtic tribes who had joined the Carthaginians to realise it was not such a good idea to oppose the Romans. Longus ignored this advice, probably keen to gain the glory of an early victory where he alone was the commander. Hannibal was of the same opinion but for different reasons: the Celtic tribes were full of animosity against the Romans, but this would diminish through a long winter, the Roman legions were untested in battle as yet and Scipio was indisposed.

The Battle of Trebbia started on 22 December 218 BC in wet and cold weather. The Romans attacked and initially made advances, but when the Carthaginians, led by Hannibal's brother Mago, made a surprise attack from their rear, the battle turned swiftly into a defeat for the Romans. Only the advancing cavalry in the centre survived, and they drove on to gain safety in Placentia. Soon after, Scipio and the remainder of his army joined them in the safety of the city. Then the winter set in and both armies regrouped.

It is at this time that the young Scipio disappears momentarily from history, only to appear again as a Tribune in the 2nd legion at Cannae in August 216 BC, a gap of eighteen months. One can assume that he returned to Rome for those months before being called again to march behind the eagle of his legion.

In the spring of 217 BC, the Carthaginians crossed the Apennines through particularly difficult marshy country. Hannibal's horses and even the lone surviving elephant that he was riding found the going hard. Due to an infection Hannibal lost the use of one eye. Once rested, Hannibal, aware of Consul Gaius Flaminius's unfortunate characteristics of unbridled pride and arrogance, moved on towards Rome, laying waste to the surrounding countryside. Soon enough he was even putting himself between the Roman army and Rome itself. What happened then was predictable. Flaminius pursued the Carthaginians, intent on glory for himself with a great victory. Hannibal prepared by setting an ambush in a valley between the shores of Lake Trasimene and the steep hills around Cortona.

On 21 June 217 BC the pursuing Roman army, having camped for the night, marched straight into the trap. In the early morning mist, the

Carthaginians and their Celtic allies closed in on them from all sides. The surprised legions fought bravely, some wading into the shallow waters of the lake to escape before being hunted down by Hannibal's North African cavalry. Within hours the victory was complete with Flaminius killed by pursuing Celts. 15,000 Romans were dead and a further 15,000 taken prisoner. Even a cavalry force of 6,000 who had managed to fight their way out to a nearby Etruscan village were soon surrounded and ignominiously surrendered to the Numidian Maharbal, commander of Hannibal's cavalry, on condition their lives were spared. At the conclusion of the battle they, with all the other prisoners, were brought before Hannibal. He then announced to them that Maharbal had no authority to negotiate with them and proceeded to put them all to death.

The Carthaginians had lost only about 1,500 men and Hannibal kept the Roman prisoners while releasing the tribes who had fought with Rome back to their homelands. He was at war with Rome, not with the other tribes of Italy. He then advanced further south towards the Adriatic Coast and arrived there about ten days later to rest and recuperate.

In the meantime, the leaders of Rome appointed Quintus Fabius as Dictator with extraordinary military powers and Marcus Minucius as his Master of Horse. Gnaeus Servilius, the other consul with Flaminius, met him at Narnia where he handed over command of his legions. Fabius now had complete command and advanced towards the Carthaginian army. Hannibal at once set out his army for battle, but Fabius did not respond, and during the following months tracked the Carthaginians without bringing them to battle. He realised Rome could not afford another battle, which they were likely to lose, against an already victorious and battle-hardened army. This policy, though scoffed at by the more belligerent Minucius, worked well.

Despite a number of skirmishes, including a dramatic nighttime escape near Capua by the Carthaginians, this remained the situation until the onset of autumn.

In order to feed his men and provide better grazing for his animals Hannibal moved further east. The Romans, temporarily under the command of Minucius, continued to harass and gained small victories by attacking groups of Carthaginians out tending their herds or foraging, but the Consul was unsuccessful in trying to draw Hannibal into a larger confrontation. All this time Hannibal was organising his troops to collect provisions and supplies for his men and horses for the winter.

It was now time for elections in Rome, and Lucius Aemilius Paullus and Gaius Varentius Varro were elected Consuls, while the previous senators would command in the field. Paullus gave strict instructions to Gnaeus Servilius and Marcus Atilius Regulus not to engage the enemy. He strongly believed that the inexperienced foot soldiers in the legions should have time to be trained up.

It was also decided to send Lucius Postumius Albinus north to Cisalpine Gaul with an army of two legions to establish Roman authority in that region of Northern Italy. Unfortunately, the name Postumius portended disaster. His army was ambushed and put to the sword by the Celtic Boii tribe in the Battle of Silva Litana. The head of Postumius was cut off, skinned, scooped out and having been plated with gold, was used as a ceremonial drinking goblet by the tribal chiefs.

Hannibal now moved further towards the Adriatic coast of Puglia and captured the small citadel of Cannae, taking large amounts of Roman stores. The two armies were now facing each other, and it looked as though there would inevitably be a confrontation. The legions awaited the arrival of Aemilius Paullus, an experienced soldier, much respected due to his victories in Illyria. In addition, it was decided to field not just four legions but double that number. There were eight legions of 5,000 infantry plus 300 cavalry in each.

Paullus, realising the ground was open and would give advantage to the superior Carthaginian cavalry, wanted to move to a better position. But Varro, with little military experience, wanted to fight then and there. Since the overall command, in true democratic fashion, alternated every twenty-four hours, and Varro was in command, skirmishes began to break out which the Romans got the better of. It was dark now and both sides withdrew for the night. On the next day, 2 August, Paullus placed most of his army on the Aufidus River, leaving about a third of his manpower on the other side, safe from enemy attack.

The next day Varro was once more in charge. This was going to be a key battle both for Rome and for Hannibal. One of the most extraordinary descriptions of ancient armies preparing for battle comes from Titus Livius, in his *History of Rome*:

> At dawn Hannibal first sent his light contingents, including the Baleares across the river, then followed with his main force, drawing up in their battle positions the various contingents as they reached the other side. On his left, near the river bank, were the Gallic and Spanish horse, facing their Roman counterparts; on his right were the Numidians, and his centre was strongly held by infantry, so disposed as to have Gauls and Spaniards in the centre and African troops on each flank. To look at them, one might have thought the Africans were Roman soldiers, their uniforms were largely Roman, having been part of the spoils at Trasimene, and some, too, at the Trebbia. The Gallic and Spanish contingents carried shields of similar shape, but their swords were of different pattern, those of the Gauls being very long and not pointed, those of the Spaniards, who were accustomed to use them for piercing rather than cutting, being handily short and sharply pointed. One must admit, too, that the rest of the turn-out of these peoples, combined with their general appearance and great stature made an awesome spectacle: the Gauls naked from the navel upwards, the Spaniards ranged in line in their dazzling white linen tunics bordered with purple.

And standing in the ranks of the 2nd Legion, his tunic immaculate and his breast-plate shining in the morning sun, stood the fearless Tribune, Publius Cornelius Scipio, drinking in the menace of what confronted him and his brothers in arms, his mouth dry with the anticipation of combat, his grip on his sword tightening and sweat pouring down into his eyes from his helmeted head.

Cannae is one of the most famous battles in history, largely because the legendary Hannibal defeated the Romans so decisively, their greatest defeat. But despite their loss, Rome came out of the situation well enough. Firstly, they had fought bravely to the last with three out of the four consuls present killed alongside their men. They had acquitted themselves well.

Hannibal realised they were worthy opponents who were not going to give up their lands easily. The only one to flee was the inexperienced Varro, who escaped with a number of survivors. Secondly, Rome did not fall and in fact, during the next few years got the better of Hannibal and his marauding Carthaginians by conducting a clever war of attrition. Cannae was Rome's worst defeat, but it came early in the history of Rome, so there was time to recover and learn, which Rome certainly did.

In the ensuing decades Rome was not only to defeat Carthage but also to conquer the rest of the Mediterranean basin and the world beyond it. The Second Punic War was a world war fought simultaneously in different theatres far apart.

The nineteen-year-old Scipio who had saved his badly wounded father from death at Ticino also endured, at the age of nineteen, the horrors and brutality of the desperate hand to hand fighting on the blood-soaked battlefield of Cannae. From the failed Roman tactics, the disgrace of Varro fleeing the field and the bravery of Paullus, though badly wounded fighting to the last, the young Scipio must have learned much. He was to marry the daughter of that fallen hero and was soon to put his experiences to good use in the service of Rome. First Scipio and the Romans had to endure their shattering defeat, many fleeing from the field, but many proud of how they had fought.

In Canusium, a number of survivors of the humiliation gathered under the command of the young Scipio. They numbered about 4,000 infantry and 200 cavalry. As they discussed their next move, a certain Philus informed them that Lucius Caecilius Metellus along with others was planning on abandoning Rome and giving up the cause. Scipio was furious and drawing his sword went straight to Metellus. Bursting in on the plotters he threatened them, 'I swear with all the passion in my heart that I shall never desert our country or permit any other Roman citizen to leave her in the lurch. If I wilfully break my oath, may Jupiter bring me to a shameful death, with my house, family and all that I possess.' At sword point Scipio then forced the waverers to swear allegiance to Rome. This they did and the danger of the moment passed.

Why Hannibal did not press home the advantage of his victory and press on to take Rome is one of the great mysteries of history. The Romans themselves considered it a miracle. One of his generals later said that he knew how to win a battle but not how to take advantage once it had been won.

Far away in Hispania, despite his military setbacks in Cisalpine Gaul, Publius Scipio, now fully recovered from his wounds, had retained the confidence of the Senate and had landed at Tarragona with a naval force of twenty ships and an army of 8,000 men. Joining forces with his brother, Gnaeus Calvus the Bald, they were opposed by Hannibal's brother Hasdrubal. Word came that the Carthaginian intended to lead an army over the Alps to join up with Hannibal in Italy. As Hasdrubal moved north the two Scipio brothers met him in full battle order early in 215 BC at Ibera and were victorious. Most of the Carthaginian troops fled and Hasdrubal retreated into the interior of Hispania. If the Scipios had not been victorious and Hasdrubal had succeeded in reaching Italy so soon after his brother, the war might have had a different result. Ibera was one of the decisive battles of the Second Punic War.

Meanwhile both the Romans and the Carthaginians struggled with the loyalties of the Spanish tribes who continually changed sides. The Scipios then won two major victories over Hasdrubal at Iliturgi and Intibili, where thousands of prisoners were taken, a thousand horses, fifty-nine standards and seven elephants. At his moment, most of the wavering Spanish tribes came over to the victors, the Romans.

But this situation was not going to last forever and within three years the tables were turned. In 212 BC Publius Scipio and Gnaeus planned to finally resolve the war in the spring of the following year. Publius was to take two-thirds of their troops to take on Mago and Hasdrubal Gisgo while Gnaeus along with the Celtiberians would oppose Hasdrubal.

Hasdrubal, realising that this Roman army was largely dependent on the Celtiberians, managed to secretly bribe them to defect from the Romans. Gnaeus quickly withdrew followed by Hasdrubal, whose troops had by now crossed the Baetis River.

At the same time Publius's army was being harassed by the Numidian cavalry of Masinissa as he marched to meet the tribal leader Indibilis at the head of his 7,500 Suessetani. As darkness approached, Publius, now surrounded by the Carthaginians as well, was soon overwhelmed in a running battle. The Romans, led by the heroic Publius, fought bravely to the last until they were overwhelmed. Later in that year of 211 BC, Gnaeus Calvus and his army were also destroyed at Ilorci near Carthago Nova.

Lucius Marcius now took command of the remainder of the Roman army in Hispania, which he described as 'a heavy burden and an anxious care', but had some success when they ambushed the camp of Hasdrubal and Mago, killing many and taking booty, including the massive Marcian Shield, with a portrait of Hasdrubal, son of Hamilcar, on it, which was hung in the Capitoline Temple.

Later in the year, Gaius Nero arrived in Tarraco with an army of 6,000 infantry, 300 cavalry and an equal number of allies, from where he advanced and soon had Hasdrubal trapped in a valley called the Black Stones. By cunning negotiations and delays, Hasdrubal orgnanised the escape of his army to escape and thereby avoided a major battle. Yet again, Rome had been deceived by the cunning Carthaginians.

It was now decided to appoint a pro-consul to take command in Spain. The still young Scipio had offered himself as a candidate for *aedilis curulis* in 213 BC alongside his cousin, Marcus Cornelius Cethegus. The Tribunate of the Plebs objected to his candidacy, saying that he was too young, but Scipio, already known for his bravery and patriotism, was elected anyway.

At the election of the new proconsul for the command of a new army to be sent to Hispania, Scipio put himself forward again.

Through his calm maturity and positive words, Scipio made such an impression that he was elected unanimously. No one had been keen to take the job until the 24-year-old Scipio stepped forward. He was a man who often implied that he was inspired by the gods. After making tactical decisions, he would indicate that this had been approved by those above. In this sense, his aura recalled the demigod status of Alexander of Macedon. Maybe because he was going to fight over foreign lands where his father and uncle had fallen, Scipio was determined to take command. This was his moment of destiny.

He sailed from Ostia in a fleet of thirty quinqueremes with 10,000 infantry and 1,000 cavalry, landing at Emporiae in north-eastern Hispania and disembarking. The first thing he did was to reassure his tribal allies of his sincerity and to thank the legions for their loyalty to his father and uncle. It was autumn and the armies on both sides were in winter quarters. All of Hispania south of the Ebro River was now under Carthaginian control and Hannibal's brothers, Hasdrubal and Mago, and Hasdrubal Gisco, were the generals of the Carthaginian forces who had already defeated and killed the older Scipios.

In the spring of 210 BC Scipio assembled his army at the mouth of the Ebro. After a stirring speech to his men in which he exhorted them, 'that each of you may say that Scipio, your beloved general, has risen from the dead or been born again', Scipio marched south towards Carthago Nova while Laelius, in command of the fleet, tracked the army along the coast. In a week, both forces had arrived outside the defences of Carthage's capital in Hispania. Taken by surprise, the city was captured quickly, thousands of people were taken prisoner, booty, war stores, supplies and weapons were taken and Scipio now had control of an excellent harbour and base of operations.

Scipio, aware of the critical importance of alliances with the Hispanic tribes, developed a humanitarian approach, rare in those times, toward prisoners and hostages. This undoubtedly helped to portray the Romans as liberators as opposed to conquerors. Titus Livius relates the tale of his troops capturing a beautiful woman, whom they offered to Scipio as a prize of war. The Roman was immediately struck by her beauty, but after being told that she was engaged to a Celtiberian chieftain, Allucius, he returned her to her betrothed, along with the money that had been offered by her family to ransom her.

This gracious act persuaded local tribal leaders to reinforce Scipio's army, and Allucius reacted by bringing his whole tribe over to the Romans, including 1,400 elite cavalry. Scipio's actions were an indication not only of his sense of honour but also of his shrewd military and political judgement. After this victory Scipio sent Licaeus to Rome with a number of important prisoners, and after training exercises with his troops he returned to his base at Tarraco.

In 208 BC, the young Roman general commanded his first set-piece battle, driving Hasdrubal from his position at Baecula on the upper Guadalquivir. Scipio, concerned that the armies of Mago and Gisco would join up with Hasdrubal making a much bigger army than he had at his disposal, had to move quickly. The battle of Baecula was decided by a determined Roman infantry charge straight towards the centre of the Carthaginian positions. Roman losses are uncertain but may have been considerable in light of an effort by the infantry to scale defensive earthworks defended by Carthaginian light infantry. Scipio then orchestrated a frontal attack by the rest of his infantry to draw out the remainder of the Carthaginian forces. Hasdrubal failed to notice Scipio's cavalry reserves moving behind his army. The resulting Roman cavalry charge, led by Scipio and the cavalry commander Gaius Laelius, ensured Hasdrubal was surrounded and his forces fled.

This was Scipio's first victory in a full engagement against an experienced enemy general. After the battle he allowed the Spanish levies to return to their tribes, another example of political acumen. The Africans who had fought for Hasdrubal were taken prisoner. The Spanish troops who had been pressganged into the Carthaginian armies were now released and crowded round the young Roman general, acclaiming him as their leader and, more dangerously, their King. Across the Roman Republic the very word 'King' was anathema and Scipio knew it. In response he solemnly responded that he was a true republican: 'If you think that I have the spirit of a King, and that a silent one, the word must never pass your lips.'

All around him, his Roman legions, Spanish allies and prisoners were astounded by his honourable words. In the distribution of the rewards of war Scipio granted Indibilis, his Spanish ally, 300 horses of his own choice as a reward for his loyalty, and a captured young African named Massiva was returned with honour to his master Masinissa, the Numidian leader, allied to the Carthaginians.

At this point Hasdrubal, despite his defeat, managed to escape and march the length of Hispania and cross the Pyrenees in the west near the Atlantic before traversing southern Gaul. There, a decade after his brother, he made the second Carthaginian army crossing of the Alps into Cisalpine Gaul. The great Hamilcar Barca had fathered two sons who marched two armies across the dangerous high passes of the Alps, Europe's most formidable mountain range.

Once in Italy, Hasdrubal advanced across northern Italy to attack the Roman defensive positions from the north. In the south of Italy, Rome, with an army led by the consul Gaius Nero, was still fighting its interminable war against Hannibal in Puglia. The Roman general now made a spectacular decision. Secretly, without his opposition knowing, he left his camp in Canusium and, having marched south as a decoy, turned north and travelled the length of Italy towards Cisapline Gaul to join up with Livius and the other consular Roman army. Once again, the Carthaginians were tricked when under the cover of darkness Nero's army joined up with that of Livius. The next day Hasdrubal was defeated along the banks of the Metaurus River. The Romans killed thousands of the enemy and in terms of numbers truly avenged the disaster of Cannae. It is said the Carthaginians lost more than 50,000 dead, including Hasdrubal who fought bravely to the end, while the Romans lost 8,000.

The next day Nero was on the way back to Apulia and within a week had returned to his camp opposite Hannibal, unbeknownst to his opposite number. Hannibal had been expecting Hasdrubal to arrive at the head of an army. Instead, the severed head of Hasdrubal was deposited at the gates of his camp. After thirteen long years fighting year after year, deep in enemy territory, this must have been the last straw for the great man. His hope of being joined by his brother in final victory over the Romans had been denied. Metaurus was a defining encounter which changed the outcome of the Punic War and should be as well remembered as Cannae. Someone once wrote that history should remember the name of Nero in a good sense rather than by its attachment to the Emperor Nero we all know.

Meanwhile in Hispania, Scipio was still engaged in his great war of conquest. Another Carthaginian commander, Hanno, had brought an army across from Africa to join up with Mago and Hasdrubal Gisgo. Scipio sent an army under Marcus Silanus to attack them before they had set themselves up in Celtiberia and the newly arrived Hanno was captured. This was a Roman victory, but Mago then marched south to Cadiz on the coast to join up with Hasdrubal Gisgo. Scipio moved west to confront them and at the same time sent an army under his brother Lucius, later Asiaticus, to capture the rich city of Oringis.

The following year in 206 BC Hasdrubal Gisgo along with Mago managed to raise a large army of more than 50,000. Scipio, now allied with Celtiberian chiefs including Indibilis and Mandonius, advanced towards them and the two armies faced each other at Ilipa, a plain near modern-day Seville. After an initial cavalry skirmish where the Numidian cavalry came off worse, the two armies faced each other in a stand-off with neither side making a move, each morning setting up in battle order, then falling out in full sight of the enemy. And each morning Scipio placed his legions in the centre with the Iberians on the wings.

Early one morning, Scipio, having ensured his men had been fed and watered, began to harass the Carthaginian outposts while advancing with the main army behind, this time with the legions on the flanks and the Iberians in the centre. This tricked Hasdrubal Gisgo who had positioned his best troops, the Africans, in the centre and the Spanish on the flanks, and he had no time to change his formation.

When Scipio launched his main attack, the light troops moved swiftly behind the legions on the wings. With his wings advancing at a faster pace than the Iberians in his centre, Scipio formed a concave, or 'reverse Cannae', battle line with his cavalry on the ends of the flanks. With the inevitable destruction of their flanks, the Carthaginian troops in the centre were further disrupted by the trampling of their elephants who were being driven towards the middle by the Roman cavalry flanking attacks. Finally, the Carthaginians began to fall back, but soon Scipio ordered the Iberians in the centre into the attack. A massacre was only averted when a huge downpour occurred, bringing matters to a close as the Carthaginians retreated to their camps.

It was a complete victory and after fourteen years of war and five years of Scipio fighting in Hispania, the Carthaginians were finally defeated.

But Scipio was ambitious for more. He realised that just as Hannibal had been pressing for victory in Rome's homeland, so he would bring the war to Africa and to the gates of Carthage itself. Firstly, he decided to form alliances in Africa and sailed from New Carthage in just two ships to pay a visit to Syphax, King of the Masaesulii. This was a high-risk gamble since, ironically, at that very moment Hasdrubal had also arrived to visit Syphax.

Fortunately, the discussions were all cordial and Hasdrubal in particular was impressed by Scipio's bearing. He realised that his main concern now was to preserve Carthaginian power in North Africa since the province of Hispania had been lost. Initially Scipio reached an accord with Syphax, but the wily old king later changed his mind, married the Sophonisba, the beautiful daughter of Hasdrubal, and fought alongside his Carthaginian in-laws against Massinissa and Scipio in Africa.

On his return to Hispania, Scipio now set out to revenge himself on those tribes who had betrayed the Romans in times past, which had led to deaths of his father and uncle. The town of Iliturgi was sacked in a brutal manner with all the inhabitants being put to the sword. Likewise, a mutiny of his own troops was dealt with at Sucro. Later that same year Scipio founded the settlement of Italica near Seville in the Roman province of Hispania Baetica, the birthplace of the Roman Emperors Trajan, Hadrian and Theodosius.

In 205 BC Scipio finally sailed for Rome in a fleet of ten ships. He was met by the Senate outside Rome at the Temple of Bellona and related to them his achievements. He pointed out to them that he had defeated four Carthaginian generals and four Carthaginian armies, captured countless cities and finally expelled the enemy from Hispania. He then paid huge amounts of money into the treasury and made a promised sacrifice to the gods. A mission was even sent to Delphi to please the gods with a gift of a great gold crown captured from Hasdrubal. It was the fourteenth year of the war and Scipio, now aged 31, was elected Consul alongside Publius Licinius Crassus, who also became Pontifex Maximus.

The ever cautious but wise Quintus Fabius had always advocated a waiting game against Hannibal, and he now spoke against the idea of Scipio invading Africa while leaving Hannibal still in southern Italy. In fairness, it was he who had fought the moderately successful delaying campaigns against Hannibal and he feared expanding the war. Scipio responded:

> Yes, Fabius, I shall have the antagonist you gave me, Hannibal himself. But he won't keep me here, I shall draw him after me. I shall force him to fight on his native ground, and the prize of victory will be Carthage, not a handful of dilapidated Bruttian forts… Italy has suffered long enough, let her for a while have rest. It is Africa's turn to be devastated by fire and sword.

Scipio's intent to bring the war to Hannibal's gates was clearly only reluctantly supported by the Senate, and he was just given command in Sicily for the time being, which might or might not become a stepping stone for an invasion of Africa. Despite this resistance, Scipio gathered resources from clients and supporters in Rome and among the Italian communities, thus allowing him to muster a volunteer army of some 30 warships and 7,000 men. The Romans had for a long time used military service in Sicily as a punishment, with the result that the garrisons in Sicily contained many survivors from the numerous Roman defeats across Italy. Scipio, who himself had suffered the ignominy of serving at Cannae, understood their disgrace was no fault of their own. Furthermore, the Sicilian garrison also contained many of the troops who had participated in the successful Sicilian campaigns of Marcus Claudius Marcellus.

From all these men, Scipio was able to muster a highly motivated and experienced army for his African adventure, and he turned Sicily into a training camp for his army. He was aware that the Carthaginian Numidian cavalry were superior to Roman cavalry, so he recruited Sicilian cavalry by exempting local Sicilian nobles from serving provided they supplied a deputy plus horse and equipment to replace them. This was in addition to most of Rome's cavalry, who were young noblemen avoiding serving in the legions.

Within months the Roman Senate sent a commission of inquiry, including Cato, to Sicily and found Scipio at the head of a well-equipped and trained army. He again asked the Senate for permission to cross into Africa. It was not only Fabius, the Delayer, who opposed the idea. In the Roman Senate there was always a tension between two schools of thought: the conservative Republicans and the more liberal Graecophiles. The first group, led by Cato the Elder, were suspicious of Scipio expanding his power and popularity and were from more modest backgrounds. They detested the aristocratic and self-confident Scipio, suspicious of his enthusiasm for Hellenistic culture. After all, Rome was a republic and the idea of a Dictator or King was anathema. The other group enthusiastically worshipped Scipio as a brave hero who would lead Rome to final victory over their arch-enemy, Hannibal.

Finally, in the summer of 204 BC Scipio gained permission to sail to Africa with four legions and landed near Utica after a calm sea crossing only delayed by unusual fog in the Mediterranean. Once they landed, the Roman army laid waste to the surrounding areas and began to besiege Utica. Carthage, meanwhile, their troops commanded by Hasdrubal, had made an alliance with the wily Syphax, despite Scipio's visit to him two years before. But Masinissa had changed sides and was now an open ally of Scipio, giving him use of his deadly Numidian cavalry. With the army of Syphax approaching, Scipio abandoned the siege of Utica and dug in on the shore between there and Carthage for the winter.

In 203 BC, he destroyed the two army camps of Hasdrubal and Syphax by attacking and setting fire to both their camps in darkness. The two leaders panicked and fled before their followers were cut down in their thousands by the Romans. This attack was prepared secretly while Scipio was still negotiating with Hasdrubal and Syphax. He had infiltrated spies into the enemy camps when talks were in progress to establish the layouts and work out where best to set the deadly fires. Though it was not a full engagement, apparently the death toll exceeded 40,000 Carthaginian and Numidian dead, and many captured. Scipio had learned these cunning and devious ways from the Carthaginians themselves. His dubious success, though less honourable than a battle in open ground, was nonetheless superbly effective.

Scipio pursued Hasdrubal and Syphax and having hunted them down, they were easily defeated in a last stand at the Battle of the Great Plains. Syphax escaped but was cornered again and finally defeated and dethroned. This ensured Prince Masinissa's coronation as King of the Numidians. Not only was Syphax put in chains but to add insult to injury, the beautiful Carthaginian daughter of Hasdrubal was taken as wife by Masinissa. After these disasters, the Carthaginians finally recalled Hannibal to Africa. To avoid Scipio's forces, he landed further down the coast at Leptis Minor and assembled an army of 36,000 infantry and 4,000 cavalry, plus 80 war elephants.

Now was to come the final clash of the war but before that, the two legendary generals came face to face. Hannibal was now about forty-four years old and Scipio ten years younger. They met on a plain between Carthage and Utica on 19 October 202 BC on the eve of the Battle of Zama.

Hannibal had sent spies to the Roman camp, and they were captured. Much to the surprise of his officers, Scipio told his tribune to release them and show them around the camp and answer any questions they might have. He then sent them back to their camp. Hannibal, surely astonished, asked for a meeting.

The two legendary commanders met the next day in the shade of a leafy grove. They had never met before, they had never crossed paths in combat before, Scipio being only eighteen years old at Trebia and only twenty and a young tribune at Cannae. Now they were commanding two armies in what was to be a history-defining fight. Hannibal was the older man, aged forty-five, Scipio was thirty-four. Both were not far off their prime of life. There seems a tone of supplication in the Carthaginian's words and a hint of anger in the answers of the Roman. Livius relates the story as Hannibal opens the conversation:

> 'How ironic it is that I first fought the Romans in a pitched battle with your father, and now fate decrees that I ask for peace with his son. The gods have a good sense of humour.'
>
> **Scipio replies:** 'This war has gone on for many years. My father and my uncle and many others on both sides have died in battle.'
>
> **Hannibal:** 'And I have lost both of my brothers, Hasdrubal and Mago, men of great bravery and ability. Perhaps it would have been better if we Carthaginians had been content with our empire in Africa and you Romans with yours in Italia. But events are more easily criticised than retrieved.'
>
> **Scipio:** 'In both of the wars that your country and mine have fought, you, yourselves, were the aggressors. In the first war it was the danger that threatened our allies, the Mamertines, and in this war the destruction of Saguntum that girded us with just and pious arms. The gods are witnesses who determined the issue of the former war and will determine the issue of this present war according to right and justice.'

Hannibal: 'You, Scipio, appear to be a general of the highest order, like myself. What I was at Trasimene, you are today. But you would do well to arrange a peace with us here and now. I suspect that your mind may be more disposed to conquest than to peace, but you should consider not only those things that have happened, but also those that may yet occur. You cannot depend upon Fortuna; she's a fickle goddess. You could lose everything you've gained over the course of years in a single hour. In nothing less than war do events correspond to men's calculation. Everything is at your disposal when adjusting a peace, but in battle you must be content with the luck the gods shall impose. Rarely does a man consider the uncertainty of events whom fortune has never deceived. You would do well to remember the example of your own general in our last war, Consul Marcus Atilius Regulus. He would have achieved utmost success and renown, if, when victorious, he had granted a peace to our fathers when they requested it, but by not checking his good fortune which was elating him, he fell with an ignominy proportioned to his elevation. It is indeed the right of him who gives, and not the one who asks it, to dictate the terms of peace, but perhaps we may not be unworthy to impose upon ourselves the fine. We do not refuse that all those possessions on account of which the war was begun should be yours: Sicily, Sardinia, Spain, with all the islands lying in any part of the sea between Africa and Italy. Let us Carthaginians, confined within our shores of Africa behold you, since such is the pleasure of the gods, extending your empire over foreign nations both by sea and land. I cannot deny that you have reason to suspect the Carthaginian faith, in consequence of their insincerity lately in soliciting peace while awaiting the decision. The sincerity with which a peace will be observed depends much, Scipio, on the person by whom it is sought. Your Senate, as I hear, refused to grant a peace in some measure because the deputies were deficient in respectability. It is I, Hannibal, who now seeks peace, who would not ask for it unless I believed it to be expedient, nor will I fail to observe it for the same reason of expedience on account of which I have solicited it. I will exert myself so that no one may regret the peace procured by my means.'

Scipio: 'I am well aware of the instability of human affairs, Hannibal. I consider the influence of fortune and know very well that all of our measures are liable to a thousand casualties. If you had come to me to ask for peace before I set out for Africa, my conduct would have savoured of arrogance and oppression if I rejected you, but now, when I have dragged you into Africa by manual force, despite your resistance and evasion, I am not obliged to treat you with respect. You have offered us nothing that we have not already gained by our victories in this war. Indeed, we must insist upon a compensation for the ships of Sextus Octavius, together with their stores that Carthage seized and plundered during a time of truce when they were washed upon your shores by a storm. If you agree to such terms, I may have matter to put before my Senate. But if these things appear oppressive, prepare for war, since you could not accept the terms of peace.'

Hannibal did not accept these terms, so it was to be war.

Despite the mutual admiration of the two commanders, negotiations failed due largely to the fundamental Roman distrust of the Carthaginians as a result of the Carthaginian attack on Saguntum, in breach of the protocols, known as the Punic Faith, that had ended the First Punic War, and a mistrust in general of their devious and therefore dishonourable military tactics such as ambushes.

On the morning of the encounter Scipio commanded 30,000 men including probably 6,000 cavalry, Hannibal 40,000 men including 4,000 cavalry. Hannibal arranged his infantry in three lines of phalanx designed to overlap the Roman lines, his Spanish and Ligurian veterans in the centre. His plan was simple. The massed elephants would advance directly into the Roman lines, creating chaos that would then be exploited by the advancing infantry and finally by the cavalry. Unusually, Scipio arranged his lines perpendicular to the advancing enemy, rather than parallel, his two Roman legions in the centre, the *hastati, principes* and *triarii* behind each other, creating avenues between each *maniple* through which the elephants would be able to charge or be encouraged along by the *velites* or other light infantry. Added to this, trumpeters blasted out and the infantry beat their weapons on their shields, creating a deafening noise which terrified the great animals and caused many to panic, some charging back into their own lines and creating mayhem. As the battle wore on relentlessly, the infantry fighting became a slugging match with the Romans slowly driving the first two lines of Carthaginians back. There was a pause before the Romans advanced again and Hannibal threw in his veterans, many of them Spaniards, in a last-ditch effort to redeem the situation before the Numidian and Roman cavalry under Masinissa and Laelius, who had finally driven off their enemy counterparts, charged into their rear and the battle was won. Hannibal now left the field and regrouped the remains of his army at Hadrumetum, from where he advised the Carthaginian senate to plea for peace. His race was run.

Scipio, aware that he might be recalled at any moment, immediately entered into peace negotiations which were agreed by the Carthaginians: Carthage was stripped of its overseas colonies, a fine of 10,000 silver talents was to be paid over 50 years, hostages were to be taken, war elephants could not be owned by the state, and its great fleet which once had dominated the Mediterranean was reduced to a maximum of 10 ships. Though both Scipio and Hannibal urged that this was an acceptable and fair peace, it was not the end of the story.

Scipio was welcomed back to Rome in triumph and was given the agnomen *Africanus*. Mindful of petty jealousies, he refused the titles Consul for Life or Dictator. For his self-restraint in putting the good of the Republic ahead of his own gain, Scipio was praised by Livius, unlike some leaders that followed him, for example Marius, Sulla and Julius Caesar himself.

In the next few years Scipio attempted to live a quiet life at his estate at Liturnum, but ten years after Zama, in 193 BC, he was one of the commissioners sent to Africa to settle a dispute between Massinissa and Carthage, which remained unresolved.

In 190 BC, when the Romans declared war against Antiochus III, the Hellenistic king of the Seleucid Empire, Scipio offered to serve with his younger brother Lucius Cornelius if the Senate made him commander in chief in Asia. The two brothers brought the war to an end when Antiochus, fielding an army twice the size of the Romans, including an equal number of elephants and advised by the exiled Hannibal himself, was roundly defeated at Magnesia in western Anatolia.

Scipio's political enemies, led by Cato, jealous of the success once again of the Scipio family, brought charges against Lucius, now Scipio Asiaticus, of corruption by accepting bribes from Antiochus. Lucius was in the process of presenting his account books to the whole Senate when his elder brother strode across, tore the books to pieces and flung them across the marble floor. Scipio then asked the accusers why they were questioning the whereabouts of an alleged 3,000 talents when Antiochus had paid 15,000 talents to Lucius as tribute after his defeat. This dramatic act forced the accusers to recant and the matter seemed closed. But it was not so, and eight years later in Scipio himself was accused of taking bribes from Antiochus. It was the anniversary of Zama when he refuted this, followed by crowds around the Capitol. Scipio once again retired to his country seat at Liternum on the coast of Campania and lived there for the rest of his life. He died in 183 BC, at the age of 53. He apparently requested to be buried far away from an ever-critical Rome with this inscription on his tomb: *Ingrata patria, ne ossa quidem habebis*. 'Ungrateful country, you will not even have my bones.'

His great rival Hannibal died in Bithynia in the same year. The playwright Seneca, who moved into his house a century later, wrote: 'He had done reverence to his African spirit and to an altar which I am inclined to think is the tomb of that great warrior.' Seneca was a Spaniard who knew well what Scipio had achieved in Spain.

Of course Scipio is considered to be one of Rome's greatest generals, if not the greatest. Skilled in strategy and battle tactics he also had 'the common touch' and could inspire his men by his oratory and his actions. He was a man worthy to follow into battle.

Cato, ironically, had his dream fulfilled fifty years later, when, long after those two famous protagonists had passed away, another Scipio, the great man's adopted grandson, Scipio Aemelianus, whose own grandfather had been killed at Cannae, led the Roman army in 149 BC into North Africa in the third and final Punic War. He besieged Carthage and in the spring of 146 BC launched the final assault on the city, systematically destroying the walls and defences and massacring the inhabitants, with 50,000 survivors sold into slavery, and ploughing over the remaining ruins.

The lands of Carthage were incorporated into the Roman Empire, becoming the province of Africa, with Utica as its capital. *Carthago delenda est* was finally achieved.

It is not without reason that Scipio is the only Roman mentioned in the Italian National Anthem. He, in all the rich history of the Italian peninsula, symbolises the purity and honour of patriotism.

From boyhood to maturity, he stands alone as a true hero. Saving his father on the Ticino River, fighting in those broken and bloodied Roman legions at Cannae, commanding the armies of Rome in Spain over the bodies of his father and uncle, and winning war-defining victories there at a tender age against a canny and formidable enemy, and, having returned to Rome, still mistrusted by politicians, gathering an army in Sicily to land on the shores of Africa and defeating perhaps one of the most brilliant commanders in history at Zama, bringing the war to an end.

2

BELISARIUS
500–565

For not by numbers of men nor by measure of body but by valour of soul is war to be decided.

In the Basilica of San Vitale in Ravenna in the apse above the altar are some of the most remarkable mosaics of the ancient world. Directly in front of the visitor and high in the curve of the apse sits Jesus Christ accompanied by angels with San Vitale to the left. Below this are two famous mosaic portrait panels. On the left stands the East Roman Emperor Justinian I the Great, with a golden halo around his head, wearing the Imperial purple, known by the ancients as Tyrian purple. On the right of the apse is a matching mosaic of the Empress Theodora surrounded by her handmaidens. Justinian stands in the centre of his group, civilians and soldiers to his right and clergy to his left, emphasising that Justinian is the leader of both church and state.

Standing next to him to his right is, apparently, his general Belisarius, with a dark moustache and thick dark hair. We do not know who the younger man next to him is. Further to the left stand a group of the *scholae palatinae*, imperial guards, behind a shield with the Chi Rho insignia. The clergy, the balding Bishop Maximian and his deacons, hold an incense burner, the Gospels, a cross and, held by the Emperor himself, the bowl to hold the bread of the Eucharist. Lurking behind Justinian and the Bishop, and seemingly a little out of place, is an unusual, plump figure, unshaven and with unkempt hair, which, purportedly, is the scheming eunuch Narses.

Gazing at these fifteen-hundred-year-old mosaic portraits is an intriguing experience. The characters appear to be real and yet one wonders whether this is really a true depiction of them. The heroic Belisarius seems almost too immaculate in his court dress and too sinister to be the honourable soldier we know him to be. Whether it is, in fact, a true depiction of him is debatable. Why was this mosaic created at a time when the Ostrogoths, whose capital city was Ravenna, ruled Italy and were being threatened by the machinations of the Eastern Roman Emperor, Justinian, and in particular by his general, Belisarius? And the image of Narses is also a mystery.

To resolve these questions, we have to look at the chronicles of the times. Belisarius, always in the shadow of the glittering Justinian, is certainly one of the most overlooked generals in history and one of the most remarkable. Most people are familiar with Justinian, few with Belisarius. The very word Byzantine conjures up images of unique architecture, of elaborate mosaics, of mystique and mystery and, of course, intrigue and complex diplomacy. What it should not imply is paranoia or suspicion, which is what this powerful and effective man had to suffer all his life at the hands of the wilful Emperor Justinian and his ruthless wife, the notorious former actress, the Empress Theodora. But one should not forget that the reign of Justinian was undoubtedly one of the high points in Byzantine history, a time of great achievements. The Empire, largely thanks to Belisarius, was much enlarged with conquests in Persia and North Africa, quite apart from the mainland of Italy and Rome itself returning to the fold two hundred years after Constantine had removed his capital to Constantinople in the East. Justinian and Theodora were famed in their time and beyond, and the Emperor is remembered for his legal edicts, the *Corpus Juris Civilia*, or *Codex Justinianus*, much of which is in use to this day. It was a time when Byzantine art and architecture flourished, exemplified by the wonderful mosaics in Ravenna and the construction of the great Christian cathedral of San Sophia in Constantinople, one of the most astonishing buildings in the world.

The association of the Byzantine Empire with matters military is not one that springs to mind; Ancient Rome, yes, Constantinople, no. Though they titled themselves the Roman Empire and were ruled by Roman Emperors, they maintained few of the virtues and disciplines of Ancient Rome. They were often referred to by their enemies as cunning Greeks, but they were more than that, peopled by many races from all over Europe and the Near East. If Belisarius had been a Roman general in the great days of the Roman Empire he would have gone down in history on a par with Julius Caesar, Vespasian or Trajan. In fact, his conquests created a Byzantine Empire as great as the Roman Empire had ever been.

Belisarius was born in the Balkans, possibly in a town called Germania. Its ruins can be found in south-west Bulgaria, near the borders of Thrace in Northern Greece. From an educated Illyrian family that spoke Latin as their mother tongue, he became a Roman Byzantine soldier as a young man, serving in the bodyguard of the Emperor Justin I who had been proclaimed in the Hippodrome as Emperor in 518 AD. It is interesting that this Emperor and his successor were both born not far from the birthplace of Belisarius, though not from the same background. Justin, too, had served in the Imperial bodyguard of the Emperor Anastasius and had become commander of the Palace Guard before he was chosen as Emperor; not an unusual sequence during the Roman Empire, several members of the Praetorian Guard raised themselves to Imperial status. As a professional soldier with scant knowledge of statecraft, and lacking the ability to read or write, Justin relied on a close group of advisers he trusted. It is said that he signed his signature for formal documents with the help of a wooden frame or stencil. His closest adviser and confidant was his nephew Flavius Petrus Sabbatius, whom he adopted as his son and gave the name Iustinianus or Justinian.

Coming to the attention of Justin and Justinian as a good officer, Belisarius was given permission by the Emperor to form a bodyguard regiment. These bodyguards were loyal to powerful individuals both domestically in Constantinople and on campaigns in the Empire. They consisted of an elite heavy cavalry unit, a so-called *bucellarius* regiment, named after the biscuit rations they tended to live on, that he later expanded into a personal household regiment 7,000 strong. These guards were always at the centre of the armies he later commanded. Armed with short lances, bows, and long swords, they were armoured as typical heavy cavalry. They could begin an attack from a distance by shooting off their arrows, then charge the enemy with their lances, and finally engage in close-quarter fighting with their swords. On campaign they were fine soldiers, in Constantinople they were enforcers of law and order, depending on who their commander was.

During the early part of his career, Belisarius, alongside another promising commander, Sittas, gained experience campaigning in the rugged borderland that lay on the extremities of the Byzantine Empire where Europe clashed with Asia on the borders of Anatolia, the northern parts of Persia and Arabia and the lands that lay to the north towards the Caucasus Mountains. On the first raid they conducted into Persarmenia and Iberia, now Georgia, they took many prisoners and were successful. Raiding again, they were confronted by Persian units under Narses and were driven off.

Belisarius had given a good account of himself and was appointed by Justinian as Governor of Dara, the fortress built in Northern Mesopotamia on a rocky outcrop overlooking the valley below, only about ten miles from the Persian border and the city of Nisibis. This territory was the southern and eastern border of the Byzantine Empire, the far side of Anatolia where Belisarius had initially been campaigning. It was here in Dara that Belisarius began his relationship with Procopius, a Christian from Caesarea in Palestine, who was to become his secretary and biographer and, possibly, judge. The year was 527 and Justinian was now the newly crowned Emperor. He ordered Belisarius to reinforce the defences at Dara and a fort was built at Mindon even closer to the Persian border. The Persians naturally objected to these military activities but were ignored by the Emperor, who promptly sent Belisarius reinforcements. Nevertheless, the Persians attacked and, after fierce fighting, drove the Byzantines back to Dara and destroyed the fort of Mindon. For his bravery and actions Belisarius in 530 was created *Magister militum per Orientum*, commander in chief of the East.

After their success at Mindon, the Persians, led by Firouz at the head of an army of 40,000 including a phalanx of 10,000 of the elite so-called Immortals, marched on Dara. Firouz was so confident of victory that he ordered a bath to be drawn for him in the city for the end of the day. The battle started at noon when Firouz calculated that the Byzantines would be weak and hungry. Nothing could be further from the truth. Belisarius and his troops fought valiantly and even the Immortals were driven off in a headlong panic. 8,000 Persians were killed and victory was complete. This was the first victory of the Byzantines over the Persians for decades. Qobad, King of the Sassanid dynasty in Persia, was shocked by these events. Advised by Almondar, the King of the Arab people to the south, he sent an army under Azarethes to cross the deserts to the west of the Euphrates and to attack the Byzantines from the south in Syria. Belisarius was surprised by this and moved swiftly with his army to Chalcis south of Antioch. He drove the Persians back to the Euphrates at Callinicum. This brilliant move was not appreciated by his army, who wanted to fight the Persians rather than just drive them away.

So the general assembled his men and asked them, 'Where would you urge me? The most complete and most happy victory is to baffle the force of an enemy without impairing our own and, in this favourable position, we are already placed.

But Belisarius's men would not take no for an answer and their blood was up. They would not be denied. The battle, which Belisarius had not wanted to fight, began on 19 April, Easter Sunday, in 531. The Byzantines had underestimated the Persians who fought bravely and drove off their enemy. Many of the men who had pressured Belisarius into a fight were the first to flee.

Only Belisarius and a small group of infantry managed to hold off the enemy until nightfall and the Persians withdrew. Many of Belisarius's men found sanctuary on islands on the Euphrates River till the following day. The battle was inconclusive, but whether it was a victory or a defeat, the Persians still withdrew to their homelands. The 83-year-old Qobad died later in the year and his son negotiated the so-called Eternal Peace with Justinian in January 532. By the terms of the peace the Byzantines ceased to occupy Dara, and Belisarius was able to return with his army to Constantinople.

During this time Belisarius met and married the widow Antonina, who was well connected in the court and a personal friend of the Empress Theodora who had just married the Emperor. Antonina's mother had been an actress and her father a charioteer, both disreputable professions, but then the Empress herself had been an actress and interestingly, Belisarius's former comrade, Sittas, now commander in Armenia, had married Comito, the elder sister of the Empress. It all appears quite incestuous and Antonina inherited the 'loose morals' of her mother, which later brought great unhappiness to the loyal Belisarius. Procopius of Caesarea, his biographer, characterises Belisarius in later works, as emotionally dependent on Antonina, who allegedly conducted a passionate affair with a younger soldier, Theodosius, which was common knowledge.

Now it was January 532 and at the opening of the public games, where, despite the fact that gladiatorial contests had been banned for a hundred years, much excitement was in the air and fighting broke out at the Hippodrome. For years there had been four tribal factions represented by their colours, red, white, blue and green, which were worn by the competing charioteers. These factions or gangs wore the colours with passion, particularly the Blues and the Greens, and they clashed with each other wherever they went in the city. This is why patricians created bodyguards to defend themselves and their families. As the violence increased, the Emperor finally had a number of their leaders put to death or thrown into prison. At the Hippodrome the crisis boiled over when the Blues and Greens joined forces to massacre the guards and release their captive friends. Their blood up, they went on a rampage into the city, crying '*Nika,* Victory,' and screaming for the resignation of the Emperor's two financial administrators, Tribonian and John of Cappadocia, and destroying everything in their way, including setting fire to San Sophia and parts of the Imperial Palace. Eventually Justinian emerged and, carrying a copy of the Gospels to symbolise his Christian authority, ventured to the Hippodrome where he made an appeasing speech to the mob. The Blues listened to him but the Greens were still not happy and continued their insurrection.

When Justinian fled back to the sanctuary of his Palace, in the Forum of Constantine the Green mob grabbed Hypatius, the nephew of the former Emperor Anastasius, and declared him Emperor, despite his protestations. Justinian, meanwhile, was considering conceding to the rebels before the formidable Theodora refused, backed up by Belisarius who had gathered his guards and decided to face the foe. His first attempt was blocked by the Palace Guards who, nervous of the outcome, were hedging their bets and waiting to watch events unfold. Belisarius with his guard then escaped by another gate and proceeded to the Hippodrome, where he attacked the Greens. He managed to open the opposite gates of the Hippodrome where Mundus, the Governor of Illyria, was in charge of another large unit of troops, and together they put the Greens to the sword. It is estimated that about 30,000 people lost their lives, including Hypatius, who was removed from his throne and executed the next day.

Now there was peace in Constantinople, the scene was set for the Emperor to put his ambitious plans into action, an invasion of the Vandal kingdom Africa with an army led by who else but Belisarius, the man who had not only defended the Empire from a Persian invasion but also ensured the continuation of the dynasty of Justinian in Constantinople. In June 533, Belisarius, accompanied by his wife Antonina, his scribe Procopius and an army of five thousand cavalry and ten thousand infantry, plus Belisarius' guard, a number of mercenaries and finally a contingent of *foederati* led by Dorotheus, *Magister Militum per Armeniam,* and the eunuch Solomon, Belisarius' *domesticus*. As praetorian prefect in charge of the logistics of the army, Belisarius had Archelaus, an experienced officer. The force is estimated to have been around 17,000 strong, with 500 transport ships and 92 warships crewed by 30,000 sailors and 2,000 marines, all under Belisarius' command.

Before departing Belisarius was blessed by the Patriarch and visited by the Emperor, and a young barbarian soldier, Theodosius, was baptised for good luck. The great fleet then cast off and glided westwards along the Bosphorus into the Sea of Marmara and sailed into the setting sun. After a voyage which took three months via the Peloponnese, the Ionian islands and Sicily and in which Belisarius had been compelled to execute two Huns for murdering another in Abydos and dealt with sickness caused by bad food, the fleet finally made land in September 533 on the African coast about 150 miles from Carthage itself.

Belisarius, having heard that the Vandal King, Gelimer, was campaigning in Sardinia, landed that same day. In the next few days the Byzantine army advanced slowly towards Carthage ensuring along the way that they stayed friendly with the locals, who already resented the rule of the Vandals. Hearing of this invasion, Gelimer at once ordered the execution of his unfortunate predecessor, Hilderic, for fear of him being set up by the Byzantines as a puppet king. This only drove many supporters of the old king onto the Byzantine side. At the village of Decimus, ten miles from Carthage, the Vandals, led by Gelimer's brother Ammatas, attacked but were driven off and Ammatas was killed. Gibamund who was supposed to lead a coordinated flanking attack on the Byzantines was also defeated by cohorts of Huns, mercenaries in the army of Belisarius. On 16 September Belisarius at the head of his troops, including the sailors moored in the harbour nearby, marched in triumph through the open gates of Carthage and due to their discipline no atrocities or pillage occurred. Quickly, Belisarius set about building up the walls and defences of the city as the nearby Arab princes came to surrender.

Gelimer wrote to his brother Zazo in Sardinia pleading for his help, which was given, and within days the two Vandal brothers joined forces in the desert near Bulla. Gelimer by now had assembled an army of 100,000 and invited the Huns in Belisarius's army as well as the Vandal inhabitants of Carthage to join him. This idea was swiftly snuffed out when the general promptly impaled a traitor, Laurus, in front of the city gates as a warning to others of a like mind. On 16 December at Tricamaron, a few miles outside Carthage, the Vandals advanced against the Byzantines. At first Belisarius's guards attacked from the centre led by John the Armenian and were repelled, then they attacked again, and again. On the third assault the Vandals broke and began to flee. They were pursued by the army of Belisarius, but Gelimer escaped while the Byzantine soldiers, finding the treasure of the Vandals in their camp, indulged themselves into the night with plunder. The next day the army of Belisarius regrouped and the treasure of the Vandals was brought into Carthage. John the Armenian was accidentally killed in the pursuit of Gelimer, who now fled past Hippo into the safety of the hills at Medeus on Mount Papua where he was besieged by Pharis and his four hundred Herules troops. After a failed attack, when Pharis lost more than a quarter of his force, Gelimer was starved into submission and eventually surrendered.

By 534, the war was over and Justinian, wary of Belisarius's achievements, now offered him two options: the Governorship of Africa or a triumph through the streets of Constantinople. If he chose the former, the Emperor would assume he was setting up a rival state, but if he chose the latter and returned to Constantinople with his many Vandal prisoners and, of course, the Vandal treasure, he could become a rival. Justinian underestimated Belisarius's loyalty. So Belisarius chose the second option and was granted his triumph, though not riding a golden chariot; to the cheers of the people of Constantinople he walked modestly in front of his chained prisoners, including Gelimer, to be received by the Emperor Justinian and the Empress Theodora as they sat on their thrones in the Hippodrome and prostrating himself beside his prisoners before the rulers of the Byzantine Empire. The modest general was also awarded the honorary title of Consul, which by now was not an indication of political power but merely a title made famous in the annals of Rome and still revered by many. The Vandal prisoners, soldiers all, were now posted in military units in faraway Persia, as was the method of the original Roman Empire.

The fabulous Vandal Royal Treasure is worth mentioning since it had a remarkable history. Originally built up from their conquests by the Romans, the captured treasure had been stored in the House of Peace in Rome before the building burned down during the reign of Commodus. It included some extraordinary objects, including the precious *menorah* and table taken from the Temple of Jerusalem by the Emperor Titus, and many Egyptian artefacts. The Vandals when they captured Rome took them for themselves. Now the treasures were all transported to Constantinople and the Jewish pieces were returned to the Jewish community in Jerusalem. Sadly, in the ensuing centuries these legendary religious objects were lost in the tides of Turkish, Muslim and Crusader invasions of the Holy City. It is interesting to wonder if the Vandal kingdom had been allowed to continue and prosper, what might have happened a century later as the Arab conquests swept west across North Africa. Might the spread of Islam have been stopped in its tracks by the stubborn Arian Christians? It is one of history's what ifs.

After his conquest of North Africa, in 535 the Emperor Justinian now commissioned Belisarius to invade the kingdom of the Ostrogoths in Italy. There the new King, Theodatus, chosen by Amalasontha, the only daughter of Theodoric the Great after her teenage son Athalaric, had died in 534, moving ruthlessly, had her imprisoned and in the following year drowned in her own bath. Justinian had seen this internal division and considered the Goths to be weak and divided. Belisarius assembled an army of 4,000 *foederati,* 3,000 Isaurians, 300 Berbers and 200 Huns, while Mundus, the general who had assisted him during the suppression of the Nika riots, moved against the Goths in Dalmatia.

In total, including his formidable personal guard, Belisarius's force numbered roughly 12,000, not large. He landed at Catania in Sicily with the idea of using it as a jumping off point for the invasion of Italy. The Emperor's plan initially was to pressure Theodatus into relinquishing his throne and to then annex the kingdom of the Ostrogoths through diplomacy and the threat of military action. This worked at first, but when Mundus, the army commander in the Balkans, lost the city of Salona as well as his son in the battle, the Byzantine army retreated and the Goths were encouraged to fight on.

In spite of this setback to the master plan, Belisarius pushed on into Sicily. The only serious resistance he faced came at Palermo, which he besieged and captured using the novel trick of sailing his ships into the harbour, raising troops in small boats up onto the masts, and firing down rounds of arrows into the besieged city. Soon, Palermo capitulated, and Belisarius controlled the whole of the island after making a triumphal entry into Syracuse on 31 December 535. But preparations for the invasion of the Italian mainland were interrupted in Easter 536 when he was compelled to cross over to Carthage once again. Disgruntled Byzantine soldiers led by a Byzantine officer, Stotzas, had mutinied and begun to lay siege to Carthage. As soon as the rebels heard of the approach of Belisarius they lifted the siege and were hunted down and attacked by the general's small force of 2,000 men at Membresa, where he won a decisive victory. Stotzas fled into Numidia and spent the rest of his days on the fringes of history.

Soon afterwards, Belisarius returned to Sicily and crossed into mainland Italy, where he advanced on Naples in November 536. Before reaching the city he had met little resistance, as a number of Gothic garrisons in southern Italy were unhappy with how Theodatus had gained the throne, and they wavered in their support. But at Naples there were strong fortifications and a loyal Gothic garrison prepared to resist the Byzantines, and Belisarius was reluctant to march north towards Rome leaving such a strong enemy presence behind him. He did not have the manpower to storm the strong fortifications, nor could he afford to conduct a lengthy siege during which time the Ostrogoths could send reinforcements. At Naples, neither bribery nor negotiation worked and he couldn't use his fleet, as he had done so effectively in North Africa, since there was strong artillery on the walls. Even cutting off the water supply by destroying the main aqueduct into the city failed, since there were so many wells within the walls. After many assaults failed, a unit of his Isaurian mountain troops found an entrance into the city via a disused aqueduct. This small force entered the city and opened the gates to Belisarius's army who, after fierce fighting, forced the inhabitants to surrender. Desperate to build up his forces, the Byzantine general showed mercy to the garrison and populace, which enabled him to gain new recruits and at the same time to save his own army from losses.

His failure to defend Naples resulted in Theodatus being deposed and replaced by a new King of the Ostrogoths, Witigis. He was to prove a worthy opponent for Belisarius. Witigis had gained power through his marriage to Matasuntha, the only daughter of Amalasuntha, who had been murdered by Theodatus. As soon as he heard news of the surrender of Naples, he sent troops to garrison Rome as Belisarius and his army approached. But as soon as they entered the city these units became aware of the pro-Byzantine attitude of the population and on 10 December 536 Belisarius, as general of the Eastern Roman Empire, marched through the *Porta Asinaria,* one of the southern gates of Rome, to reclaim the Eternal City for the Empire. It was a historic moment and it must have affected such an educated man as Belisarius, who had been brought up on the proud history of Rome. To have recaptured the legendary city which had fallen to the Ostrogoths some sixty years before and been superseded by Constantinople for more than two hundred years, was a significant moment. Lenderis, the Gothic commander of the garrison, was taken prisoner and transported to appear before the Emperor Justinian in Constantinople to surrender the keys of Rome. Justinian was now ruler of the ancient and symbolic capital of his Empire, as well as Constantinople, a fact which few emperors could claim.

As soon as Belisarius entered the ancient city he began to organise the defences. The disused moat around the walls was dug deeper and the broken walls were hurriedly built up again during the winter months as news came that Witigis was assembling a formidable army of more than 150,000 men to march south from Ravenna. This huge force first appeared before Rome on 10 March 537.

Knowing they would approach from the north, Belisarius had built up the Milvian Bridge across the Tiber just outside Rome and placed a garrison there. He was well aware that the bridge was famous for being the site of Constantine's historic victory over Maxentius in 312 and must have prayed that he, too, would benefit from Divine intervention. On seeing the enormous Gothic army approach, the garrison fled, but, as they approached the city walls Belisarius himself opened the gates and led the defenders out in a fierce counter-attack, despite the fact that he was a prime target for the Goths who recognised him and his distinctively marked bay horse. Eventually, the Goths withdrew, but all Belisarius and his men had achieved was to give the enemy a bloody nose, no more.

The siege now began in earnest with nothing to defend the weak fortifications but the small Byzantine army of 12,000 men plus groups of Roman citizens formed into cohorts who defended particular sections of the walls and made foot patrols with dogs that guarded the great trench around the walls at night.

This heroic Byzantine defence against the enormous Gothic army was to last a full year until 21 March 538. Though Belisarius inflicted heavy casualties by launching a number of successful sorties, made more effective by the lack of Gothic military discipline and the experience of the Byzantine officers, it is still a mystery how Belisarius achieved this defence for so long. It can only be put down to his remarkable gifts as a tactician and inspirational leader, remembering it was he who often led these dangerous counter-attacks outside the protection of the city walls. Even when Witigis tried to increase the size of his patrols to prevent these raids, Belisarius sent out bigger patrols that encircled them.

When the Goths attacked with siege engines, Belisarius ordered his archers to shoot at the oxen pulling the siege equipment. Whenever the Goths retreated from a certain section of the wall, Belisarius launched an attack on their rear, inflicting more casualties. Still hugely outnumbered, Belisarius tried to end the siege with attack after attack. Even when he tried to break the siege by emerging from the city with virtually a small army, Witigis had enough numbers to absorb the attack and then to counter-attack.

It was now December 537, and a truce was agreed upon for three months while a Gothic embassy was allowed to journey to Constantinople and demand terms. In the meantime, Belisarius was not idle and took over two important fortresses north of Rome, Albano and Civitavecchia, making Wittigis's army more vulnerable if they were to retreat northwards again. Belisarius made sure one of his officers, John the Bloodthirsty, was in command of Albano and controlling the province of Picenum in the event of Witigis breaking the truce. Fearful of all this activity, Witigis, already losing the siege, decided to make one last attempt on the wall which ran along the Tiber where it was much less of an obstacle. He bribed some of the defenders to give the guards drugged wine, but the plot was revealed and Belisarius brutally punished the traitors. With even this attack failing, Witigis decided to end the siege after he heard that John the Bloodthirsty had advanced further and captured Rimini, not far from Ravenna.

On 21 March 538, Witigis finally began to withdraw his army and, as soon as half of his men were on the Tuscan side of the Milvian Bridge, Belisarius emerged from the city and attacked. It was another victory for the Byzantine general as hundreds of the enemy were trapped on his side of the river and were either killed, captured or drowned trying to escape. Witigis now had to retreat across Italy to his capital, Ravenna. He still had enough men to place in garrisons along the way: 4,000 at Auximus near Ancona, 2,000 for the city of Urbino and 3,000 at other strong-points. Hildiger, another of Belisarius's senior officers, was now deployed at the head of 1,000 cavalry to harass the retreating Goths and, on reaching Rimini, to order John the Bloodthirsty to quit the city with his cavalry. John refused and remained in Rimini where Witigis duly arrived and laid siege. The King of the Ostrogoths was keen to succeed at Rimini after before the walls of Rome he had been humiliated.

In June 538, Belisarius advanced north through Italy, capturing as many Gothic fortresses as possible. This campaign was to last nearly two years. It was a war of attrition where the Byzantine general had to preserve the numbers in his army as much as possible by using his considerable powers of persuasion and negotiation. Some cities swiftly surrendered at the mere mention of his name, but just as many did not. He was encouraged with the news that 7,000 Byzantine reinforcements had landed near Ancona under the command of the Imperial eunuch, Narses. This was a two-edged sword, as Narses was a dangerous man, the Domestic in the Palace of Justinian and Theodora, working solely on their behalf and, doubtless, under orders to observe and curtail the alleged ambitions of Belisarius. Narses was a diminutive and deformed figure in contrast to the powerfully built and handsome general, and evidently his motives were devious. He insisted to his troops that he had a special relationship with the Holy Virgin who could always advise him when to make his moves. He was the very antithesis of Belisarius. One was loved by his men, trusted and admired, while the other commanded through fear and the knowledge that he alone was acting for Justinian. Neither general was named overall commander, so Narses was a constant thorn in Belisarius's side.

The two generals finally met at Fermo near Rimini. A plan was agreed to take Rimini by tricking the Goths into thinking they were going to be attacked by numerous Byzantine armies plus the Byzantine fleet, now under Hildiger, which was sailing up the coast. This was achieved by a method the Carthaginians had used centuries before against the Romans in the Campania, where many torches were lit at night, some on the horns of cattle, to give the impression of a larger army. At dawn the following day, the Goths gave up the siege and fled towards Ravenna.

At the same time Belisarius had also sent a force of 1,000 men under the command of Mundilas to occupy Milan and they were now in turn under siege by a Gothic army under Uraias, nephew of Witigis. Narses deliberately blocked Belisarius sending troops to save Milan, so, under Martin and Uliaris, a smaller force was sent to save the city. Meanwhile the time-wasting Narses insisted on besieging Urbino. Once there he, along with John the Bloodthirsty, abandoned the siege and proceeded to take the easier pickings of Emilia.

Belisarius took the surrender of Urbino in December 538. He now moved towards Orvieto, which was still in Gothic hands and was too close to Rome for comfort. The news from Milan was dire; the inhabitants had surrendered to the Goths and their allies the Burgundians. The city was destroyed, thousands raped and murdered and Matin and Uliaris had failed to help them. Uliaris clearly was not a very effective soldier. It was he who had mistakenly killed John the Armenian in North Africa. Belisarius refused to allow either officer into his presence when they returned to his camp.

It was now March 539 and winter was drawing to a close. Justinian recalled the scheming Narses to his court. Once more Belisarius was left as sole commander in chief in Italy. He continued to lay siege to more strategic cities, including Osimo, controlling more and more of the peninsula. Finally Witigis, desperate for support, sent out embassies far and wide, even as far away as the Persian Empire, knowing them to be the traditional enemies of the Byzantines, while Belisarius now set up siege forces around Auximum and sent troops to Fiesoli, starving both cities into submission by late in the year. He led the siege of Auximum himself. Knowing he couldn't storm the city, he tried to cut off the water supply but this failed. Always full of novel ideas, he paraded the captured leaders of the Fiesoli garrison in front of the walls and the garrison duly surrendered after seven months.

Central Italy was now finally secure, so Belisarius moved his army to surround the Ostrogothic capital of Ravenna by the end of 539. The grain shipment to the city hadn't been able to enter, so as the Byzantines approached the city the grain ships were also captured. The desperate Gothic nobles, led by Witigis, now offered the throne of the Western Empire to Belisarius himself. Belisarius feigned acceptance and entered Ravenna via its sole point of entry, a causeway through the marshes, accompanied only by a unit of his trusted *bucellarii*. He also prepared the grain shipment to enter the city if they surrendered. Soon afterwards, he proclaimed the capture of Ravenna in the name of the Emperor Justinian. The Goths' offer had, of course, raised suspicions in Justinian's mind and, doubtless at the behest of Theodora, Belisarius was summarily recalled in his moment of triumph.

In 540, after five years of campaigning across the length and breadth of Italy, from the slopes of Mount Etna in Sicily to Ravenna on the shores of the Adriatic Sea, Belisarius once again returned to Constantinople with a barbarian treasure and a barbarian King and many of his soldiers as prisoners. This time he was not accorded the privilege of a triumph. Ironically, the seemingly hopeless request by King Witigis of the Goths to the King of Persia to attack the Byzantines had worked, though too late to save the Gothic kingdom in Italy.

In the ensuing weeks the Persians led by their King Nushirvan invaded the Byzantine provinces in Syria. He was a follower of Mazdakism, a form of Zoroastrianism, the ancient religion of Persia. He quickly took Sura, destroying the city and massacring the people. He then laid siege to Hierapolis and stood ready to attack Antioch, the greatest city of the region, which had been destroyed by a catastrophic earthquake fourteen years before in 526 but rebuilt magnificently, largely due to the efforts of the Emperor.

Justinian's general Buzes had fled when the Persians first attacked. He was replaced by Germanus, his nephew, who wavered in his proposed defence of the city, saying his presence as a member of the Imperial would merely encourage the Persians to attack. In defiance, the people of Antioch, emboldened by the presence of 6,000 newly arrived reinforcements, arrogantly sent a message to the Persian King which enraged him, and he promptly attacked the city. Within days Antioch was taken and another massacre took place before the Persian King entered the burning city and demanded a tribute from the Emperor. He then advanced to Seleucia where the Orontes River reaches the sea and, as was the Magian way, bathed alone in the sea and sacrificed to the sun. Next he turned to the ancient city of Apamea and duly captured it, despite the belief of Thomas the local bishop that the city's ownership of a piece of the Holy Cross would protect it.

His conquest of Syria now complete, Nushirvan turned for home, demanding a ransom from the city of Chalcis as he passed, and crossed the Euphrates back into Mesopotamia. The Persian King, having hardly encountered a Byzantine soldier in his whole campaign, now set his sights on Edessa where, rather than a siege, the citizens agreed to a large ransom, thereby ensuring their own safety but also the release of their fellow citizens who had been taken prisoner in Antioch. But now the disreputable Buzes reappeared, took the ransom for himself, and allowed the Persian army to go on its way. Fortunately for the prisoners, whose hopes of release had been raised then dashed, on their arrival in Mesopotamia the King built them a city, one day's journey from Ctesiphon, along with a circus and public baths where they could reside and live out their lives. All these disastrous events for the Byzantines had taken place while Belisarius was languishing in Constantinople waiting for his call to arms for the rest of 540, and only in the spring of 541 was he confirmed as Commander in the East and permitted to join the army at Dara, a place familiar to him.

Finding the army unpaid and in disarray, he began to mould them into a fighting force. After all, his reputation went before him and he brought with him many of the Gothic warriors who had been taken prisoner by him in Italy. They were doughty fighters who put a backbone into his forces. He now led this new army eastwards and approached Nisibis on the borders of Persia. This city had to be taken first to secure his retreat route if he moved deeper into Persia.

Belisarius ordered a camp to be set up at a good distance from the city in leafy meadows full of natural springs to wait for the enemy to emerge. Two of his officers, Peter and Nicetas, disagreed and left the main force and camped closer to the city. Belisarius warned them that the Persians would attack by emerging from the city gates. Belisarius was familiar with these tactics, which he had used successfully in Rome. This is exactly what happened. As the troops were unsaddled, out of their armour, and preparing to eat, they were duly attacked. Belisarius at once saw what was going on and drove the Persians back behind their walls.

Now the general, keen to avoid long sieges, bypassed Nisibis and marched thirty miles towards the next Persian stronghold at Sisauranum. While he besieged Sisauranum, he sent Arethas, the Bedouin leader, reinforced with 1,200 Byzantine cavalry to raid the rich lands beyond the Tigris. The assaults on Sisauranum were initially repulsed and suffered losses, but soon the city ran out of supplies and the garrison surrendered.

At this point, an altogether unheard-of phenomenon hit Belisarius. Not only was he fated to face fierce enemies while dealing with untrustworthy leaders, but also his armies now fell victim to the bubonic plague, the first recorded outbreak in history in the Middle East, later to be known as 'Justinian's Plague'. A third of the general's forces caught the fever, many dying, and he elected to withdraw from the battlefields of Mesopotamia. Some take the view that he should have marched onto the Persian capital, Ctesiphon, thereby capturing the trophies and treasures of yet another enemy of the Byzantines, making a trio of conquered Kings, the Vandals, the Ostrogoths and the Persians. But this time discretion, or rather practicality, was the better part of valour.

Belisarius returned to Constantinople for the winter, but, during the early spring of 542 Nushirvan invaded again. This time, he planned to conquer Palestine and, in particular, take the treasures of Jerusalem. Outnumbered by the Persians, Belisarius decided to wage the next campaign more by guile than brute force, a familiar practice for him due to necessity rather than desire. As Nushirvan advanced, Belisarius sent an embassy to meet his emissaries accompanied by a large force of highly trained troops dressed as though on a hunting expedition. The Persians, tricked into thinking this was just a small unit at their leisure ahead of a much bigger army, retreated. Belisarius now sent cavalry units to police their retreat and, though the Persians took some fortresses, they were pushed back within their frontiers. Many think their retreat was possibly through Nushirvan's fear of catching the plague in Byzantine territory. Once again, Belisarius returned to the capital having secured the Eastern frontiers of the Empire.

In Italy much had changed since his departure three years before, and the Goths led now by a charismatic new King, Totila, had made great gains against the inefficient and corrupt Byzantine leaders. And the truth is that if the paranoid Justinian had just left his loyal general to complete the job, the peninsula of Italy would have been secured for the Eastern Empire for a considerable period. Totila had been proclaimed King of the Goths in the autumn of 541. He took full advantage of the fact that the Plague of Justinian had decimated the Roman Empire and that Belisarius, whose name struck fear in the Goths, was occupied on the Persian frontiers. The two current Byzantine generals, Constantinian and Alexander, laid siege to Verona, one of the main Gothic strongholds, but were driven off and defeated at the Battle of Faventia in the spring of 542. Totila then advanced into Tuscany where he laid siege to Florence. Other Byzantine generals, John, Bessas, and Cyprian, marched to its relief but at the Battle of Mucellium, later in the year, their numerically superior forces were defeated again.

Totila now marched south, and at Naples he allowed the city to surrender on terms in 543 and was considerate in his treatment of the defenders. He had learnt from Belisarius that this policy sometimes brought benefits. Having taken Naples, Totila attempted to make peace with Justinian, which was refused. In an attempt to gain the support of the citizens of Rome he ordered copies of this refusal to be posted all over the city. But the Romans remained loyal to the Emperor, so Totila marched north and once again, the great city was besieged.

After much prevarication by Justinian, Belisarius was eventually reappointed to take command in Italy in 544. But due to the plague and a reluctance to serve the Empire by many families, he could only raise about 4,000 men, hardly an army. Anyway, most able men fit for military service were still needed to police the vast Eastern borders, even though there was now a five-year truce in place. The plague was not selective and even the Emperor himself fell ill but miraculously survived.

Since Belisarius couldn't assemble a large enough army to transport by sea to Italy, he first marched into Thrace to recruit more men, then across Macedonia to Salona on the Adriatic, from where he sent troops and supplies to the beleaguered Otranto in the heel of Italy, forcing the Goths to call off the siege. He then sailed further up the Adriatic to Pula in the extreme north-east of the Italian peninsula from where he could safely organise his small army. Totila, on hearing of the arrival of the legendary Byzantine, sent spies to his camp ostensibly as emissaries from Genoa who reported that the ageing Belisarius commanded a small and weak army.

They were accurate in what they said. Belisarius could be said to be in his old age by now and, indeed, his army was modest in number. Totila, now outside Rome, captured and sacked the small town of Tivoli, putting all its citizens to the sword in order to terrify the inhabitants of Rome. In response, Belisarius now crossed to Ravenna and appealed to both the Goths and the occupying Byzantines to acknowledge the authority of the Emperor. This was met with no response. Clearly, the peninsula of all Italy was in chaos.

Totila, still tentative when faced with the reputation of Belisarius, though knowing about his small army, was still cautious and leaving the siege of Rome he marched north across the Apennines to besiege Osimo and to confront Belisarius. The reputation of the Emperor's great general went before him and never failed to strike fear in the hearts of his opponents; but knowing he was outnumbered, Belisarius avoided a direct confrontation and Totila, having captured Osimo, Assisi and Spoleto, returned to the walls of Rome.

Belisarius now sent John the Bloodthirsty to the Emperor pleading for more troops and moved south to Dyrrachium on the Illyrian coast opposite Apulia. He was playing a waiting game and as soon as support arrived he sent John the Bloodthirsty at the head of a light cavalry division to land in Southern Italy, and from there to make his way across the Apennines to Rome, while he sailed round the coast to Portus, the port of Rome. Once there he devised a novel plan to sail up the Tiber with two specially devised ships built with a wooden castle on board to destroy the besieging Gothic defences. This plan came very close to success and was only spoiled by other unauthorised attacks against his orders, which alerted the enemy and obliged him to retreat. His desperate attempts to relieve Rome came close to success but ultimately failed.

His last throw of the dice to save the city was a letter he drafted to Totila. It is a document which guarantees him a place in history as a civilized man as well as a great general. It could have been written by many generals to preserve beautiful historic places, be they Baghdad before the Mongols in 1258, Constantinople before the Crusaders in 1204, Monte Cassino before the US Air Force in 1944, Dresden before Bomber Command in 1945, or even Rome itself in 450 before the Vandals. The words of Belisarius, written fifteen hundred years ago, still stand the test of time:

> While the creation of beauty in a city which has not been beautiful before could only proceed from men of wisdom who understand the meaning of civilization, the destruction of beauty which already exists would be naturally expected only of men who lack understanding, and who are not ashamed to leave to posterity this token of their character. Now among all the cities under the sun, Rome is agreed to be the greatest and the most noteworthy. For it has not been created by the ability of one man, nor has it attained such greatness and beauty by a power of short duration, but a multitude of monarchs, many companies of the best men, a great lapse of time, and an extraordinary abundance of wealth have availed to bring together in that city all other things that are in the whole world, and skilled workers besides. Thus, little by little, have they built the city, such as you behold it,

> thereby leaving to future generations memorials of the ability of them all, so that insult to these monuments would properly be considered a great crime against the men of all time; for by such action, the men of former generations are robbed of the memorials of their ability, and future generations of the sight of their works. Such then, is the facts of the case, be well assured of this, that one of two things must necessarily take place: either you will be defeated by the emperor in this struggle, or, should it so fall out, you will triumph over him. Now, in the first place, supposing you are victorious, if you should dismantle Rome, you would not have destroyed the possession of some other man, but your own city, excellent Sir, and, on the other hand, if you preserve it, you will naturally enrich yourself by a possession the fairest of all; but if in the second place, it should perchance fall to your lotto experience the worse fortune, in saving Rome you would be assured of abundant gratitude on the part of the victor, but by destroying the city you will make it certain that no plea for mercy will any longer be left to you, and in addition to this you will have reaped no benefit from the deed. Furthermore, a reputation that corresponds with your conduct will be your portion among all men, and it stands to wait for you according to you decide either way: for the quality of the acts of rulers determines, of necessity, the quality of the repute which they win from their acts.

Despite the moral compass of the Byzantine general, his words were ignored. After more than a year besieging the city, Totila entered Rome on 17 December 546 when his men, helped by Isaurians, those agile mountain men from the Taurus Mountains who had probably switched sides from the Byzantines, scaled the walls at night and managed to open the Asinarian Gate. Rome was now put to the sword. But Totila, who had planned to level the city, as he had done with other captured towns, destroyed only a third of the ancient walls. Perhaps he had taken note of the words of Belisarius after all.

Totila took communion in St Peters' where he was greeted by Pope Pelagius, though simultaneously, outside the doors of the cathedral, Byzantine soldiers and Roman citizens were being murdered by his troops. The leader of the Goths now sought peace, sending messages to the Emperor Justinian. He received a curt reply that he should negotiate with Belisarius, since only he spoke for the Emperor in Italy. Totila then left in pursuit of the Byzantine forces in Apulia before marching north to finally evict the Byzantine presence from the Italian peninsula.

The Eternal City now lay deserted and desecrated for the next forty days, before Belisarius, taking matters into his own hands, fiercely drove off Gothic units blocking his path and in February 547 marched once again into Rome, a decade since he had done the same. Once again, he rode past the legendary monuments, the broken pillars of the ancient forum and past the menacing Colosseum where only stray dogs and sedentary cats observed him. Once again, he sent the keys of Rome as trophies for his Emperor in Constantinople.

Though Rome was now a ravaged city, Belisarius had once more to ensure its defence. He organised the rebuilding of the damaged walls by any means possible and he deepened the ditches again and fortified them with pointed stakes. It was only a month before the enraged and vengeful Totila, by means of forced marches across the diagonal of Italy, appeared before the walls to retake the city he had so proudly captured not so long before. Immediately, the King of the Ostrogoths attacked but was driven back after two days of fierce fighting in which Belisarius personally took part. After resting for some days, Totila attacked again, but for a third time he was driven off and retreated before moving off into Southern Italy to engage with the Byzantine cavalry forces of John the Bloodthirsty.

Belisarius was now left with an occupying army, or really just a bodyguard, of 300 infantry and 700 cavalry. Rarely in history has a general commanded such a diminutive army and after a short time it was agreed that he should join up with John the Bloodthirsty's troops in Apulia. Belisarius now marched out of

Rome for the last time and took ship southwards where he joined his Byzantine colleagues. But with unfavourable winds he was held up and could not land, so in 548 John's cavalry were heavily defeated in Calabria. Further action to defend the port of Cortone was considered pointless and within a few weeks Belisarius was summoned to return to Constantinople.

As he sailed away from Italy, his thoughts might have been similar to Hannibal's some seven hundred years before. They had both ventured into the peninsula of Italy, won great victories but ultimately failed, though the Byzantine had captured Rome twice, which would have irked Hannibal. And they both sailed away to face ignominy at home, despite the fact they had both been made immortal by their deeds. Edward Gibbon wrote of Belisarius, 'In these campaigns he appears a more consummate master of the art of war than in the season of his prosperity, when he presented two captive Kings before the throne of Justinian.' How he had managed to survive in Italy, let alone conquer, was an extraordinary achievement rarely matched in history. When Belisarius finally arrived back in Constantinople, he learned that the Empress Theodora had died of the plague and for the next years he appears to have enjoyed the fruits of his labours as Chief of the Imperial Guard and General of the East.

But in 559 once again Constantinople was threatened when barbarians under Zabergan invaded the Byzantine Empire from the north and threatened the capital. Belisarius was recalled by Justinian and managed to raise an army of his old veterans plus citizens and refugees from the invading barbarians. He advanced towards the enemy and, by tricking them at night into thinking he was leading a much larger army, moved against them in a narrow gorge and drove them off.

Once again, Belisarius was a hero in Constantinople and his retirement with his now forgiven wife Antonina continued peacefully for another three years before he was falsely accused of being involved in a conspiracy against Justinian. The accusations were ludicrous, but the paranoid Emperor allowed them to continue to trial. The so-called conspirators were tried in front of the Prefect of Constantinople, who ironically was none other than Procopius of Caesarea, the former scribe and loyal companion of the general who had written a masterful history of the times and travelled with him on most of his campaigns, but, for some unknown reason, had fallen out with him. The defendants were all found guilty and sentenced to death, though Justinian allegedly had mercy on his loyal general and commuted his death sentence to blinding, a common punishment for patricians throughout Byzantine history. That such a brutal punishment was meted out without cause on such a loyal man is beyond comprehension. Those were different times. After some period of time begging on the streets, some of his fortune was returned to him and he was allowed to live out his days in his own home on the Asiatic side of the Bosphorus near where he was probably buried.

The Emperor Justinian the Great and his general, Consul Belisarius, both born in the same regions of the Balkans as Alexander the Great himself, together increased the size of the Byzantine Empire by nearly a half. They died within a few months of each other in 565. Justinian is remembered for the great Christian cathedral, Hagia Sophia, and the hugely important *Corpus Juris Civilis*, Belisarius is not remembered as he should be for his conquests, consummate military skills, fierce loyalty and personal bravery, which stand in history as impressive as any ancient religious building or books of laws. It is not for nothing that he is known as 'The Last of the Romans'.

3

BOHEMOND OF TARANTO, PRINCE OF ANTIOCH

1051–1111

> His stature was such that he towered almost a full cubit over the tallest men. He was slender of waist and flanks, with broad shoulders and chest. He was neither slim of form nor heavily built and fleshy, but perfectly proportioned; one might say that he conformed to the Polyclitean ideal... The skin all over his body was very white, except for his face which was both white and red... His eyes were light blue and gave some hint of the man's spirit and dignity.
>
> Anna Comnena, the *Alexiad*

The Crusades were some of the most dramatic and thought-provoking conflicts in human history. In their thousands, European emperors, kings, lords and knights, each with their private armies, descended on the Holy Land in pursuit of their Christian beliefs to pray at the Holy Sepulchre in Jerusalem and attempt to capture the Holy Places for Christendom. The fact that these Holy Places were also sacred to Judaism and Islam was at the root cause of the conflicts which continued on and off for the better part of five hundred years. Indeed, conflict about control of these Holy Places continues to the present day. The only successful crusade, or armed pilgrimage, if you want call it that, was the First Crusade called by the French Pope Urban II in a rousing speech made in the autumn of 1095 at Clermont, France, calling on the leaders of Christendom to free the Holy Places for pilgrims to visit safely. This followed a plea by the Eastern Orthodox prelates at the Council of Piacenza for help. Urban called the Crusade at this particular time for a number of reasons: to exercise his tenuous authority over the Christian kings of Europe, to help the Eastern Christian Church of Constantinople against the threat of the Moslem Turkish invasions, to facilitate the need for pilgrims to reach the Holy Land, and to establish Christian control in any form over the city of Jerusalem.

Many great leaders of the day rallied to the cause, the most willing of these and the best positioned geographically were the legendary Normans of the South. And the most renowned of this ambitious band of adventurers was Bohemond of Taranto, the first son of the infamous Robert Guiscard.

Deep in the south of Italy there is a small cathedral in a town called Canosa di Puglia, the Canusium, where the youthful Scipio Africanus repaired after the disaster at Cannae just ten miles away. Attached to the southern wall of the sturdy building is a strangely oriental-appearing mausoleum. Its magnificent green bronze doors are decorated with Arab designs and inscriptions and open to reveal a plain room supported by two simple columns, in the middle of which is a stone sarcophagus. Looking carefully in the windowless light, you can pick out nine crudely-carved letters: BOAMUNDUS. Their simplicity challenges the witness in this silent place to discover who this man was. Though a thousand years have passed since the body of Bohemond, Count of Taranto and Prince of Antioch, was laid to rest here, one cannot fail to be moved. On the doorway to the tomb is an inscription in ungrammatical Latin:

Magnanimus Sirie jacet hic sub tegmine princeps
Quo nullo melior nascetur in orbe deinceps.
Grecia victa quater, pars maxima Partia mundi

Ingenium et vires sensere diu Buamundi.
Hic acie in dena vicit virtutis arena
Agmina millena, quod et urbs sapit Antiochena.

Here lies the magnanimous prince of Syria
No better prince will be born in the world.
Greece vanquished four times, Parthia, the largest part of the world, experimented long with the genius and strengths of Bohemond.
Here with a troop of ten he vanquished armies of a thousand
And this the city of Antiochus knows.

The tomb of the great Bohemond is a haunting place. As you emerge into the harsh sunlight of Puglia from the relative cool of this mysterious tomb of a mysterious Norman warrior, some matters need explaining. Bohemond de Hauteville was a Norman, one of that illustrious band of brothers who changed European history a millennium ago, the greatest of whom, in British terms, was undoubtedly William the Conqueror. Bohemond was born in Calabria, the toe of Italy, in roughly 1055, a decade before the Battle of Hastings. His mother was Alberada of Buonalbergo, a high-born woman of Norman stock. This date enables us to envisage his costume and bearing from the very informative Tapestry of Bayeux, or more correctly Embroidery. There you can see the costumes, headdresses, footwear, weapons and military uniforms of the day. There is no reason to believe that the cousins of the men who fought at Hastings wore different clothes as they ventured into the Italian peninsula.

Most important to remember is that he was a member of the remarkable Hauteville family, originally from the Contenin peninsula in southern Normandy. He was the eldest son of Robert Guiscard 'The Cunning', Count of Apulia and Calabria. Because he was born in the family castle in San Marco Argentano, not surprisingly he was christened Mark, but his father called him Bohemond, the Giant, after a mythical monster. Nicknames were popular in the family; his father was known as the Weasel, his brother, the Accountant, and his cousin, Iron Arm. The name stuck, and his later deeds matched his physical presence. His father had arrived in Italy in 1049 with a small band of companions but in a short time had established himself as an accomplished warrior and a wily politician. In early medieval society, that was a formidable combination.

The Hauteville family's achievements in Southern Italy and beyond were truly remarkable. Like all the Normans, they were only two generations from their ancestors, the Vikings, or Norsemen, the legendary men from Scandinavia who had crossed the Atlantic Ocean and plagued Europe and the Mediterranean during the ninth century. Having sailed up the Seine into France, many had settled in the agreeable countryside of lush Normandy and within two centuries had conquered England, Southern Italy and Sicily. Initially, they had arrived as itinerant mercenaries, then began to set up their own fiefdoms. Unlike Duke William's conquest of England, the Normans of the South fought no decisive battle to gain control, rather land-grabbing piece by piece until the whole of Southern Italy and Sicily became one kingdom.

The forefather of this formidable and prolific family was a little-known Norman lord named Tancred of Hauteville who fathered twelve sons and a number of daughters with two wives. Ten of his sons emigrated to Southern Italy. Being nobles of modest means, Tancred's sons like many of their contemporaries had no alternative but to seek their fame and fortune as 'free lances', or soldiers of fortune. Southern Italy, the Mezzogiorno, was an ideal destination where the Byzantine Empire was weak and the Lombard lords not well established. Furthermore, the Church of Rome was keen to gain control in Apulia and Sicily where the Eastern Orthodox Church still held sway, not to speak of the strong Arab Moslem presence in Sicily. The determination of these Christian knights was further enhanced by the presence of a place of pilgrimage, a shrine to the Archangel Michael, the great adversary of Satan, established on Mount Gargano on the 'spur' of Italy. What more appropriate Holy Warrior could there be for the war-like Normans?

While Bohemond was still a young child, his father, due to consanguinity, separated from his mother Alberada and married the formidable Sikelgaita, a Lombard of noble birth, sister of the Prince of Salerno, and by all accounts an Amazon in bearing. Bohemond was now technically a bastard but, fortunately, in a short time, his mother remarried another cousin, Richard of Hauteville, which ensured that the young Bohemond was raised in knightly ways, always remaining his father's favourite son and serving under him. As the years passed, he grew into a powerfully built young man and before long was campaigning at his father's side throughout the south of the Italian peninsula. He had by now grown into the giant physical specimen that the contemporary historian, Anna Comnena, daughter of the Byzantine Emperor, later described.

In 1073, when Bohemond was probably just shy of twenty, Robert was taken seriously ill. Sikelgaita, a schemer as well as a warrior, summoned Robert's men to Bari to acknowledge that her eldest son, the young teenager Roger Borsa, the 'Accountant', would be his father's heir. What Bohemond thought of this arrangement, no chroniclers of the time venture a guess, but he must have realised at that moment that he would have to think differently about his future if the callow Roger was to be the next Count of Apulia. Anyway, Robert Guiscard survived his illness and, for the moment, the problem went way, but Bohemond realised that he would have to carve out a kingdom for himself in the future.

Once these southern lands of the *Mezzogiorno* had been brought under the control of the Roman Catholic Church, Robert Guiscard, now lord of Apulia and Calabria, and his cousin, Roger, ruling Sicily, began to look further afield to enlarge their lands. Like many of his tribe, he had great ambition and a restless *wanderlust*. Apulia and Calabria were not enough for him. In 1081, he ordered the still youthful Bohemond at the head of an army to cross the Adriatic Sea and make a landing in Epirus. This time Guiscard was going to invade the Byzantine Empire, which ruled much of Greece, the Balkans, Anatolia and the Middle East from Constantinople. Bohemond crossed the treacherous Straits of Otranto and captured Valona on the Epirus coast, then sailed north, avoiding contact with a well-defended Corfu, and landed at Butrinto. Guiscard arrived in the latter half of May with his troops and the combined Norman army then laid siege to Dyrrhachium, the most important Byzantine city on the coast of Epirus, with a window towards the West.

The Byzantine Emperor, Alexius I Comnenus, on succeeding to the throne had to decide which of his enemies he had to deal with first: the ever-advancing Turks who were a threat from central Anatolia, or the Normans of Southern Italy who were constantly impinging on his fiefdoms there. Now they were attacking in Epirus on the Greek mainland. Alexius, an experienced soldier himself, judged the Normans to be the most immediate threat and led an army towards the Adriatic coast, where he arrived in the autumn of 1081. On 18 October, the Byzantines advanced against the much smaller Norman army. Guiscard commanded the Norman centre, with the formidable Sichelgaita, in full armour, next to him. Bohemond commanded the inland left flank. This was his first experience of a pitched battle with two large armies facing each other on open ground. The armies were quite unused to the sight of the other, the Byzantines, wearing unfamiliar chain-mail, supported by ranks of Turkish bowmen, and the Normans clad in their familiar steel helmets, some with nose-guards, tapered great shields and massive swords. At first the Emperor's men led by the formidable Varangian Guard, mainly made up of exiled Anglo-Saxons, wielding their giant two-edged axes, forced the Normans into retreat into the sea. According to Anna Comnena, this crisis for the Normans was averted by Sichelgaita herself:

> Directly, Sichelgaita, Robert's wife, saw these soldiers running away, she looked fiercely after them and in a very powerful voice called out to them in her own language, 'How far will you flee? Stand and acquit you like men!' And when she saw that they continued to run, she grasped a long spear and at full gallop rushed after the fugitives; and on seeing this they recovered themselves and returned to the fight.

At that moment, Bohemond's flank with units of crossbowmen wheeled to help avert the crisis and soon the danger had passed, with the Normans now in the ascendant. The retreating foot soldiers of the Byzantine army were forced to take refuge in the nearby chapel of St Michael. The Normans set fire to the building, killing all of them. The Anglo-Saxon soldiers who had sought happier hunting grounds far from England had once again met their nemesis in the form of the all-conquering Normans. Bohemond had now taken part in a victory in battle against a formidable enemy. It is worth remembering that in this same battle the Emperor Alexius, already a seasoned campaigner, saw for himself what formidable warriors the Normans truly were. And Bohemond was the quintessential Norman commander.

After a siege through the winter months, Dyrrhachium was captured on 21 February 1082. The Normans then began to advance on the Via Egnatia, the ancient road that had connected Rome to Constantinople. It was along that same road that Mark Antony and Octavius had marched in relentless pursuit of Brutus and Cassius after the murder of Julius Caesar.

The Normans now marched deep into the rugged country of Illyria to Kastorias, before Guiscard was compelled to return to Southern Italy, where there was unrest among some of his Greek citizens. In addition, the German Emperor Henry IV had invaded Italy once again and Pope Gregory VII had to summon Count Robert for help. Bohemond, now in charge of the whole Norman army, advanced deeper into Macedonia, defeating the Byzantines at Ioannina and Arta. At the beginning of November 1082, as winter closed in, Bohemond laid siege to the city of Larissa. This winter siege took its toll both on the defenders of the city and on the attackers. It was fully six months before Alexius could raise an army and advance against the Normans, and it was summer before he decided to drive off the besieging army. But the poor morale and lack of military experience of the Byzantine troops necessitated Alexius using guile rather than brute force to defeat the Normans.

Feigning a full attack, complete with false Imperial flags and trumpets, the Byzantines drew the Normans into a counter-attack and at once withdrew to a position where Alexius and his best troops were waiting. It was a trap and, inevitably, Bohemond's aggressive impulses led him into it. As the Normans advanced, they were surprised by a flank attack from the Byzantine infantry. They drove them off but were surprised by their use of caltrops, deadly metal spikes, which impeded their horses. The next day, the Byzantines again attacked with mounted archers. The Normans formed a phalanx with their great shields. But this tactic fell apart when their standard bearer was killed and they were forced to retreat. Alexius had succeeded in driving off the invading Normans.

In the heat of summer and far from home, the Norman soldiery became restless. Without pay and often bribed by the Byzantines, many of these mercenaries, for that is what they were, soldiers of fortune, deserted, so Bohemond wisely cut his losses and retreated to the coast before returning to Apulia.

The following year, 1084, the restless Normans again harassed the Byzantines when capturing the fortress of Corfu and driving off the Venetian fleet which had arrived in support of their Byzantine trading partners. But an epidemic, probably typhoid, broke out in the Norman army and Bohemond himself fell seriously ill before returning to Apulia before Christmas that year.

Six months later on 17 July 1085 Guiscard died in Cephalonia while on campaign off the Greek coast. He was sixty-seven years old. Sikelgaita and her son, Roger Borsa, swiftly returned to the Italian mainland where his succession was confirmed by the Norman barons. For the next decade the Bohemond was left frustrated and quarrelled frequently with his half-brother, despite their holding a meeting at their father's tomb in Venosa. Borsa now held the title of Duke of Apulia and Calabria, succeeding his father, and there was nothing much Bohemond could do about it.

In October 1095, a momentous event changed history. Pope Urban II, a Frenchman, having been approached for help by the Eastern Church at the Council of Piacenza earlier in the year, made a legendary speech at Clermont calling for the leaders of Christian Europe to join a crusade and put a stop to the Muslim maltreatment of Christian pilgrims to the Holy Land. Though he may have heard rumours, it appears Bohemond was not aware of these momentous events for a whole year. It was not directly from the Pope, nor wandering preachers, that the Normans of Southern Italy heard of the crusade, but from French crusaders who had already taken the cross. In October 1096, Prince Hugh of Vermandois, younger brother of King Philip of France, travelled through Rome leading his troops into southern Italy on his way to Bari, seeking sea transportation to Dyrrhachium.

The Hauteville family, including Roger of Sicily, Borsa and Bohemond, were at full strength besieging Amalfi when the Crusaders passed by. Bohemond listened intently to their words: 'We are well-armed, we wear the badge of Christ's cross on our right arm or between our shoulders, and as a war-cry we shout all together "God's will (Deus vult), God's will, God's will!" which is what the believers cried after the Pope's summon to arms in Clermont.' Apparently inspired by the Holy Ghost, Bohemond ordered the most valuable red cloak he owned to be cut up and made into crosses to be sewn onto their white tunics, and most of the knights who were at the siege joined him, full of religious fervour.

Another, more sceptical opinion of Bohemond's motives comes from contemporary chronicler Goffredo Malaterra, who viewed Bohemond as a potential usurper of the legitimate inheritance rights of Duke Roger Borsa in Apulia:

> Bohemond previously, along with his father Guiscard, had invaded the Byzantine Empire, and had always wanted to conquer it for himself. Seeing a great multitude of people travelling through Apulia but lacking a leader, he hastened back, and wishing to be the army's leader and to make them his followers, placed the badge of this expedition, namely the cross, on his garments. The warlike young men of the whole army, both from Borsa's army and Count Roger's were keen on anything new, as is the custom nowadays, and when they saw Bohemond's cross and were summoned by him to follow his example, they eagerly flocked to do so. Hence they

> assumed the cross, and immediately bound themselves by a vow to make no further attack on any Christian land until they had reached the land of the pagans.

The Norman siege of Amalfi faded into nothing as many of the besieging soldiers slipped away and joined Bohemond's army. His time had come.

During the ensuing weeks he returned to his lands to prepare himself for the great pilgrimage. His nobles, led by his formidable nephew, Tancred, did likewise. It is estimated that he raised an army of about seven hundred knights plus maybe five thousand infantrymen. This force, though comparatively small in number, was made up of experienced and ruthless soldiers, fresh from numerous battles, sieges and campaigns all across Sicily, Apulia and Calabria. Furthermore, they were led by two formidable commanders, Bohemond and Tancred, who they would willingly follow to the ends of the earth in pursuit of Christian righteousness, treasures and land.

Late in 1096 they crossed the Adriatic from Bari and landed at various points along the coast of Epirus. This time, unlike their previous landings there, they came as allies and were met by John Comnenus, nephew of the Emperor, and the local governor. During the next few months they made the difficult winter crossing over snow-covered mountains, fast flowing rivers and through hostile inhabitants, towards Thrace, the north-eastern part of Greece, where they arrived on 1 April 1097.

Bohemond, realising he needed to have the ear of the Byzantines before the other Christian leaders arrived, hurried ahead of his army and was admitted to the presence of the Emperor Alexius on 10 April. Alexius was well aware of the abilities and strengths of Bohemond; after all, they had met in combat on a number of occasions. He knew he was a dangerous man, ambitious, wily and unscrupulous, formerly an enemy, but now an ally in their common cause of freeing the Holy Land from the control of the non-believers. He was popular with his men, who trusted him implicitly. He also had charm and good looks which Anna Comnena, the teenage daughter of the Emperor, did not hesitate to remark on, despite the fact that she distrusted him. Some years later she wrote:

> Bohemond's appearance was, to put it briefly, unlike that of any man seen those days in the Roman world, whether Greek or barbarian. The sight of him inspired admiration, the mention of his name terror. I will describe in detail the barbarian's characteristic. His stature was such that he towered almost a full cubit over the tallest men. He was slender of waist and flanks, with broad shoulders and chest, strong in the arms; in general he was neither slim of form nor heavily built and fleshy, but perfectly proportioned – one might say that he conformed to the Polyclitean ideal. His hands were large, he had a good firm stance, and his neck and back were compact. The skin all over his body was very white, except for his face which was both white and red. His hair was lightish-brown and not as long as other barbarians; in fact the man had no great predilection for long hair, but cut his short, to the ears. Whether his beard was red or of any other colour I cannot say, for the razor had attacked it, leaving his chin smoother than any marble. However, it appeared to be red. His eyes were light-blue and gave some hint of the man's spirit and dignity. He breathed freely through nostrils that were broad, worthy of his chest and a fine outlet for the breath that came in gusts from his lungs. There was a certain charm about him, but it was somewhat dimmed by the alarm that his person as a whole inspired; there was a hard, savage quality in his whole aspect, due, I suppose to his great stature and his eyes; even his laugh sounded like a threat to others. Such was his constitution, mental and physical, that in him both courage and love were armed, both ready for combat. His arrogance was everywhere manifest; he was cunning, too, taking refuge quickly in any opportunism. His words were carefully phrased and the replies her gave were regularly ambiguous. Only one man, the Emperor, could defeat an adversary of such character, an adversary as great as Bohemond.

Clearly, whether as a friend or as an enemy, Bohemond was no man to trifle with. One wonders what hyperboles Anna Comnena would have used had he been a proven ally. In any event Bohemond, aware of the power of the Byzantine Emperor, quickly gave his oath of fealty and even requested that he be appointed the Grand Domestic of the East or Commander in Chief of the Crusading army. Alexius prevaricated here but made tempting promises to Bohemond. Once the agreement had been made between them, Alexius quickly organised for Bohemond and his army to cross over the Bosphorus into Asia where the great crusading army was being assembled – and where they might cause less trouble than in the streets of Constantinople.

To complete a journey across the great expanse of Anatolia, from the borders of Europe deep into the Middle East, the first objective of the Crusaders was to take Nicaea, the capital of the Seldjuk Turkish Sultan, Qilij Arslan, situated on the Ascanian lake only two days march from Constantinople. There was no way they could risk leaving this great fortress in enemy hands blocking their safety route back to Christian Constantinople. By early May 1097 the crusader armies were in position around the forbidding Byzantine-built walls of the ancient city where the Nicene Creed, that triumph of Christian theological thinking, had been formulated seven hundred years before.

None of the Crusaders had ever seen such a giant fortress: the walls were four miles around with two hundred and forty towers. Duke Godfrey of Lorraine alongside his younger brother, Baldwin, and Count Robert of Flanders, positioned his army opposite the northern wall, The Normans of the South led by Bohemond and Tancred took the eastern wall and Count Raymond of Toulouse with his Provencal army took the southern wall. Duke Robert of Normandy, Prince Hugh of Vermandois and Count Stephen of Blois reinforced them. The Sultan immediately attempted to relieve the city, where his wife and children were trapped, and there was heavy fighting before the Turks finally were driven off. The crusaders then used their siege guns to lob the decapitated heads of the enemy into the city as a warning.

By mid-June, the crusaders planned to storm the fortress. But they were outwitted by the Emperor Alexius, who was keen not to let the crusaders take control of Nicaea, so sent a flotilla of boats, dragged overland from the shores of the Bosphorus by oxen, which were launched quietly into Lake Askania. At daybreak on 18 June they set sail across the lake towards Nicaea's waterfront walls. Crewed with heavily armed Imperial turcopole mercenaries, the vessels floated ominously into view of Nicaea's defenders. On the landward side, a heavy assault by siege towers and catapults was taking place. The defenders, realising they were facing a catastrophe, quickly surrendered; but it was to the Byzantines rather than the menacing and barbaric crusaders. When this became known to such men as Tancred, all across the crusader armies there was resentment at not being able to sack the city and benefit from pillage.

Alexius meanwhile was monitoring events well behind the frontlines, from the safety of a gigantic palace-like marquee, complete with central cupola, which took twenty camels to transport. His ambassador to the crusader leaders was the extraordinary-looking Arab-Greek general, Tatikios, who had fought against Bohemond's father, Robert, in the 1080s, and who stood out by virtue of wearing a false nose made of gold.

The frustrated crusaders were now well rewarded by Alexius in his elaborate tent with fantastic treasures taken from the Turkish leaders of the city. In return for these gifts, many of the lesser crusaders were compelled to pay homage to the Emperor. The hot-blooded Tancred, who had avoided taking an oath in Constantinople, demanded more than his share of the spoils and was upbraided by the Emperor's brother-in-law. The Norman, as though in a bar-room brawl, threatened him and an unruly scene was only averted by Bohemond, who sharply reproved his nephew, forcing him to reluctantly pay homage. This did not augur well for the future relationship between the crusaders and the Byzantines. The truth is that the crusaders distrusted the Byzantines with their mysterious Eastern Orthodox Christianity, unimpressive military prowess and diplomatic trickery, while the Byzantines considered the crusaders brutish barbarians only useful to oust the Turks from their borders. They both had a point.

Now, in high summer, not an ideal time to travel in the Near East, the march began across the harsh Anatolian plain towards Antioch more than a thousand kilometres away. Bohemond, in command of the leading army, camped for the night in desolate country only two days out from Nicaea, near a place called Dorylaeum.

At sunrise the Turks attacked with mounted archers sweeping in to release their arrows at the ambushed crusaders. Icy calm, Bohemond placed all the non-combatant pilgrims in the middle of his men, getting them to bring up water and food when needed, having first dispatched a messenger to call his co-crusaders to come swiftly to his aid. His men clustered behind their great Norman shields as best they could, save one foolhardy knight who charged out into the enemy lines and was ignominiously driven back. It was this same unnamed character who had loutishly slouched with his feet up on the Emperor's throne in Constantinople and had been admonished by Bohemond. Once a fool, always a fool.

From dawn to midday, the Turks harassed the Normans until the supporting armies of Duke Godfrey and Prince Hugh arrived on the battlefield. The Turks were taken aback by the arrival of these forces, thinking they had trapped the whole crusader army. The crusaders quickly formed up in full battle order in the blazing midday heat, with Bohemond, Robert of Normandy and Count Stephen of Blois on the left, Count Raymond and Robert of Flanders in the centre and Duke Godfrey and Prince Hugh on the right. They must have presented a formidable sight with their pennants, flags, and shining armour bright in the sun. Then, just as the Turks began to advance a shout went up: someone had seen another army, led by the intrepid crusader the Bishop of Le Puy, appear on the hills behind them. This was too much, and the Turkish army panicked and fled, leaving their camp in its entirety with all the treasures of the Sultan. Once again, the crusaders were rewarded for their efforts. They had won a great combined victory and cleared the road ahead, since any opposition now feared them. But if it had not been for Bohemond and his battle-hardened Southern Normans holding out valiantly against enormous odds on that first morning, it is doubtful if the Turks would have been defeated.

Now Bohemond and his fellow leaders made the great journey across the plains of Anatolia and through the gorges of the Taurus Mountains down into the Cilician Plain on the shores of the Eastern Mediterranean, where the coastline turns southwards towards the Holy Land. The achievement of reaching Antioch by mid-October was remarkable in itself, considering they had travelled in the heat of summer across such barren country with little food or forage for horses, often encountering poisoned wells and sometimes being harassed by swift and sudden attacks by Turkish cavalry units. Some support was given by the Byzantines, with few troops but the reassuring presence of the experienced Tatikios, who had made this journey before. Despite their hardships, many of the crusaders and the pilgrims amongst them felt they were now truly on their way to the Holy Land. As they marched into northern Syria they passed the site of Alexander the Great's victory over the Persians at Issus thirteen centuries before, and as they slowly descended into the plain of the Orontes river they saw the mighty walls of Antioch before them, built by the Emperor Justinian

Bohemond must have wondered whether this legendary city could be where he could make his mark on history. Currently it was a vulnerable place vacated by Byzantines and occupied by local Turkish warlords. But its geographical location at the crossroads of Europe and Asia gave it an imposing strategic position and maybe he could make it strong again, even recreate the Seleucid Empire south into the Holy Land, west across Anatolia and east into Asia.

Bohemond was a man with great ambitions and, thus far, few opportunities to achieve them. His nephew Tancred was right behind him in every move he made. Antioch had been one of the great cities of ancient times, founded in 300 BC by Seleucus I Nicator of Syria, one of Alexander the Great's captains, the Diodachi, and named after his father Antiochus. During the Roman Empire it had been the third city in the world after Rome and Alexandria and St Peter had founded his first bishopric there, where those who followed Jesus Christ were first named Christians. In recent times the city had fallen on harder times with its capture by the Turks and a series of earthquakes, but it was still a formidable fortress on the corner of northern Syria at the crossroads where the Byzantine and Turkish Empires met. Trade from the Mediterranean into Asia could make the city rich.

The crusaders prepared themselves for a long siege and Bohemond brought to bear all his military and political experience to bring about the surrender of the city, not to the crusaders, but to him personally. He planned to emulate what he had seen Alexius achieve at Nicaea not too long ago. The Turcoman governor of the city, Yaghi-Syan, expected the crusaders to attack immediately, and the bellicose, one-eyed Count Raymond suggested this. But the other leaders listened to Bohemond who proposed they wait for Tancred and his men to join them from Alexandretta, plus possibly the Byzantines with their formidable siege engines and forces, and even a Genoese fleet rumoured to be in the region. The siege was to last nine months through the hard winter of 1097-8. Though the Genoese fleet had arrived at St Symeon, just ten miles away, bringing men and armaments, by December starvation amongst the men and their horses was setting in and rations were running short.

So Bohemond and Count Robert of Flanders set out on a foraging expedition towards Hama at the head of an army. The following night, Yaghi Syan attacked the remaining crusaders and there ensued a desperate fight in which at one moment the crusaders had almost forced the open gates and at the next they themselves were facing defeat. Meanwhile, Bohemond was taken by surprise by a relieving Muslim army led by the Emir of Damascus. Count Robert's army was quickly surrounded, but Bohemond charged the enemy at their moment of victory and drove them off. They retreated towards Hama and Bohemond, realising he was deep in enemy territory, turned back.

Arriving back in Antioch he learned of the desperate battle before the walls where Raymond had almost lost his life. There had also been an earth-tremor which had unnerved the crusaders, always looking for signs. In the following weeks starvation set in, decimating the army and killing off many of the horses. Many deserted, including Peter the Hermit and William the Carpenter, both charismatic preachers of the crusade. Tancred hunted them down and they were brought before Bohemond, who chastised them with brutal threats. Realising their position was desperate, it was agreed that their spiritual leader, Bishop Adhemar, should make a plea for help to the West. Then the Emperor's representative Tatikios abruptly left the crusade and took ship to Cyprus, ostensibly to get help. The story goes, which there is no reason to disbelieve, that Bohemond summoned him one night telling him that there was going to be another Turkish attack encouraged by the Emperor and that the rumour going about was that the crusaders were going to kill him in revenge. Tatikios promptly left and once he had gone, Bohemond declared he had betrayed them, as had the Emperor, and therefore the Crusade was free from any obligation to the Emperor.

In early February another Turkish army, under Emir Riwan of Aleppo, approached and again Bohemond saved the crusading armies when he, at the head of seven hundred knights, put the enemy to flight. Once more the occupants of Antioch came out and attacked the crusaders in savage fighting.

Finally, Bohemond, always conscious that cunning was as good a quality as courage in medieval warfare, made secret contacts within the city and on the night of 2 June, with Kerbogha, Atabeg of Mosul, reported to be on his way with a large army, Bohemond made his move. Bohemond had bribed an Armenian convert to Islam, named Firouz, who commanded the Tower of the Two Sisters, to let a small band of crusaders including Fulcher of Chartres into the city. Firstly, he called a meeting with his fellow leaders telling them his plan. He needed their help. The crusader army, in a big show, made a fake advance eastwards, ostensibly to meet Kerbogha. That night they crept back under the city walls and once Firouz let them in, the crusaders scaled the walls and entered the city, opening the gates to the main body of crusaders. A savage massacre followed, and within hours Bohemond's purple standard was flying high above the city. Only the citadel continued to hold out.

Kerbogha, Atabeg of Mosul arrived the next day and laid siege to the city. The crusaders were now the besieged rather than the besiegers. Rather than be starved into submission, in habitual fashion, Bohemond persuaded his fellow leaders to counter-attack immediately. Within weeks the crusaders advanced out of the city and put the enemy to flight. On their return the Arab commander of the citadel refused to surrender to anyone but Bohemond, which he duly did.

But there was a problem. The crusaders had all taken an oath to the Emperor to return the city to Byzantine rule. Bohemond now argued that their oaths to Alexius were invalid. He had not come to help them in their hours of need and his representative, Tatikios, had abandoned them and fled to Cyprus.

Bohemond was the man that most of the knights and foot soldiers trusted as their leader. They believed he should have the city. After all, he had planned its capture, it was to him that the citadel had surrendered, it was he who had driven off the attacking Turks with no help from the Byzantines. But Count Raymond did not agree. In Constantinople he had bonded with Alexius, and along with Bishop Adhemar did not want to give up the idea of the crusade as Western Christendom fighting alongside Eastern Christendom against a common enemy. Pope Urban II would want that.

By taking Antioch for himself, Bohemond threatened that whole idea. Hugh of Vermandois was sent as an emissary to Alexius to explain the situation. The crusaders still believed the Emperor was on his way to support them, not knowing that he had already turned back after his meeting with Stephen of Blois, who was returning to France.

The exhausted army rested at Antioch until 1 November before advancing to the Holy City. Hugh only arrived in late autumn in

Constantinople and by then, with winter setting in, the earliest the Emperor could be expected in Antioch would be in the spring. Meanwhile relations between Raymond and Bohemond continued to deteriorate, though Bohemond was clearly in the strongest position, especially as the ageing Raymond and Bishop Adhemar both fell sick. Some knights had ventured off to join Baldwin, who had taken Edessa, east of Aleppo, as his personal fiefdom. With the summer heat setting in, disease was rife and eventually Bishop Adhemar died on 1 August 1098. The whole crusader army was disquieted by his death; he was the personally appointed emissary of the pope on the crusade and was a worthy Christian priest respected by all, even Bohemond and his men, but also a good soldier who had been hugely instrumental in the victory at Dorylaeum. Most importantly, he gave a religious credibility to the whole crusade and often kept the political squabbles between the main protagonists from boiling over.

Finally, on 13 January 1099, fifteen months since they had arrived before the walls of Antioch, Count Raymond of Toulouse, barefoot as a true Christian pilgrim, set off on the final part of the journey towards Jerusalem leading his fellow Provencals. Robert Curthose, Duke of Normandy, followed, accompanied by Tancred, probably acting as Bohemond's eyes on what was to occur in Jerusalem. Duke Godfrey of Lorraine and Count Robert of Flanders set off some weeks later. Bohemond, the greatest warrior and the most effective commander of them all, stayed behind. Bohemond was now to become the Prince of Antioch. For the time being he remained there, with Baldwin doing likewise in Edessa. These two warlords, both born without inherited lands, Bohemond as illegitimate, Baldwin as a younger son, had now staked their claims in these harsh new lands.

Six months later, on 17 July 1099, Jerusalem fell to the crusaders amidst scenes of fearful massacre as the blood-soaked Christian crusaders knelt in prayer at the Church of the Holy Sepulchre. Far away in Rome, Pope Urban, who had started the great undertaking, died before learning of his triumph.

Before his death he had appointed Archbishop Daimbert of Pisa as Papal Legate to the Holy Land, replacing the unfortunate Bishop Adhemar. Daimbert sailed for the Middle East with the Pisan fleet, which promptly went to Bohemond's aid in his attack on Lattakie in Syria, the best port for Antioch, controlled by the Byzantines. Count Raymond, along with Robert of Normandy and Robert of Flanders, realising that if their aspirations were to be fulfilled they would need the help of the Byzantines, summoned Daimbert to Jabala. On his arrival, they complained that Bohemond's ambitions were endangering the whole crusading movement. As a result, Bohemond withdrew to Antioch where he installed Daimbert as the Latin Primate. Robert of Normandy and Robert of Flanders now sailed home via Constantinople, where they were cordially received by Alexius. What was clear at this point was that some of the crusade leaders had come on the journey to free Jerusalem as pilgrims, and others had come to stay.

In the weeks before Christmas, to fulfil his original vows, Bohemond travelled with Daimbert and Baldwin to Jerusalem, where they prayed at the Holy Sepulchre and spent Christmas Day at Bethlehem. He had now fulfilled his duty as a Christian.

In the summer of 1100, he made a fatal blunder. Asked for help by Gabriel, the Armenian lord of Mitelene, against the constant attacks of the Danishmend Turk Gumushtekin, Emir of Siwa, he rode northwards with Richard of Salerno and a few hundred knights, deep into the rugged wooded ravines of the upper Euphrates in central Anatolia. His decision was impulsive, as had been many of the decisions in his life, but this time it did not pay off. He and his small band were ambushed in terrain where the powerful impact of a Norman charge was ineffective. Aware that he was in mortal danger, he sent a messenger to Baldwin in Edessa advising him of his plight. Bohemond and Richard of Salerno were taken prisoner while many of his companions, including Bishop Cyprien of Antioch and Bishop Gregory of Marash, were promptly executed. The survivors were marched northwards to the Turkish fortress of Niksar, the former capital of the legendary Mithradates,

King of Pontus, the great opponent of the Roman Empire during the 1st century BC

Within days, Baldwin of Edessa set off with an army to save Bohemond. He attacked the Turks outside Mitelene, breaking the siege, but the enemy had already fled north taking Bohemond and Richard with them. Baldwin pursued them for three days but had to break off the rescue attempt, fearing his small party might also be ambushed in the rugged passes of the Pontus Mountains. Little is known about what happened to Bohemond during those desperate three years chained up in a remote fortress far from help. The imprisonment of Richard the Lionheart a century later springs to mind. Even great commanders can be brought low.

Endless negotiations for Bohemond's ransom were conducted between Gumushtekin, his captor, of the Danishmend Turks, the constantly interfering Byzantine Emperor Alexius, and Baldwin of Edessa. As soon as the news reached Alexius of his enemy's imprisonment, he sent emissaries offering 260,000 dinars as a ransom. Word soon got out to the Turkish Seljuk Emir in Anatolia. He warned Gumushtekin, leader of what he considered a junior branch of the Turks, the Danishmends, that he would want half of the ransom. The bartering continued until finally the frustrated Bohemond, chained in his dungeon, took control. He demanded to see his captor and Gumushtekin complied. Never was a prisoner more the captor than the captive. Bohemond realised that the Danishmend Turks were forever in the shadow of their more successful cousins based in their capital of Nicaea. They resented them and Gumushkin objected to having to give half of the ransom away.

Bohemond solved the problem. He, by way of his allies at Edessa and Antioch, Baldwin and Tancred, would undertake the ransom of 130,000 dinars himself. The deal was done and in March 1103, Bohemond and Richard of Salerno were released.

Bohemond now travelled back to Antioch and once more triumphantly entered the city that, just five years before, he had claimed as his own fiefdom. Talking with the ever-loyal Tancred, who had ruled the city in his absence, he quickly became aware of the impossibility of raising even small groups of warriors, let alone a full army. The Principality of Antioch, as were all the crusader enclaves, was constantly under threat either from local Turkish or Arab leaders, or the Byzantines. He determined to return to Europe once more to call men to arms as reinforcements in support of those brave men who had campaigned on the First Crusade.

In fact, there were many who had abandoned it, in particular Count Stephen of Blois, later to become the father of a King of England, who on his return from the crusade was so chastised by his formidable wife, Adela, the daughter of William the Conqueror, that he was compelled to go on the next crusade called by Bohemond. All crusaders had taken a vow when going on a crusade to liberate the Holy Land from the oppression of the Muslims and, equally important, to kneel at the tomb of Christ. Only then could they call themselves true pilgrims.

Bohemond set off for Apulia in 1104 and, with the blessing of the new Pope Paschal III in Rome, travelled north to France, the land of his ancestors, where he regaled his hosts with tales of adventure in the Holy Land where the good fight could be fought and land could be acquired. He even showed them relics he had acquired on his travels. This charismatic giant of a man, handsome and with a commanding voice but also aware of courtly manners, must have been hard to resist. The King of England, Henry I, is supposed to have banned him from coming to his shores for fear of him marching off with many of his best knights. At the court of King Philip of France, Bohemond met and wooed Constance, the beautiful sister of the king, and they were married in a great ceremony in Chartres Cathedral. Bohemond also found a suitable wife for his nephew Tancred, Cecile of France, Constance's younger sister. They travelled south together to Apulia and soon Constance gave birth to a son also called Bohemond. The continuance of the house of Antioch was assured.

In 1107, with his newly recruited troops, rather than returning to the Holy Land Bohemond chose once again to wage war on his old nemesis, the Emperor Alexius. On 9 October, having put things in place in Apulia, he set sail once more for Epirus. Landing at Avlona he again besieged Dyrrachium, but this time the city would not surrender and his starving army suffered a serious setback when an epidemic broke out, and soon Bohemond, surely now exhausted by his endless campaigning, realised there was no way forward militarily. He had underestimated the resilience of the Byzantines. The Emperor invited the now ageing Norman warlord to negotiate with him at Diabolis further inland on the Via Egnatia. The tables had turned in the more than twenty years that had passed since Guiscard and Bohemond's great victory at Dyrrachium.

At the negotiations, Bohemond was at once accused of betraying the oath he had taken in Constantinople to Alexius in 1097. His response was that this had been nullified by the fact that in 1098 Alexius had himself broken his promise of support for the crusaders when he failed to help them at Antioch.

The Treaty of Diabolis of 1108 was a final humiliation for Bohemond. Firstly he had to become a vassal not only of Alexius but also his son when he inherited would be paid a retainer to defend the Empire whenever required. In return he was recognised as the Prince of Antioch by the Byzantines and was also granted the fiefs of Antioch and Aleppo, the first of which he already controlled, and the second he would have to conquer. In return, he should return various Cilician cities on his borders to the Byzantines. Furthermore, he had to allow Alexius to appoint a Greek Patriarch in Antioch, ending his quest to impose the Latin Church in his Principality. The treaty was a disaster for Bohemond, nullifying much of what had achieved. Now more than fifty years old, it seemed as though his battered body had lived more than twice that long, so he once more crossed the Adriatic back to Apulia, dying in Bari in 1111. His death was his last strike at the Byzantine Empire, since the terms of the Treaty of Diabolis only applied to him and not his successors. Antioch, under the rule of Tancred, Roger of Salerno and Bohemond's son, Bohemond II, was to remain a Western enclave.

Bohemond of Taranto, Prince of Antioch, was truly one of the great men of his age. If he was less successful than William the Conqueror or Robert Guiscard, his father, the other two great Norman conquerors, he played for higher stakes than the former and with lesser means at his disposal than the latter. If he had not been captured at Mitelene and had succeeded in his final attack on the Byzantine Empire, who knows what he might have achieved? After all, from the West he controlled Apulia and to the East he controlled Antioch. Maybe he might have created a new Seleucid Empire stretching from Southern Italy to Baghdad and beyond. He certainly had the vision and capability of achieving things beyond the ability of most men.

4

ALBRECHT WENZEL EUSEBIUS VON WALLENSTEIN 1583–1634

In Wallenstein were embodied the fateful forces of his time.
Theodore Rabb

Albrecht Wallenstein is one of the more sinister characters in European history. There is something of the night about him. Fine paintings and lithographs of him are few and far between and those that exist accentuate his saturnine features, his black hair in a widow's peak, his menace. He was tall with dark and glowering features, dressing normally in black with a flash of crimson on a sash or a plume. He ruled by fear rather than by persuasion and became one of the central figures of the bloody Thirty Years' War. Though born into an impoverished Protestant noble family, he rose to become the supreme commander of the Catholic Imperial Army of the Holy Roman Empire and one of the richest and most influential men in Germany during the war.

Albrecht Wallenstein was born on 24 September 1583 in Heřmanice Castle in Bohemia, twenty years before the death of Elizabeth I of England, to place him in time. His parents both died before he became a teenager. From early childhood he was fluent in German and Czech, though he preferred to blaspheme in Czech.

His uncles had him educated at schools run by the Protestant Bohemian Brethren according to his parents' religion, and in 1599 he began to attend the Protestant University of Altdorf near Nuremberg in Franconia, where as a young student he joined in the drinking, duelling, and murderous brawls, leading to a brief period of imprisonment in the town jail. Another more concerning tale of his youth tells of how he assaulted his manservant so badly that not only did he have to pay a large fine but also was ordered to purchase the poor fellow a new set of clothes. After a brief time in Altdorf, Wallenstein began to travel in Europe, as many students did in those days, studying intermittently in Bologna and Padua. It is sometimes said that it was while he was in Italy his obsession for horoscopes began, though this is more likely to have occurred when he began his association with the celebrated astronomer Johannes Kepler in Prague.

Aged twenty, in 1604 Wallenstein enrolled as a soldier in the army of the Emperor Rudolf II, commanded by Giorgio Basta. In the campaign in Western Hungary, Basta and his army were excessively brutal in their dealings with the Turks and in particular with Protestant rebels fighting against the Hapsburgs. During this time Wallenstein must have realised that to reach high office in the service of the Hapsburgs, you had to be a Catholic. Within two years he had returned to his studies and enrolled at the Catholic University of Olomouc in Moravia, run by the Jesuits, founded less than twenty years before in an attempt by the authorities to push back against the large majority of Protestants in Bohemia and Moravia.

In 1606 he graduated and soon after converted officially to Catholicism. Whether you accept that this turnabout was brought about by the Virgin Mary apparently saving his life when he fell drunkenly from a window in Innsbruck, or that he was an intelligent Protestant masquerading as a Catholic for his own future ambitions, is moot. Certainly, Wallenstein was no Catholic saint with a Road to Damascus conversion.

In 1607, Wallenstein, now 27 years old, was made a chamberlain at the court of the Archduke Matthias, later to become Emperor in

1612. He also became a chamberlain to the Archduke Ferdinand II of Styria, the father-in-law of Matthias and Maximilian, the younger brother of the Emperor, based on recommendations by the influential aristocrat Karel of Zierotin. Two years later, Wallenstein, now a well-connected young courtier, married the older wealthy widow Lucretia of Víckov, who owned substantive lands in Moravia. She died five years later, and Wallenstein used his new wealth to win favours. He commanded a unit of two hundred cavalry for Archduke Ferdinand in his campaign against Venice in 1617, relieving the fortress of Gradisca in Istria from a Venetian siege.

The following year, 1618, the Thirty Years' War broke out, one of the most devastating wars in European history, in which tens of thousands of innocent civilians died either by the murderous brutality of mercenary armies or by fire or starvation; harvests were trampled upon and cities sacked. It was effectively the military and political result of the theological arguments that had torn Europe apart during the previous hundred years, which were not even fully resolved even when hostilities finally ended in 1648. The Civil War in England which followed was an addendum to those political and religious arguments which had torn Europe apart.

Wallenstein was in Bohemia when hostilities first broke out and was murdered sixteen years later in 1634, fourteen years before the brutal wars finally ended. He was to play a major role in three of the four main alignments of the conflict. This ruthless commander did as much as anyone to set the merciless tone of the conflict.

When the Estates of Bohemia rebelled against Ferdinand II in 1618 and elected Frederick V of the Palatinate, the leader of the Protestant Union, as their new King, Wallenstein associated himself with the Catholic cause and the Habsburg dynasty. Clearly it was a choice of Catholicism or Protestantism, but for many nobles this was not a theological question, but rather a decision as to where the ultimate power lay. Count Jindrich Mathias Thurn led 10,000 troops into Moravia to secure their loyalty to the rebellion and was one of the Protestant leaders involved in the defenestration of the Imperial representatives in Prague after they had refused

Protestant requests for freedom of worship. Nobles who wished for a rapprochement with Ferdinand now faced a choice.

Zierotin's son-in-law, Georg von Nachod, commanding the Moravian cavalry, and his brother-in-law, Wallenstein commanding the infantry decided to take their regiments into Austria. But von Nachod's troops rebelled and he fled for his life. Now Wallenstein's second-in-command demanded that he gain permission from the people of the Estates before marching. Wallenstein's response tells us much about his character. He cold-bloodedly killed the officer by stabbing him through and through with his sword. If nothing else, he was not a man to be trifled with.

Leaving Bohemia, he marched his regiment to Vienna, taking with him the Moravian treasury. There, however, the authorities told him that the money would have to go back to the Moravians – but he had shown his loyalty to Ferdinand, the future Emperor, who was shortly to succeed the ailing Matthias. Wallenstein now equipped a regiment of cuirassiers and won distinction under Charles Bonaventure de Longueval, Count of Bucquoy, in the wars against the Protestant leaders Ernst von Mansfeld and Gabriel Bethlen, the Hungarian Prince of Transylvania. Wallenstein recovered his Moravian lands, which the rebels had seized in 1619 and, after the decisive Battle of White Mountain outside Prague on 8 November1620, in which he did not take part, though his regiment did, he was in a position to seize all the lands belonging to his mother's family as well as confiscating vast tracts of Protestant land. He accumulated sixty-six separate estates, many through illegal seizures, which were designated firstly an Imperial County Palatine in 1622, then an Imperial Principality in 1623 and finally the Dukedom of Friedland in 1625.

In 1623, Wallenstein was married for the second time, to Isabella Katharina, daughter of Count Karl von Harrach, an influential courtier to the Emperor, which gave him a still more elevated status. His two marriages had made him one of the wealthiest men at the Hapsburg court. He now owned a quarter of the land in all of Bohemia, in addition to large holdings in Moravia. Furthermore, he was an efficient and profitable administrator of the Duchy from his capital at Jičín, sending a large representation to Prague to emphasize his nobility. Judging by this enrichment, one might add the words ruthlessly ambitious. He also lent large amounts of money to the Emperor, which put him in a very strong position both financially and politically. To reinforce his loyalty to the Austrian Empire and the Catholic faith he founded a Jesuit school in Jičín and built a cathedral there in the style of Santiago de Compostela.

In order to help the newly elected Emperor Ferdinand II in his alliance with the Elector Maximilian of Bavaria against the threat of the Northern Protestants, and to produce a balance in the army of the Catholic League under the man from Brabant, Johann Tserclaes, Count of Tilly, Wallenstein offered to raise an army of 50,000 men for the imperial service following the sinister *Bellum se ipsum alet*, in German *Der Krieg ernahrt den Krieg*, principle, and finally reached agreement on this, though with a smaller army of 20,000, on 25 July 1625. *Bellum se ipsum alet* is the policy of planning for an army to live off the land as it campaigns in foreign territories. In effect it is a licence for rape and pillage under the guise of legality and practicality. It is often proposed as a way of being economical and efficient, enabling fighting units to move faster without having to wait for supplies. It was a precedent which the Nazi Wehrmacht was to utilise in Russia in the Second World War.

The two Catholic armies were to coordinate operations against Mansfeld with Wallenstein now *de facto* a general, on a par with the Count of Tilly. Like Oliver Cromwell twenty-five years later, Wallenstein was not a soldier by profession as he was now a rich man, but he became a general and a good one.

In the autumn of 1625 Wallenstein crossed the border into Germany and marched north on his first military campaign. Now he was to be tested and could answer his critics at Court in Vienna, who considered him nothing more than a boastful *parvenu*. The Protestant armies in the north were commanded by King Christian IV of Denmark, Christian of Brunswick and the Luxembourger, Ernst von Mansfeld. On 25 April 1626 von

Mansfeld and his army attempted to make a crossing of the Elbe at Dessau. Von Mansfeld's troops, surprised by the efficiency and determination of Wallenstein's men, whose artillery was very effective, lost a third of their number and retreated into Brandenburg pursued by the Imperial army. Wallenstein had won his first victory.

Later that summer Christian of Brunswick died of wounds and Christian of Denmark was decisively defeated by Tilly. Wallenstein now cleared Silesia of the remnants of von Mansfeld's army, which broke up and fled south. Von Mansfeld died far south in Bosnia in a desperate attempt to get support from the Turks in 1627.

Wallenstein's troops now ravaged and burned much of Silesia and Brandenburg while the general himself took Magdeburg, after Tilly had heavily defeated Christian of Denmark at Lutter in Thuringia. Those months in Germany were always remembered for the bad harvests, the accompanying famines, and the return of the plague in many cities and, of course, the rape and pillage being carried out by the invading armies. Twenty-eight thousand people died in Wurttemberg alone. The people of Brandenburg wrote to their Elector, '"Is there no God in heaven that will take our part? Must we look on while our houses and dwellings are burnt before our eyes?'

The Elector wrote to Wallenstein pleading for clemency but was ignored, and a deputation from Halle were thrown in jail in chains and threatened with death if there were more complaints. By New Year 1627, Wallenstein had increased the size of his army to one hundred and forty thousand and had an eye on attacking Holstein and Mecklenburg on the Baltic coast.

Complaints were flooding into Vienna from all sides, and when Wallenstein got wind of them he threatened to resign immediately, knowing this would not be accepted. Eventually he met Hans Ulrich von Eggenburg, the Imperial adviser, at Bruck in Brandenburg where they discussed the Baltic campaign and agreed that taxes from Bohemia would finance the army there. The Catholic League led by Maximilian of Bavaria called a meeting in Wurzburg in January where they threatened to withdraw support for the

Emperor unless Wallenstein's power and the barbaric behaviour of his armies was curtailed. Of course, nothing was achieved and during the spring and summer Tilly drove Christian's army back into Denmark while Wallenstein prepared to winter in Jutland. Later, Wallenstein travelled south to Bohemia once more and had a meeting with the Emperor at Brandeis. He pledged that he could finance the army for at least the next six years in a campaign to take over most of the states of northern Germany and, in addition, pay for a fleet of more than twenty ships, to be matched by the Spanish, to challenge the existing naval powers in the Baltic.

The result of this promise was that on March 11 1628 Ferdinand bestowed on Wallenstein the duchy of Mecklenburg, the hereditary dukes having suffered expulsion for supporting the Danish king. This award of a major territory to someone of the lower nobility shocked the rulers of many German states. Wallenstein was now an independent prince on a par with the rulers of Wurttemberg and Hesse.

Who else could now be deposed, the concerned onlookers mused? The Spanish ambassador in Vienna wrote: 'The Duke is so powerful that one must be almost grateful to him for contenting himself with a land like Mecklenburg. The Emperor in his goodness, in spite of all warnings, has given the Duke such power that one cannot fail to be anxious.'

The Electors of Germany now met in the early spring of 1628 in Mulhausen, and led by Elector Maximilian of Bavaria sent a demand to the Emperor Ferdinand indicating that they would not sign off on the election of his beloved son as King of the Romans, a formalisation which more or less guaranteed his succession as the next Emperor, if Wallenstein was to continue as commander of the Imperial armies.

Wallenstein by now held the grandiose title 'Admiral of the North and Baltic Seas', formalising the Imperial plan to become a sea power in the north of Europe. Alliances were formed with Lubeck and Hamburg, and Wallenstein sent an army to attack the seaport of Stralsund. The burgers of the city offered eighty thousand thalers for him to withdraw, but he refused, arriving in front of the city walls on 6 July 1628. The city had signed a defence agreement with Sweden and twice resisted attacks by Wallenstein. By the end of the month he had given up the siege.

This was his first military setback and, more importantly, was more of a morale boost for his opponents rather than a military defeat. Someone wrote of the Hapsburgs, 'Eagles cannot swim,' alluding to Hapsburg designs in the Baltic. Christian of Denmark, ever the optimist, landed with an army in Pomerania but was intercepted and roundly defeated by Wallenstein at Wolgast on 2 September 1628. Following the winter, the Peace of Lubeck was signed on 22 May 1629 by Christian of Denmark and Wallenstein, which effectively ended the second chapter of the Thirty Years' War.

Wallenstein now attempted to aid the army of the Polish-Lithuanian Commonwealth led by Herman Stanisław Koniecpolski against the Swedes, but he failed to engage any major Swedish forces which may have had a bearing on Swedish actions in the years that lay ahead.

Although Wallenstein was now technically the victor, his situation was looked upon with concern by allies and enemies alike, since he now controlled vast tracts of northern Germany and an enormous army with no clear objectives. He was even draining his ally's armies by offering more money to Tilly's rank and file to join his army. His power was still growing.

It's difficult to ascertain exactly what motivated this enigmatic man. Was he a German or Austrian nationalist eager to unite the Holy Roman Empire under one leader? Surely not, he was a Czech, a Bohemian. And should that notional leader be the Hapsburg Emperor or Wallenstein himself? He is hard to read as an individual, mysterious, with his adherence to the stars, remote in his dealings with other men, calculating rather than emotional, harshly practical, lacking in human kindness and in the end unlikeable. Maybe it was just blind ambition and pursuit of power that drove him on across the wasteland of Germany that he was largely responsible for creating. What becomes clear though, is that he was something of a visionary: his grand plan was perhaps to create a powerful political entity in Central Europe, incorporating much of Germany and the Austrian Empire, with his beloved Bohemia at the centre of it, a cohesive Catholic overarching power prepared to face any threats from the powers of Western Europe or the Ottoman Empire in the east.

The bottom line was that over the course of the fighting Wallenstein's ambitions and the abuses of his forces had earned him a host of enemies, both Catholic and Protestant, princes and non-princes alike. He was now a renegade general commanding an out-of-control army. The political situation further deteriorated when the Emperor, a fervent Jesuit-raised Catholic, on 6 March 1629 issued the Edict of Restitution, which effectively reversed the 1555 Peace of Augsburg where an accord had been reached by which Protestants and Catholics could live side by side.

In June, the Electors of Germany, including Ferdinand, Elector of Bohemia, convened at Regensburg. Wallenstein adroitly moved his headquarters just ten days before, three hundred miles south to the nearby town of Memmingen. The main concern of the Electors, led by Maximilian of Bavaria, was that Wallenstein had too much power and should be removed.

For centuries the Holy Roman Emperor title had almost been honorary without much effective power, but now, backed by Wallenstein's brute military force, the Emperor might be able to depose Electors or Princes of the Empire at will. Though this suspicion was not mentioned, the delegates confirmed that there would be no agreement to the nomination of the King of the Romans until Wallenstein was dealt with. They feared he was the mailed fist in the velvet glove of the Emperor. None of the protagonists except Ferdinand, had even met the Czech prince, so much of their suspicion and animosity was based on hearsay. The publicity and rumours that surrounded the menacing Bohemian were not positive.

Finally, in mid-August, Ferdinand acceded, and it was agreed that Wallenstein should be dismissed. The news came out at the end of the month and emissaries were sent to Memmingen. Surprisingly, the general accepted the status quo calmly and wrote later: 'I am glad to my innermost soul that what they have decided in Regensburg, as it means that I can escape from this great labyrinth.' The story goes that on hearing the news Wallenstein laid out his horoscopes on a table and saw they indicated Maximilian's signs dominated Ferdinand's at that moment and there was nothing he could do about it. It was in the stars.

Another more practical consideration for Wallenstein was the lack of funding both for his armies and his personal entourage. It was becoming increasingly difficult to raise money in such chaotic times across the Empire, and after a few days of the Regensburg decision his banker, Hans de Witte, committed suicide after having to face bankruptcy Wallenstein was used to being rich and financial problems would now impede him.

It was during these days that Gustavus Adolphus, King of Sweden, landed on German soil in Pomerania on 6 July 1631 to take up the mantle of leadership of the Protestant cause which was now, in theory, at the mercy of Wallenstein's brutal armies and the Emperor Ferdinand II's blatantly pro-Catholic Edict. The Swedish king landed with 13,000 men and was at once joined by the Straslund garrison of another 4,000. Senior officers in the Imperial army were only advised of Wallenstein's dismissal in mid-September and a number of regiments were dissolved. Many units in Pomerania switched sides to a new employer, Gustavus Adolphus, whose army now increased to 40,000 men. Soldiers in those times served whoever could pay them, regardless of their religious preferences. The Catholic Electors, meanwhile, content that they had got rid of Wallenstein, miscalculated that the war would continue only in the north. Within a year the Swedish army had taken Mainz in central Germany and six months after that they were in Munich.

Wallenstein, now sick with gout and other ailments, retired to Jičín, his capital of the Duchy of Friedland, having taken the waters at Karlovy Vary, living there in his gloomy palace in 'an atmosphere of mysterious magnificence', like a latter-day Achilles in his tent before Troy. Letters were sent to him from the Emperor requesting his presence in Vienna, but he failed to respond. Maybe, despite his ambitions, by now in his late forties, he had had enough of politics and soldiering in hostile territories and could contentedly rule over his duchy.

Now another chapter in this brutal war took place. On 17 September 1631, King Gustavus Adolphus allied with Protestant Saxony won a great victory over Count Tilly at Breitenfeld outside Leipzig. In the battle the Imperialist army, fresh from further atrocities in Saxony, were soundly beaten by the Swedish army and suffered 27,000 casualties. The Swedish tactics and rapid artillery fire caused Tilly's troops to break and flee. It was the first out-and-out victory for the Protestants in the Thirty Years' War. The Imperialist army was utterly defeated; some kind of poetic justice against an army that on 20 May and the following days had brutally sacked the Protestant city of Magdeburg on the Elbe in an orgy of violence, rape, murder and arson, killing 20,000 people out of a total population of 25,000, probably the worst atrocity of the war.

The following year, Gustavus Adolphus continued on his triumphant way. He received a setback against Tilly at Bamberg on 9 March but defeated him at Rain am Lech on 15 April 1632, where Tilly was mortally wounded by a stray shot. The Protestant advance into Bavaria and Bohemia required a vigorous response. The Protestant cause now had a clear leader in the Swedish King and the Emperor Ferdinand had no choice but to recall Wallenstein. In December 1631, Wallenstein, now titled the Duke of Friedland and Zagan, had set out for Znojmo, some miles north of Vienna, where he met Prince Eggenberg, Ferdinand's loyal adviser. He was promptly appointed commander in chief from 15 December for a period of three months, a limited time to reorganise and galvanise an Imperial army to face the King of Sweden. Doubtless from his palace in Bohemia Wallenstein had heard of the atrocities committed by troops on both sides all over Germany and in particular at Magdeburg. Indeed, he had probably witnessed such incidents frequently while on campaign. While he was no man to shrink from violence, he was also a man who rewarded efficiency and an ill-disciplined army was not an efficient army.

Ironically, during this time Wallenstein was to learn lessons from his enemy, the King of Sweden. Gustavus Adolphus had now instituted stern discipline by giving rewards for bravery and harsh punishment for disorder, thievery, and cowardice. Wallenstein likewise set up strict discipline within the new army he had raised. In the spring of 1632 he was ready and, remarkably, had raised an army of 100,000 men to match the threat of Gustavus Adolphus and his allies. His first priority was to protect his rear before he marched into Bavaria to confront the enemy, who had occupied Munich and laid waste to most of the countryside around it. In a number of confrontations in May and June, Wallenstein with a large advantage in numbers drove Hans Georg von Arnim, his former officer, out of Bohemia and Silesia, and occupied Prague. Now Wallenstein, along with Pappenheim's army in the north, was a serious threat to Gustavus Adolphus deep in southern Germany. The Swedish King, having defeated and killed Count Tilly in April, advanced towards Nuremberg while Wallenstein prepared to face him.

The Bavarian troops occupying Nuremberg under the Elector Maximilian now broke out to join Wallenstein's army. It was the first time that the two Catholic generals had met, and it would be interesting to know what was said between them since Maximilian had been the most vociferous opponent of Wallenstein at Regensburg and had had him removed from command. Now he was reliant on him.

Gustavus Adolphus was now effectively trapped, and knowing the disaster had occurred at Magdeburg when he had abandoned that city the previous year, he decided to stand his ground at Nuremberg. Now the time had come for the confrontation between the two great generals of the age. And the menacing Wallenstein had the whip hand with an army twice the size that of Gustavus. Instead of investing the city, he set up camp on high ground to the west on the large site of an old castle, the Alte Veste, which looked over the whole city and its surroundings. Wallenstein knew there was a long history of large armies failing to defeat smaller armies if they were behind strong defences. Gustavus himself had not bothered to attack Regensburg and Ingolstadt earlier in the summer, knowing them to be well defended. So Wallenstein, more cautious in his military tactics than in his politics, dug into his own fortress and waited.

In late August a relieving army of 30,000 led by Count Oxenstierna, the Swedish Chancellor, entered Nuremberg. Wallenstein did not intercept them for a reason. If he had, there might have been a chance for Gustavus to attack him in the rear, so he watched and waited for the Swedes to make the first move. Wallenstein was always a calculating man. Many generals before and after him were of a similar disposition, the art of generalship being that unusual combination of caution and daring, preparation and instinct. The boot was now on the other foot. It was for Gustavus to work out how to attack a well-prepared army behind strong fortifications, much like his opponent had faced just two months before. The difference was that time was not on his side, since there were simply too many troops in the city and supplies were running out.

On 31 August, the Swedish army began operations by simply bombarding the Imperialist redoubt with their superior artillery. This continued during the following day but by dawn on 2 September the Swedes had moved some units north of Wallenstein's camp. The Imperialist army prepared for battle, but none came. Instead, Gustavus planned to attack on the well-defended eastern flank of the Alte Veste. His attacks from the north and the east began on 3 September, and the battle raged all of that hot day. The defences and men of Wallenstein's army threw the Swedes back and by the end of the day the attack had failed with Swedish losses of 1,000 killed and double that number seriously wounded. Wallenstein wrote to the Emperor: 'All officers and soldiers, infantry and cavalry alike, behaved as bravely as I have ever in my life seen in a battle.'

During the next few days the Swedish army, losing dozens of men due to desertion to the Imperialists, withdrew west to Bad Windsheim thirty miles away while Wallenstein rode north, not pursuing his defeated opponents. Maximilian, of course, urged

Wallenstein to administer the coup de grâce, but Maximilian was not a soldier and the general knew that the Swedes were still strong and it would be dangerous to pursue them.

Satisfied with his success, Wallenstein moved north, obliging Gustavus to follow him, and joined the notorious Heinrich Holk in Saxony, hoping to force the Elector John George I out of the war. Leipzig was captured in early November and Wallenstein decided to establish winter quarters there, believing the Swedes would not risk giving battle. However, next day the Swedes, learning that Gottfried Pappenheim's legendary unit of 2,200 cavalry and 3,500 infantry had advanced to Halle, decided to attack, realising they had a numerical advantage. This left Wallenstein with 13,000 to 15,000 men, facing an estimated 18,750 under Gustavus, who was advancing quickly from his base at Naumburg with additional units from Saxony and Hesse-Kassel.

Late in the afternoon of 15 November, the Swedes ran into an Imperial outpost at the Rippach stream, about three miles south of Lützen. Seeing the danger, Wallenstein sent a messenger with orders to Pappenheim to return as quickly as possible. Pappenheim only received the note after midnight, but he immediately set off through the night with his cavalry, leaving the infantry to follow.

The Swedes halted outside the town and camped in battle order, while the Imperial troops worked through the night building defensive positions along the main Lützen-Leipzig road. The ground they occupied was mostly flat except for their right flank, which Wallenstein anchored on a low hill next to three windmills, supported by his main artillery battery. Fortunately for Wallenstein there was a heavy mist in the morning, which was present on and off for most of that damp November day and the Swedish attack was delayed until mid-morning. This was a blessing for the painfully sick Wallenstein, who could hardly get himself into the saddle. This delay also gave Pappenheim more time to reach the battlefield. Although Bernhard of Saxe-Weimar made little progress against Wallenstein's right, Gustavus overran a line of musketeers holding the ditch along the Lützen-Leipzig road, crossed it, and then swung round to outflank the Imperial left.

At around midday, Pappenheim, at the head of his more than 2,000 cavalry, finally arrived. Despite their lengthy cross-country journey, they went straight into the attack, driving the Swedish infantry back to their starting positions, with Pappenheim seeking out King Gustavus to personally engage with him. Both sides suffered heavy casualties in the brutal fighting. As so often in this conflict, senior officers suffered as much as their men, and Pappenheim, who in the initial onslaught was trying to reserve Gustavus for himself, was mortally wounded and died later in the day as he was being evacuated. At the same time, Heinrich Holk led his cavalry in a furious charge at the Swedish centre, driving them back.

By now it was early afternoon and smoke from burning buildings blew across the battlefield, mixing with the mist and making visibility even worse. King Gustavus was in the thick of it with his staff officers trying to give support to the infantry but, unable to see where he was, became surrounded by an Imperial cavalry unit, was shot three times and came off his horse. The badly wounded animal was later seen galloping around the battlefield, a worrying sight for the Swedes. Their reserve under General Dodo Knyphausen managed to hold the line, providing time for their colleagues to reform and for the panic to die down on news of the possible death of Gustavus. There was a brief lull in the fighting early in the afternoon and on being advised of the Swedish king's demise, Wallenstein was sceptical.

The battlefield was by now full of dead and severely wounded troops, and the Swedes were only able to recover the half-naked body of their King under a pile of corpses as the light fell. Pappenheim's remaining cavalry were leaving the field, telling the advancing infantry from Halle that the battle was lost. The twenty-eight-year-old Bernhard of Saxe-Weimar now took command of the Swedish army and ordered another attack. A colonel who argued against him was promptly shot, and this time the attack on the Imperial left was successful and the Via Regia, as the main road was called, was crossed once again and some of the Imperial guns were captured and turned on Wallenstein's men. With darkness falling, the two armies locked in that deadly struggle finally separated and Wallenstein had to leave the field without his baggage and artillery, since most of his horses had been taken by fleeing troops. Though Pappenheim's infantry, numbering just under 3,000, finally arrived on the battlefield after dusk offering to go into battle, giving Wallenstein a numerical advantage, he ordered them to cover his retreat.

Although the Imperial casualties of more than 5,000 killed or wounded were lower than Swedish losses of around 6,000, Wallenstein decided he could not hold Leipzig and withdrew into Bohemia, leaving behind over 1,200 wounded, who were taken prisoner. During this retreat, the Imperialists were harassed by Saxon peasantry angry at the destruction of their crops and suffered significant additional casualties. Wallenstein's withdrawal and the capture of his artillery train resulted in the Swedes claiming a victory that drove the Imperial army out of Saxony, but most of all Lutzen is remembered for the death of Gustavus Adolphus, and the truth is the battle had no victor; but the Protestants had lost their greatest talisman.

In January 1633, a document was drawn up by the Emperor's closest advisers looking at options for the future in this savage war. Wallenstein, now 49 years old and crippled with a number of ailments, mused as to what lay in the future: 'I long for peace as much as for my own salvation, but nevertheless I am now making greater preparations for war than I have ever done.'

In 1632 he had driven Gustavus Adolphus from Saxony and prevented him from invading Imperial lands. He had put an end to the apparent invincibility of the Swedish King. He also realised that the Edict of Restitution was always going to be an unacceptable thorn in the side of the Protestant majority in Germany. So now he returned to Prague and positioned his troops in Bohemia. He sent money to the widow of his friend Marshal Pappenheim and made payments to some of his wounded officers and men.

Almost as if to perpetuate his own myth, Wallenstein also put into place the so-called Blood Tribunals in Prague. In a number of trials, twelve officers, including a senior colonel, and five other junior officers were publicly executed on 14 February 1633, despite pleas by some of his senior men for him to show mercy. A further thirty junior officers were sentenced to death in absentia. The trials were ostensibly fair but, in spite of the fact that this custom was prevalent in all armies at this time, it merely added to the stories of cruelty and violence that still hang around the name of Wallenstein. He was his own worst enemy. Rumours that had always existed about him now circulated more vigorously: about his dark temper, that he would have no officers come into his rooms with jingling spurs; that he would have straw laid on nearby streets to muffle the sound of carriage wheels rattling on cobblestones; that he had dogs, even cats and cockerels killed wherever he lodged on campaign and had a servant hanged for waking him in the night; and that he demanded the punishment of any visitors who talked too loudly. In the light of what was to happen to him later, his paranoia was terrifying but explicable.

In those opening weeks of 1633 he kept himself to himself, only allowing close friends and confidants into his presence, his servants, his brother-in-law Adam Trcka, and the brutish one-eyed Danish commander Heinrich Holk, whose Holk's Horse, – 'notorious even in an age of atrocities' – had been responsible for many war crimes during the conflict, and who was to die of the plague six months later, abandoned by his terrified servants at the side of the road.

In April 1633, the Heilbronn League was formed, led by Axel Oxenstierna, which consolidated the Protestant forces following the death of Gustavus Adolphus. Count Mathias Thurn was appointed commander of their forces in Saxony and in March Imperial delegates met Georg of Hesse-Darmstadt, who represented the Protestant Electors of Brandenburg and Saxony. They wanted the withdrawal of the Edict of Restitution and the Emperor to accept the existence of the Calvinists within the Empire. Furthermore, they wanted the eviction of all Swedish forces from Germany.

At the same time, Thurn sent Johann Bubna to warn the Imperial court of the possibility of the Generalissimo, as Wallenstein was now known, claiming the throne of Bohemia and negotiating a peace in defiance of the Emperor, surrounded as he was by such fervent Catholics. Wallenstein reacted with shock and anger at the suggestion, calling it a 'gross villainy' to betray his Emperor. In fact, during all these months of 1633 when various plans for peace were mooted by the Electors, the Swedes and the French, Wallenstein never even toyed with idea of being made King of Bohemia, which was quite within his capabilities. He would eventually be charged with treason, but there is simply no evidence that this cautious and essentially practical man would have countenanced a betrayal of his overlord and employer.

In June, Wallenstein, though now a sick and tired man, raised his armies once again and moved with them into Silesia. Though his force of 35,000 was larger than that of von Arnim, he set up his headquarters at Schweidnitz not far from Breslau, where talks had been planned to take place. He was accompanied by Trcka, Gallas and three Protestant colonels, while on the Protestant side was the Brandenburger and Wallenstein's former confidant, Hans George von Arnim, along with Duke Franz Albrecht of Saxe-Lauenburg. The veteran officers, after years of campaigning all across Germany, came together amicably, realising that most people were tired of the violence and the presence of foreign troops. They agreed that 'hostilities between the two armies should be suspended and that the forces should be used in combined strength against anyone who should attempt further to disturb the state of the Empire and to impede freedom of religion.'

These men were soldiers, practical and realistic, who were well aware of the effects of all this campaigning. On 12 August Count Schlick was sent as an envoy from Vienna and on 22 August a further month of truce was agreed. He was also tasked to find out the political positions of Generals Galas and Piccolomini in the event of Wallenstein retiring. Imperial officials Questenburg and Trautmansdorff attended the talks, attesting that Wallenstein and the Protestant Electors would enforce the status quo. But in November it was realised that the Electors were still reluctant to move against the Swedes, and Wallenstein would likewise not break with the Emperor. The truth is that von Arnim, wanting to create a 'third power' in Germany, comprising the Protestant Electors and

Wallenstein, to dictate terms to the Emperor Ferdinand II and to Oxenstierna the Swedish leader, who was living in a fantasy world.

Wallenstein was now exasperated with the endless negotiations. In the campaigning of 1633, his apparent unwillingness to attack the enemy or come to the help of Maximilian in Bavaria caused concern in Vienna. He expressed frustration at Ferdinand's refusal to revoke the Edict of Restitution. By this time the dimensions of the war had grown more pan-European, and it seems as though Wallenstein was looking at all his options. Historic records tell us little about his secret negotiations, but some sources indicated he was preparing to force a just peace on the Emperor in the interests of a united Germany. With this apparent plan, he entered into negotiations with Saxony, Brandenburg, Sweden, and France. Apparently, the Habsburgs' enemies tried to draw him to their side. In any case, he gained little support. Anxious to make his power felt, he resumed the offensive against the Swedes and Saxons, winning his last victory at Steinau on the Oder in October. He then resumed negotiations.

In December, Wallenstein retired with his army to Bohemia, around Pilsen. Vienna soon convinced itself of his treachery, a secret court found him guilty, and the Emperor looked seriously for a means of getting rid of him. A successor in command, the future Emperor Ferdinand III, was already waiting in the wings. Wallenstein was aware of this plan to replace him but felt confident that when the army came to decide between him and the Emperor, the decision would be in his favour. But on 24 January 1634 the Emperor signed a secret document removing him from command. The anti-Wallenstein clique in the Vienna court had finally got their way. It consisted of Prince Hans Ulrich von Eggenberg, Maximilian von Trauttmansdorff, and the Spanish ambassador, Oñate, who had made up his mind that everything depended upon not allowing Wallenstein to 'leap the ditch' and settle things by his own action. Ferdinand's son, the King of Hungary, was also admitted to the deliberations of the commission, keen as he was to take over the title of commander in chief of the Imperial armies.

A month later, on 18 February, a document charging Wallenstein with high treason was signed and published in Prague, the seat of Wallenstein's power. The Generalissimo was to be arrested and brought dead or alive to Vienna. This was effectively a death sentence, and Wallenstein suspected it was coming. Up to this point the battle-hardened campaigner had always harboured a secret contempt for the ineffective priests and peacocks of the Hapsburg court and of their Emperor, the blindly Catholic Ferdinand II. The chips were now down and five days after the decree was made public, the Generalissimo began the move with his entourage from Pilsen to Cheb, fifty miles away, maybe hoping to meet the Swedes under Prince Bernard of Saxe-Weimar there.

But matters were now moving fast and the sick Wallenstein, during the difficult and uncomfortable journey in a sled, was not fully aware of these sinister goings on behind his back. Apart from his loyal companions, he was surrounded by a group of mercenary soldiers, loyal only to their ruthless officers. The first stop was at Mies, only fifteen miles from Pilsen. Here a Colonel Walter Butler and his regiment of 900 dragoons joined the escort. The second night was spent at Plana, where Butler was separated from his men by being billeted in the castle. From there he sent a message via his chaplain to General Piccolomini reaffirming his loyalty to the Emperor, while Wallenstein sent Colonel Breuner with a message to Eggenberg and Trauttmansdorff at the Court that he was ready to resign and retire to private life. But it was too late.

Breuner was arrested in Pilsen but his message reached the Emperor, who indicated he had not changed his mind. This was made clear to Generals Matthias Gallas and Ottavio Piccolomini. The latter had nervously only advanced to Pilsen with his 3,000-strong cavalry division after Wallenstein had left. These plotters were clearly still fearful of the Generalissimo's power. The garrison town of Eger must have been familiar to Wallenstein. He had set off from there against Christian of Denmark in 1625 and against Gustavus Adolphus in 1632. He was now installed in the city. Lieutenant Colonel John Gordon had been ordered to close the gates to him but had refused, evidently obeying his commander in chief, and put him in his own quarters in the main square. Accommodation was also organised for Wallenstein's entourage including General Christian von Ilow, Lieutenant Field Marshal Adam Trcka and Count Wilhelm Kinsky and their wives and, unfortunately, Colonel Butler. Most of the military escort camped outside the gates, while 700 troops remained within the walls.

It was at this moment that a copy of the Emperor's edict of January 24 was handed to the Generalissimo. He was shocked and vented his fury at those around him, not unreasonably threatening the House of Austria. Major Walter Leslie, another of the garrison officers, was to witness this outburst and use it against him. The next morning, Ilow harangued the officers and forced them to sign allegiance to their commander in chief, which they duly did. But these mercenaries, for that is what they were, Butler, Gordon and Leslie, already knew that the Generalissimo had been dismissed and was now technically a rebel. They hatched a plan which they shared with other officers of Butler's regiment, a Major Geraldine and Captains Devereux and Macdonell. Gordon, as garrison commander, now invited Wallenstein's staff officers to a dinner in the castle, the invitees to be Ilow, Trcka, Kinsky and Captain Henry Niemann, Ilow's adjutant. The assassins hid in nearby rooms.

As the dinner progressed, on a signal, fourteen men of Butler's regiment burst into the banqueting room with Geraldine crying out 'Vivat Ferdinandus Imperator' MacDonell responded with 'Et tota Domus Austriaca.' The conspirators all shouted 'Who is a good Imperialist?'

The guests were stabbed or hacked to death. No firearms were used so as not to create too much noise. Only the burly Trcka managed to break out of the darkened room but was murdered at the gates. Now Butler led his men silently and swiftly over to Wallenstein's quarters on the town square and Devereux, with six troopers, entered the great house, ran up the stairs, killing one servant on the way up, kicked down Wallenstein's door and entered his darkened room. Their commander in chief, Wallenstein, was standing there in the darkness in his sleeping attire, and, for a split second, Devereux stood face to face with him before stabbing him fiercely with his already drawn partisan pike, upwards from below the lungs, killing him instantly. His bleeding body was rolled in a carpet and dragged down the stone staircase of the house, his skull apparently bouncing loudly on the stairs. The men who committed this heinously brutal crime were quite used to violence of any sort. They were not men of religion or profound political thought, they were killers for hire to the highest bidder.

No personality occupies a place in the history of the Thirty Years' War, at once so characteristic of that war and so unique in itself, as that of Wallenstein. But his greatness – if such it was – lies not in his achievements either as a leader of armies, though the 'general without victories' description of him was not fair since he defeated both Mansfeld and Gustavus Adolphus. Nor does it lie in his consummate insight and capacity as a politician, who could make use of all circumstances and opportunities and would not permit himself to be used by any of his fellow players in the great game. It lies rather in the innermost purposes of his statesmanship, and above all in his supreme ambition to become the Peacemaker of the Empire, which he was fully capable of achieving, in the interests of that Empire as a whole, to liberate it both from threats from foreign powers and from the internal dominion of the Reaction, the Counter Reformation, in all its ugly manifestations. Here he showed a far-sightedness due to the inspiration of a grandiose self-reliance, reinforced, maybe, by his readings of the stars.

The Peace of Prague, signed on 30 May 1635 by the Emperor Ferdinand II and the Elector John George I of Saxony, differed from the settlement which Wallenstein would have concluded on behalf of, or even without, the Emperor. He would have been fully justified, since that Emperor and his Spanish and Bavarian allies signed treaties which France and Sweden enforced at Munster and Osnabruck, and bitterness remained within the Empire about the Peace for many generations.

Moreover, the progress in religious freedom secured by the Peace which ended the war could not have been achieved had it not been for Wallenstein's sword. Not only did his deeds secure future security for the Holy Roman Empire but also for the existence and survival of the Protestants of Germany. The principle of *cuius region, eius religio,* whose realm, their religion, was re-established as a paradigm and without the actions of Wallenstein who, like so many of the combatants, had started out as a Protestant and converted to Catholicism or vice versa, it might have taken many more decades to be established.

Unlike many of the protagonists in this book, the tall, dark and menacing Albrecht von Wallenstein was a forbidding and in some ways abhorrent figure. But that's not to say he wasn't a formidable diplomat and soldier, despite those negative qualities, often prerequisites when playing for such high stakes as he, uncompromising, obstructive, cunning and ruthlessly ambitious.

The 'lean and hungry' Cassius in Shakespeare's *Julius Caesar* remarks to the ever honourable Marcus Brutus,

> Men at some time are masters of their fates.
> The fault, dear Brutus, is not in our stars,
> but in ourselves, that we are underlings.

Wallenstein, never an underling, would have well understood these words. He might have been intrigued, even amused, by the bard's reference to the stars.

5

DOGE FRANCESCO MOROSINI 1619–1694

> He dressed always in red from top to toe and never went into action without his cat beside him.
>
> Jan Morris

In the centre of Venice stands the Museo Correr, founded by the eminent Venetian art collector Teodoro Correr. At one time it was the Imperial Palace of Napoleon and is situated on the southern side of the Piazza San Marco, directly opposite the Basilica of San Marco. Inside the museum there is an unusual exhibit. It is an embalmed cat with a mouse between her paws. Her name, apparently, was Nini, and she was much loved by the Venetian Francesco Morosini, so much so that he took her on board his flagship with him wherever he campaigned.

You don't normally associate Venice with generals. Merchants, yes, traders, yes, manufacturers, brokers, money lenders and bankers, yes, but men of war, no. The success and wealth of the Venetian Empire was built on these mercantile skills, but for them to thrive there had to be peace, and to maintain peace you needed military and political dominance, or at least parity.

The Venetians achieved this with a chain of strong points and fortresses all over the eastern Mediterranean. And these places had to be defended and supplied with an effective and feared fleet. So many of the great Venetian military leaders were, in fact, admirals and generals where one supported the other and combined operations were the norm. Armies fighting on the mainland or islands had to be supplied by sea, and the fortresses and conquered lands had to be defended by land. So, Venetian military commanders had to be capable both on land and sea.

The greatest exponent of this was the Admiral and General Franceso Morosini, known as *Il Pelepponasiaco*, The Peloponnesian, and the owner of the cat. He was born in Venice on 26 February 1619, the third son of the future Procurator Pietro, of the parish of Santa Marina, and of Maria Gabriele, in Calle dei Botteri. He was just one year old when his mother drowned in the Brenta River, trying to rescue her husband who had fallen into the water. In 1627, Pietro remarried to a widow, Laura Priuli, into whose palazzo near the Campo Santo Stefano the family moved. Morosini's father was rich, influential and ambitious, keen to gain more and more honours for himself and for the family.

Franceso from an early age must have been aware that the Morosini family had produced four Doges, two cardinals and a number of generals and admirals over the centuries. They had first appeared in the tenth century before the Crusades had even begun, when they saved Venice from being handed over to the Holy Roman Emperor Otto II by the Caloprino family. Domenico Morosini was elected Doge in 1148, extending Venetian power in Istria and along the Dalmatian Coast. A hundred years later, Marino Morosini was also elected Doge in 1249. Michele Morosini was elected in 1382 and during that time Antonio Morosini contributed to a controversial history of Venice, which the authorities insisted on his amending. At the end of the sixteenth century Andrea Morosini was commissioned by the Senate to add to an official record of the Republic during his lifetime. So the Morosini name punctuates centuries of Venetian history.

As a teenager, Franceso was sent to a new college, San Carlo in Modena, which a number of young nobles attended. The atmosphere of this school attended by young men from a number of different states in Italy, linked in many respects to the feudal and military world, ended up accentuating his inclination towards martial and competitive pastimes rather than the arts of discussion and debate on which the government of Venice, *La Serenissima*, was based. His fellow students were all of the ruling class, and for a young Venetian in this situation, the natural career to follow would be naval.

This was his destiny. It is recorded that he first embarked on a Venetian ship commanded by his cousin, Pietro Badoer, as a *sopracomito*, meaning captain of a galley, but this was the general rank of an officer in the navy and did not necessarily denote that he was in command of the ship. He would probably have first gone to sea in one of the two great annual convoys where dozens of vessels large and small voyaged south as far as Methoni, to the Venetian Modon on the extreme south-west of the Peloponnesian peninsula before venturing out into the Mediterranean. The fortress there was known in common parlance as, 'The Eye of Venice', since from there any hostile naval force would be spotted at that point where one left the security of the Adriatic, Venice's relatively safe home waters.

These convoys and expeditions were highly organised. They were led by an experienced admiral and a fleet navigator both appointed by the Republic. The ship's secretary on each galley scrupulously kept records of all details on board. Even trading ships had chaplains, doctors and a company of gentlemen archers drawn from Venice's influential families as their first experience overseas. Morosini would undoubtedly have started his career in such a fashion. Whether he was allowed to wear his favourite bright red doublet and breeches at this point is not known. The advice given to one such young man by his elder brother was not to get involved in gambling, to move fast when the boarding drum sounded in port, not to eat too much when ashore, and certainly not to consort with ladies of the night in foreign ports.

On 10 June 1640, he was actually given command of a galley and distinguished himself in a number of actions against Barbary corsairs in the Adriatic. Three years later during the War of Castro, a small town just outside Rome, he was part of a Venetian naval unit which, in support of the Farnese Duchy of Parma, fired on Papal strongholds on the Italian Adriatic coast at Cesenatico, Senigallia and Rimini. In 1645, the War of Candia broke out between the Ottoman Empire and the Venetian Empire. This conflict, which lasted a quarter of a century, was to shape Morosini's career until the end of his life.

On 1 October 1645 he was promoted to *Capitano delle Galeazze*, on 7 July 1647 *Governatore dei Condonatti* and on 29 September *Capitan del Golfo*. Such rapid progression makes plausible his participation in the operations in defence of the Cretan ports of Rethymno and Suda in the summer of 1646, as indicated by the sources and much literature, although the same documents and the detailed history of the war of Candia by Andrea Valier sometimes confuse his name with that of other Morosini family members engaged in the long conflict, such as Daniele, Giorgio, Taddeo, and Tommaso. And the position of *Capitan del Golfo*, to which Morosini had been elected, taking over from Alvise Mocenigo, appointed *Capitano Generale da Mar*, involved the command of the fleet operating in the Adriatic, which would make his presence in the Aegean less likely. Either way, he was still *Capitan del Golfo* when, on 17 January 1650, he was promoted to commander of the great galleys, enabling him to operate in a wider area and participate directly in the defence of Crete, or Candia as it was known by the Venetians.

By the beginning of the seventeenth century the Republic of Venice had ruled the island for more than four hundred and fifty years, back to the decade after the terrible events of the Fourth Crusade in the early years of the thirteenth century when Constantinople had been brutally sacked by Venetian and other crusaders, and Byzantine possessions across the eastern Mediterranean had been distributed amongst its conquerors.

The growing power and reach of the Ottomans from 1453 onwards was inevitably to lead to a confrontation between the Ottoman Empire and the Republic of Venice. As trade had been Venice's lifeblood since her inception, the merchant Republic, annually wedded to the sea in an elaborate and spectacular ceremony known as La Serenissima, always endeavoured to maintain cordial relations with the most powerful Empire in the eastern Mediterranean. But there was always an incipient rivalry between the two ill-matched powers, and it only takes a small spark to ignite a firestorm.

The Cretan War or *La Guerra di Candia* took place between 1645 and 1669. In 1651, the Venetians had temporarily given up their annual blockade of the Dardanelles through which any important Ottoman fleet carrying troops and supplies would emerge to reinforce their possessions across the Aegean Sea. By this time Franceso was an experienced Venetian captain who had been patrolling these waters for ten years. Many of the horizons, lines of mountains, bays and headlands were familiar to him. Likewise the sound of the wind in the rigging, the smell of the livestock clustered round the kitchens, the constant murmur of conversation below decks and in calm weather the measured beat of the lines of oars. These oarsmen were not slaves, they were citizens of the Republic of Venice and they were proud to pull their weight as the great galleys with their ensigns of red and gold depicting the Venetian winged lion fluttered in the wind. From afar, a Greek farmer or a Turkish janissary with some education must have thought these great galleons looked like the triremes of the ancients, be they Greeks on their way to Troy or Romans venturing towards the hostile coasts of Asia Minor.

By 1651 Francesco Morosini had been promoted to *Capitano delle Galleazze* which effectively was the rank of vice-admiral, commanding a number of warships. On 21 June of that year, Hazam Ali the Ottoman commander sailed unopposed through the Dardanelles with a formidable fleet of fifty-three galleys and more than sixty smaller vessels. Alvise Mocenigo, the Venetian captain-general and a scion of another influential Venetian family, commanding twenty four galleys, twenty-eight ships and six galleasses, was patrolling the waters off Negroponte, the Venetian name for Euboea, when he heard that the Ottoman fleet was moving south from Chios to Patmos. Anxious to stop the enemy reaching Crete, Mocenigo sailed south towards Santorini, which had been suffered a devastating volcanic eruption only the year before.

On 8 July the Ottoman fleet closed with the Venetians and Girolamo Battaglia commanding five ships was put under severe attack. Soon Luca Barbaro, the *Capitano delle nave*, came to his aid. Then Mocenigo, with the main fleet, approached and the Ottomans retreated northwards. Two days later, the Venetians caught up with them between Paros and Naxos and attacked. The brothers Tommasso and Lazzaro Mocenigo, each commanding a galleas, attempted to attack some Turkish galleys still taking on water at Paros. Then Hozam Ali himself trapped them with six galleasses and other ships. Tommasso was killed and Lazzaro wounded before Morosini, commanding his small flotilla, counter-attacked and the enemy fled. This was a decisive action which was a precursor of what Morosini was going to become: a brave and decisive commander. Lesser commanders might have left the Mocenigo brothers to their self-inflicted fate.

After Morosini's rescue of the Mocenigo galleasses, the Venetian fleet broke the Turkish line and their galleys fled, leaving their sailing ships to fend for themselves. The Venetians captured about a dozen enemy ships and burned five others, capturing nearly a thousand prisoners. Admiral Mocenigo now withdrew to the harbour of Candia where he was joined by four Papal and four Maltese galleys. But Morosini's triumph ended up generating deep jealousy between the rising star and his superior, Alvise Mocenigo, advanced in years and, on occasion, too cautious. So Mocenigo, first expelled him from the consultation of military leaders, then accused him of having disobeyed orders and imposed on him forty days under arrest. Morosini at once replied, and on 5 August addressed the Senate, claiming merit for the victory and criticising the lukewarm efforts of the ageing Captain General. In September Alvise Mocenigo gave up the baton of Captain General to his successor, Leonardo Foscolo. Hozem Ali returned to Istanbul by the end of the year and was removed as Grand Admiral in October 1652. For the next two years the Ottomans did not attempt to break out of the Dardanelles due to constant internal strife in the Seraglio.

For the time being, Morosini seemed to be depressed by these military rivalries and later in 1651 his father advised those in power that he wanted to apply to be a Ducal Counsellor. But Mocenigo made an official retraction of the charges he had made against his young rival, and in February 1652 Morosini was appointed *Provveditore generale d'Armata*, Superintendent General of the Fleet. For the rest of that year, and also in 1653, there were no major actions but only raids on the Aegean coasts, where Morosini was patrolling the waters from Gallipoli to the Cyclades.

Fighting resumed in the late spring of 1655, when the Venetians sent a squadron to blockade the Straits to prevent Turkish ships from sending aid to their troops engaged in Candia. On 13 May there was an encounter off the Dardanelles in which Morosini took part with eight galleys. Despite the Turks suffering many losses, they managed to gain the open sea and reach Crete. Just to confuse any student of this period of history, there was another Captain Franceso Morosini, at this encounter, who was killed in this so-called First battle of the Dardanelles: '...il capitan del Golfo Francesco Morosini colpito da moschettata vi rimanesse estinto', 'killed by a musket shot'.

A short time later Mocenigo died while the military campaign was underway, and Morosini took over the supreme command and continued to harass the enemy in operations where the galleys powered by oarsmen had greater manoeuvrability. Then he engaged in a war of destruction in the Greek Archipelago, capturing Turkish ships, making sudden landings and spoiling the food depots intended to supply the enemy army.

In 1655 Morosini began the year with an attack on the island of Aegina, near Athens, which was used by the Ottomans as a supply centre for operations in Crete. But, at the beginning of the campaign, on 5 May the new *Capitano general do Mar*, Girolamo Foscarini, died of a fever. A week later Morosini was dismissed from the command of naval operations and appointed *Provveditore generale delle armi* at Candia. Clearly this was a demotion.

On 10 June 1655 Lorenzo Marcello was made *Capitano general do Mar*. He was one of the proponents of the strategy of bottling up the Ottoman fleet in the Bosphorus by blocking their exit through the Dardanelle Straits.

However, a year later, on 26 June 1656, Marcello was killed in the successful Third Battle of the Dardanelles and it seemed as though Morosini would become *Capitano Generale* again. But in the Senate he still had plenty of opponents, and the honour fell to the thirty-two-year-old Lazzaro Mocenigo, who in the battle had covered himself in glory after being badly wounded and losing an eye. It was he who had returned to Venice with news of the victory aboard one of the captured Ottoman ships. But fate once again intervened and on 1^{h} July 1657, the young hero, leading a squadron of twelve vessels, drove thirty-three enemy ships through the Sea of Marmora to the very walls of Constantinople before a random shot from a shore battery scored a direct hit on his powder magazine, blowing up the ship and collapsing the mast, which killed him instantly. He was one of the few senior admirals to have taken part in each of the four Dardanelles actions.

His death marked the end of the blockade strategy, and this time the title of *Capitano Generale da Mar* finally fell to Morosini, who was promoted on 30 August 1657 and handed the poisoned chalice of defending the city of Candia in its death throes. His first plan was to recapture Canea, a nearby island, but the operation ended in failure and Morosini blamed this on the *Provveditore d'Armia*, Antonio Barbaro, with whom he had clashed since 1651. Barbaro had been a supporter of Alvise Mocenigo when he had accused him of embezzlement, of which charge he was found not guilty by the *Quarantia*, the Council of Forty, the supreme court of Venice.

In keeping with his strategy for the war, the years that followed were not marked by major battles but only by raids on the Aegean islands and the Peloponnese. But with the Ottoman fleet free to roam the seas and re-supply their forces in Candia, it would only be a matter of time before the outpost of Venice would be swamped by sheer weight of numbers. The only thing that could swing the balance decisively would be support from the rest of Christian Europe, but for decades, if not centuries, most had been loath to support what they perceived as an opulent and monopolistic Venice. Often their support was too little, too late.

In the summer of 1660, Candia had been reinforced by a French contingent of four thousand men led by the Italian Prince Almerigo d'Este. They arrived too late in the summer to be effective and after a failed attack on the Turkish lines many fell sick with dysentery, including their leader. After a few weeks they returned home without having achieved anything except deplete rations in the starving city. It was a similar story with a German group of two thousand volunteers.

After these disasters and, without proper support, Morosini became demoralised and on 30 August 1660 resigned his post, leaving the navy. Two months later he became the *Podesta*, Chief Magistrate, of Padua. This office, removing him from Venice, sounded like a step backwards. In June 1663 he was elected *Provveditore* in Friuli. At this time the Ottomans were once again threatening the Austro-Hungarian Empire and Venetian defences of their land borders were essential. After Friuli, Morosini was put in charge of the strategic town of Palmanova and in 1665 became the Councillor of Castello, another mainland town. He was then elected *Provveditore d'Armata* in December 1666, a postion he refused, considering it a demotion after being *Capitano general da Mar*. He was again offered the post on 29 September 1666 and accepted, so as not to exclude himself from higher promotion. It was important politically that he gave the Senate the satisfaction of being obeyed, particularly at a time when the Grand Vizier, Ahmed Köprülü, was preparing his final offensive against Candia with a massive build-up of troops. Another problem for Venice was that the Anglo-Dutch war of 1664-7 meant those two maritime powers, who normally would charter vessels to the Republic, were unable to do so at this critical time. In fact, faced with this increased threat, on 2 January 1667 Morosini was appointed *Capitano generale da Mar* for the second time, and with the approach of summer he returned to Candia to face Köprülü.

The Ottomans were not his only opponents, since his old enemy, Antonio Barbaro, was general superintendent of the whole island of Candia, which inevitably caused friction between the two men. Barbaro favoured more naval actions while Morosini took crews and artillery from the galleys to strengthen the defence of the city.

On the night of 8/9 March 1668, Morosini won a decisive naval victory near Standia, an island used for anchorage just off the Cretan coast. It was a victory that earned him the title of Knight of St Mark. Late in the same year another group of aristocratic French soldiers of fortune under the Marquis de Montbrun arrived. They included the Duc de la Feuillade, the Duc de Chateau Thierry, the Duc de Caderousse, the Marquis d'Aubusson, the Counts of Villemor and Tavanes, the Prince of Neuchatel and many other young noblemen. It was a veritable Gallic Burke's Peerage.

It was a bad time. Not only had a Venetian engineer, Andrea Barozzi, defected to the enemy the year before, giving them details on the underground fortifications of the city, but during the previous summer Morosini had lost six hundred officers and seven thousand men during the fighting and by disease. Immediately on the arrival of the blue-blooded reinforcements, Morosini ordered them to man the ramparts in defence. The Duc de la Feuillade, maybe he should have been titled the Duc de la Folie, refused to obey and instead on 16 December led a pointless and foolhardy attack on the Turkish lines. Out of a force of nearly three hundred men, forty were killed including the two Counts, and sixty severely wounded. Within a week the French volunteers had gone, many dying of the plague on their journey home.

The following year Louis XIV, persuaded by the Venetian Ambassador, Giovanni Morosini, a kinsman of Francesco's, sent a more formidable fleet under the flag of the Papacy carrying six thousand men, three hundred horses and fifteen cannon, which who landed at Candia on 19 June 1669. The commanders of this army, the Duc de Beaufort and the Duc de Noailles, were shocked at state of the besieged city with the stench of death, ruined buildings, collapsed houses caused by mined tunnels underneath, rubble, and used cannon balls lying everywhere in the streets.

Despite Morosini's plan to recapture Canea, a nearby strategic stronghold, with their help, once again the French rushed into a pointless offensive less than a week after arriving and once again, they were driven back with severe losses. Two weeks later a French warship approaching the harbour was blown out of the water and within a month of arriving de Noailles advised Morosini that he was re-embarking and leaving. On 21 August the French fleet along with other allies from the Empire, Malta and the Papal States set sail and the Venetians were left alone in the smoking ruins of Candia. The Grand Vizier now ordered another attack, which was repulsed, and Morosini with just three thousand six hundred able-bodied soldiers realised that the game was up. They could not hold out another winter.

As well as a military commander the fifty-year-old Morosini was also a political beast. He remembered that even in 1647, ten years later in 1657 and again in 1662, the Senate in Venice had not avoided the discussion of a negotiated peace over Candia. Now in 1669 he had no choice in the matter and the horrific brutalities inflicted on the surrendering castle commander of Famagusta, Andrea Bragadin, one hundred years before, must have preyed on his mind, and he was aware that there could also be a massacre of all the inhabitants if a peace was not negotiated. But the Grand Vizier, Ahmed Koprulu, admired Morsini's bravery and judgement and the treaty signed on 6 September 1669 was as good as could be expected. The Venetians could leave the city in twelve days, longer if the weather was intemperate, even taking imported artillery with them, and Venice would retain the Grabousa islands, Suda and Spinalonga.

Exactly three weeks later, the keys of Candia were handed to Koprulu and the banner of St Mark was lowered from the citadel of Candia after twenty-two years of siege, one of the longest in history, and four hundred and sixty five years of occupation stretching back to the aftermath of the disastrous Fourth Crusade in 1204. In the final two years of the siege the human losses had been appalling: seventy thousand Turks, thirty-eight thousand Cretans, and twenty-nine thousand Christians had died. It was a long-remembered loss for Christendom. Ironically, on 20 September 1669 the Senate, still unaware of the conclusion of the war, had conferred on Morosini the title of *Procurador de Supra*, the second highest honour in the Republic after the Doge.

Morosini must have realised that his enemies in Venice would plot against him on his return. He was hardly the returning conqueror and despite his new position charges were soon brought against him by his old opponent, Antonio Correr, the *Avogador di Comun*, the State Prosecutor, which included cowardice, treason, speculation and corruption. The arguments made by the appointed inquisitor, Francesco Erizzo, were vigorously pursued for months, but finally the battered soldier was exonerated of all blame by the Senate. Of course, the powers in Venice were dismayed at the loss of Candia, their most important and profitable possession, and they needed to find a scapegoat. There were discrepancies in the financial assessments, but Candia had been under siege and no one individual could be held responsible for all financial irregularities in time of war.

Though many have described Morosini as being out of favour during the years following his heroic defence of Candia, the facts are that the real powers in the Republic continued to value his abilities. He was entrusted with military appointments virtually non-stop during the ensuing years. He was appointed *Provveditore all'Armar*, responsible for the provisioning of the fleet crews and armaments, from 7 November 1671 for one year, then from 18 July 1676 for another year and from 23 January 1683 for another. He was also *Provveditore alle Artiglierie*, responsible for artillery supplies, from 28 October 1679 for another year.

On 5 March 1681 he was selected to supervise Venice's mainland fortifications. Along with his contemporaries, Andrea Corner and Andrea Valier, he inspected the western fortresses of Peschiera, Legnago, Orzinuovi and Cremona, where the works designed by Bartolomeo Grimaldi were being carried out. He was elected *Provveditore generale* for Friuli on 15 July 1683, when the Ottoman offensive against Vienna was more pressing, the first place the Ottomans might attack if they were successful against the Hapsburg Empire.

A few months later, after the Ottomans had been defeated by the Austro-Hungarian Empire, Venice declared war on the Porte, as the Ottoman rulers and government was called, and on 11 March 1684 Morosini was once more elected *Capitano generale da Mar*, the highest military post in the Republic. Contrary to his war-like image, in the Senate he was never in favour of all-out war but believed in the interruption of Turkish supplies from Anatolia to the Balkans and in the bolstering of security for Venetian trade, the lifeblood of *La Serenissima*. Maybe it was his moderate approach that secured him his promotion.

Instead of following the old and disastrous policy of blockading the Dardanelles where Venice had signally failed, Morosini decided to concentrate his efforts on objectives closer to home and easier to enact. His plan was firstly to take the strongholds around the whole coast of the Peloponnese, the great southern peninsula of Greece named after the mythical King Pelops and which the Venetians named the Morea (meaning in their language, *mora*, a mulberry leaf, which grew prolifically there and whose shape it resembled), then the mainland of the peninsula itself.

The war that now began was probably the most successful in the history of the Republic. The achievements are really down to one man, whose sheer strength of character managed both to command a successful conquest and at the same time to deal with the machinations of Venetian politics. Typically, at one moment Francesco Morosini had been cheered to the rafters for his valiant defence of Candia and the next he had been accused of betraying his country's interests when he concluded the peace in a hopeless cause. He had been acquitted after what must have been a humiliating and depressing trial and during the next fifteen years he no longer patrolled the high seas of the Adriatic and the Aegean, his services no longer required or his genius recognised. Like all great military men, his character played a key role in his public career. He had spent twenty years of his life until he was in his mid-forties at sea in the service of the Venetian fleet where he had built a formidable reputation. He was strong-minded and courageous, not obstinate or rash, he was cheerful, physically strong, he could walk with kings and had not lost the common touch. Maybe he was not a great strategist, but he was a good administrator and tactician, two key qualities of a military commander. He had to deal with the complications of land-based and naval operations, which are notoriously difficult to meld. He was often held back by a jealous Senate and command of combined operations was always difficult when at sea, where he sometimes took immediate opportunities rather thinking of the bigger picture. Commanders overseas, often out of contact with their government, have to take small victories when they appear rather than follow a cautious approach when long delays can bring frustration and criticism. They have to take their chances, but at the same time be able to recognise what is a chance.

Francesco Morosini was now sixty-four years old, a legend and a wily and experienced man of the world. He still wore his signature all-red costume with red tights and red velvet jacket, and he was always accompanied by his black cat (or rather, a black cat).

The fleet he sailed with consisted of 68 fighting ships including 6 galleasses, 30 ships of the line and 30 galleys, plus a myriad smaller vessels. The vessels and men were mostly Venetian, but by July 1684 when they departed, they had been joined by auxiliary vessels from the Papacy, the Grand Duke of Tuscany and the Knights of Malta. Aboard were a battalion of Papal soldiers and a battalion led by the Knights of Malta, resplendent in their red satin tunics with white crosses.

They joined an army of 8,000 men, which the Senate quickly realised needed to be augmented by the recruitment of mercenary soldiers from all over Europe. After all, the security of Venice against the encroachments of the Muslim Ottoman Empire was of concern to all the Christian peoples of Europe. By invading Greece, Venice thought that the increased revenue from a subjugated Morea would substitute for their losses in Candia, which for centuries had produced a large part of their exports. Morosini was not after the glory of conquering the legendary cities of Sparta and Athens but realised that the rich farmlands of the Morea might bring increased revenue for Venice, some of which could cover the costs of foreign arms and armies.

The land campaign started in July when Morosini, having conferred with his fellow commanders at Corfu, attacked Santa Maura, which surrendered on 6 August 6 after a sixteen-day siege. It was a perfect jumping off point for military operations in the Morea. It was also situated strategically between Corfu and Cephalonia, commanding the entrance to the Adriatic and the Gulf of Corinth. In the weeks that followed his troops raided into Arcanania, burning villages and taking prisoners, and on 29 September captured Preveza, the equally important stronghold and port, where some fierce fighting took place before the Ottomans surrendered. The citadel was found to be full of ammunition, powder, cannons and many guns, a great bonus for the Venetians.

Morosini had now secured his lines of communication with Venice at the head of the Adriatic and now planned his attack on Morea itself. But during the winter that followed, the plague struck and many in the army died, including General Count Strazoldo, the hero of Debrezin in Hungary, who had played a key part in the capture of Preveza.

The Senate, aware of this danger, decided to employ more foreign troops. Mercenaries, in the guise of Christians fighting the Muslim threat, were sought in Germany where Venice had an alliance with the Emperor. Agreements were made with a number of German rulers and both Brunswick and Saxony agreed to send whole regiments including their commanding officers, a total of two thousand four hundred each. The Duke of Brunswick, later the Elector of Hanover, signed the agreement in December 1684 and by June 1685 they had joined Morosini at Dragomestre. Ismael Pasha had now marched more troops into Morea and taken hostages to ensure the co-operation of the local Greek towns.

Early in the spring of 1685 Morosini sailed against the old port of Corone further south on the west coast of the Morea. He arrived on the island of Sapienza and met the leaders of the Maniots, the inhabitants of the Maina Peninsula, who were naturally opposed to any foreign occupation, particularly by the Turks. In talks with them, he was promised support if he arrived with a an army. They said if he captured the cities of Mistra and Leondari, the coastal fortresses of Zarnata, Kielapha and Passava would then be obliged to surrender.

Morosini then landed his army of some nine thousand five hundred men from Venice, Germany, the Papal States and Tuscany, plus the 120 Knights of Malta, and surrounded Corone. This was truly an army of the Christian Holy League. The Ottoman garrison put up a desperate defence and only raised the white flag on 10 August. While the terms of surrender were being discussed, a Turkish cannon accidentally opened fire, killing a number of Venetians. The reaction was violent in the extreme and the inhabitants of the town were massacred with few exceptions. Within the next few months many other towns fell to the invaders. The Venetian-led army now crossed the Gulf of Maina to the mainland where they quickly took Zarnata on 10 September when the Ottoman governor was persuaded to surrender with the offer of a large pension and a guarantee of safety in Venice itself.

Morosini now encouraged the Maniots to join him in the capture of Kalamata, defended by 6,000 infantry and 2,000 spahis. Twenty-six years before, Morosini had taken Kalamata capturing fourteen cannons, making many of his prisoners slaves and razing the town. Again he threatened Kalamata, but the local Capitan Pasha rejected his proposals. Meanwhile a Saxon contingent of more than three thousand troops had just arrived under the command of the splendidly named Hannibal von Degenfeld, which encouraged Morosini. He ordered Kalamata to be attacked immediately. The Saxon commander, aware of the determined defenders and formidable defences, tried to delay but was overruled by the nineteen-year-old Prince Maximilian of Hanover, who said they had orders which should be followed. Degenfeld complied and the soldiers of the Holy League defeated a much larger contingent of Ottomans outside the town. Kalamata duly fell and the castle was demolished, but this time Morosini spared the inhabitants.

The heavily armed Ottoman forts of Kielapha and Passava quickly capitulated and Maina was evacuated by the Turks. Garrisons were placed in Zarnata and Kielapha to keep watch over the potentially rebellious Maniots and to control the key ports of Armyro and Vitylo from which most local produce was exported. It should not be forgotten that the Venetians were merchants and traders by choice, not warriors.

Morosini and his combined force now wintered at Corfu, Santa Maura and Zante. The Hanoverian contingent who had served from April 1685, by the end of the year had lost two hundred and fifty men in fighting and more than seven hundred from disease, not an unusual statistic then, nor indeed for the next two hundred years of campaigning for all armies across the world. The plague was to take many more lives during the next two years.

As the following year, Count Otto William von Konigsmark, a Swedish Field Marshal, the uncle of the legendary beauty Maria Aurora, hired at the enormous salary of 18,000 ducats, arrived to command the land campaign and met up with Morosini at Santa Maura to plan their strategy. It was decided to continue with the conquest of the Morea. They had to move fast since the Turks soon counter-attacked in April and laid siege to Kielapha but were driven off by the Venetian fleet under Venieri. Three thousand more recruits arrived in the spring, mainly from Hanover, and the whole army now numbered in excess of ten thousand. This was now virtually a crusade. The new army took time to assemble and they were only ready to campaign after some months. On 3 June, Konigsmark took Pylos, Old Navarino, which quickly surrendered. He now moved on the Ottoman fortress of New Navarino, which had been built a hundred years before by the Ottomans after their defeat at Lepanto. The Turkish commander Sefer Pasha agreed to surrender in four days but was killed in an accidental magazine explosion. The fortress surrendered and three thousand prisoners were taken. Nearby Mithoni, later known as the Eye of Venice, was then attacked and capitulated on 10 July. The town was looted and many prisoners were taken, some of whom became slaves. The Hanoverians objected, not to the taking of slaves, but because they were not allocated enough of the loot. Though they resented Morosini for this and his harsh discipline, they could only admire him for his bravery. At Mithoni, dressed in his distinctive bright red costume replete with breast-plate glinting in the Grecian sun and accompanied by other gaudily dressed Venetian officers, he stepped too close to the enemy lines. They were promptly fired on and all fled, save Morosini, who stood there fearless. Those who witnessed his raw courage admired him and tales were told of the fearlessness of their commander.

Now combined operations were in full swing as the army was transported round the whole peninsula to the eastern coast and was put ashore at Port Tolon, just along the coast from Nauplia. After taking the hill of Palamidi, which they later built into a formidable fortress above the town, the Venetians laid siege to Nauplia. But the town was well provisioned and the local *Seraskier* had an army of four thousand cavalry and three thousand infantry just inland at Argos. The fighting was intense and the undermanned Hanoverian artillery officers had to make local Greeks pull their cannons into their emplacements. Many of the Turks retreated to Corinth, but the town kept on fighting hoping help was near, despite artillery fired from Palamidi into the town. The plague once more decimated the Venetian army. Of the 1,550 Hanoverians under arms, 1,200 were sick or wounded. The Turks counter-attacked on 29 August with initial success, but Morosini landed 2,000 more men, many of them Venetians and Slavs, who fought tenaciously. The battle was turned by the cool head of Konigsmark. Nauplia surrendered on 3 September 1686 and 7,000 prisoners were taken. Disease was the main problem for Morosini – though he also had to had to deal with complaints that the Hanoverians had too many servants! The Saxons had left at the end of the previous summer but had been replaced with recruits from Hesse and Wurtemburg. The Hanoverians also increased their numbers with 1,200 new soldiers.

In 1687, Mehmet Pasha arrived in Patras to reinforce the garrison with ten thousand troops. Campaigning did not start until July when Morosini's forces landed west of Patras while the fleet sailed past Lepanto on the night of 22 July. The fighting was brief and the Turks were taken by surprise, vacating Lepanto and Patras and the two strongholds defending Corinth. The victory was swift and complete and the news was sent immediately to Venice. Messengers arrived in *La Serenissima* on the morning of 11 August and the whole city rejoiced. The humiliation of Candia had been avenged. The Great Council suspended its' session so members could attend a service of thanksgiving at St Mark's Basilica, and the Senate ordered a bronze bust of Morosini to be placed in the Armoury of the Council of Ten in the Doge's Palace with the inscription: 'FRANCISCO MOROCENO PELEPONNESIACO ADHUC VIVENTI, SENATUS.' Morosini, now known as the Peloponnesian, in the vernacular Venetian Italian 'Peleponnesiaco' rather than 'Peleponnesiano' in standard Italian, was awarded another knighthood by the Council.

His portrait was placed in the Great Hall, something never done before. Konigsmark was awarded 6,000 ducats in a golden bowl and his salary raised to 24,000 ducats per annum, a huge sum, the Prince of Hanover was presented with a golden sword, and many officers were well rewarded.

Castel Tornese, Salona, and Corinth were captured on 7 August by a regiment of Hessians after being abandoned by the Turks. Those that were not taken prisoner fled to Mistra and Monemvasia, the only two cities still in Ottoman hands in the Morea. As they retreated, they massacred local Greeks in their way, and the Greeks soon learned to retaliate.

Morosini now wanted to attack the key Ottoman fortress of Negroponte, on modern-day Euboea, which would give him control of all Greece south of Thermopylae and a strategic naval post from which to interdict any Ottoman ventures into the Aegean. His fellow commanders, including Konigsmark, disagreed, arguing that it was too late in the year to undertake such a difficult challenge. So Morosini shrugged and calmly decided to take Athens where they could overwinter.

On 21 September the Venetian fleet entered the ancient port of Piraeus, known to them as Porto Leone, after the great marble lion which had stood on the dockside for centuries. Konigsmark with his army of ten thousand, including eight hundred and seventy cavalry, camped in the olive groves along the Sacred Road to Eleusis, looking south towards the Bay of Salamis. It was the birthplace of the great patriot and playwright Aeschylus, who had fought at the Battle of Marathon. Their objective, the legendary city of Athens, was less than seven miles away. This splendidly arrayed Venetian army, made up mainly of German, Italian and diverse European soldiers of fortune, was now treading on the hallowed land of the ancients.

Athens, with no proper defences, was quickly occupied and a siege of the Acropolis began. The occupying Turks, soldiers and civilians alike, had all taken refuge on that sheer hilltop that had dominated the skyline of the ancient city for centuries, adorned with the immaculate white marble Parthenon and Temple of Minerva.

An early attack was initiated against the Propylaea where the Turks based their defence, and on 25 September a mortar bomb hit and blew up a small powder store. The attackers now set up two mortar batteries, one near the Mouseion Hill and one near the Pnyx Hill, both under the cover of the Areopagus. Two more were positioned in the town itself north-east of the Acropolis. A Turkish deserter revealed that most of their ammunition had been placed inside the Parthenon. It is said that a young German lieutenant from Luneburg in the late afternoon of 26 September adjusted his sites and fired his mortar in a wide parabola from the Mouseion Hill with deadly accuracy, through the ancient roof of the classic edifice. There was a dull thud as the projectile hit the stone floor within, then a massive explosion as the ordinance store of the Ottomans ignited.

The familiar sound of the cicadas suddenly ceased. The centre columns of the peristyle collapsed, the walls fell inwards, bringing the architraves and cornices with them. Many sculptures were of course defaced and some totally destroyed. Three hundred Turks were killed, soldiers and civilians, since the whole of the Turkish population of Athens at that time had taken refuge on the Acropolis. As night fell, in the darkening Attic sky was the dwindling smoke of the fire that had swept through the Parthenon. The cicadas began to sing again. An attaché of Otto Wilhelm

Königsmarck wrote later: 'How it dismayed His Excellency to destroy the beautiful temple which had existed for three thousand years!' Morosini, in his despatches, described it as a 'fortunate shot'. The remnants of the Turkish garrison surrendered two days later when it became clear that no help would arrive, since Konigsmark had divided his army into two, blocking any Ottoman troops advancing from Negroponte or Thebes.

The Turkish garrison were allowed to depart for Smyrna and on 4 October. They embarked at Piraeus. Some were baptised as Christians and allowed to remain. The Venetian Count Tomeo Pompei was named commandant of the Acropolis and German troops in Athens made one mosque into a Lutheran church and another into a Catholic church. It seemed as though the conclusions to the Thirty Years' War had been applied to Greece.

The service of three Hanoverian regiments had expired and they departed from Piraeus on 26 December 1687. As he departed, the Lieutenant from Luneburg who had fired the devastating shot might have gazed back towards Athens, perhaps more in relief that he was going home than guilt at the destruction he had wrought. In their campaigning across the Greek mainland, the Germans, a key part of the Venetian forces, had lost 88 officers and 2,900 men, more from the plague than from enemy fire. Another 1,400 volunteers had already arrived to replace them.

Morosini decided that after wintering in Athens he would attack Negroponte in the New Year. A further advance into Attica would be pointless, particularly since the Ottoman *Seraskier* in the area commanded 2,000 cavalry. The ancient city, dominated now by the ruined Parthenon atop the Acropolis, became a ghost town. More than five thousand inhabitants chose to leave while many of the servile class of Albanians were forced into military service by the Venetians.

During the first few weeks Morosini attempted to plunder the ruins of the Parthenon. On 19 March 1688 he ordered his engineers to take the ancient statues of Neptune and the Chariot of Victory, both by Phidias. This was a disaster as they were damaged further and proved impossible to move, otherwise they would have ended up adorning a piazza in Venice. Instead, Morosini took four lion figures, in particular the mysterious statue that had stood on the quay at Piraeus for centuries, now in front of the Arsenal in Venice. Allegedly, the lion was sculpted in the time of Alexander the Great and had stood in Piraeus for nearly two thousand years. The enormous lion, about nine feet high, was clearly a fountain at one time. It looks more Mesopotamian than classical Greek. A further mystery are the strange runic inscriptions carved on its body, which may have been incised by Viking raiders in the ninth century, or possibly by Norsemen serving under Byzantine Emperors in the Varangian Guard: early examples of graffiti.

On 23 March 1688, Doge Marcantonio Giustinian, the intellectual linguist who had been in his earlier days the Venetian Ambassador to France during the siege of Candia, died. Venice's great champion, despite the usual naysayers, Francesco Morosini was at last elected to the highest office in the Republic and became Doge at the age of sixty-nine. He was honoured in Poros where the Venetian fleet was wintering. He was also advised that the Senate were making efforts to raise more volunteers in Europe to come to his aid. Inevitably, these troops arrived slowly and it was only on 8 July that the fleet sailed from Poros for Negroponte with a force of thirteen thousand men and naval strength of another ten thousand. Negroponte, called this by the Venetians but there was no 'black bridge' there, had six thousand defenders and the defensive walls were formidable and extensive, having been designed and built by the Venetians themselves. There was a fortified bridge over the narrow Euripus River that divided the island from the mainland. Perhaps it had once been black. The fort of Karababa stood menacingly overlooking the narrows.

Konigsmark wanted to attack from the mainland side, capture Karababa and cut off the town from any possible Ottoman reinforcements from Thebes. but Morosini decided to attack from the island side where he could put more troops ashore. In retrospect, Konisgmark was probably right since during the siege the garrison were continually supplied, could evacuate sick and wounded, and could reinforce from the landward side.

The outworks of the fortress were manned by Turkish janissaries who fought fiercely in the blistering heat of July and August, and it was only on 30 August that they submitted. The Venetians captured thirty cannon and five mortars. Since the main Venetian army was camped near unhealthy marshland, their main problem was not combat losses – they outnumbered the Turks by two to one – but disease, either the plague or probably malaria, which spread rapidly. On 15 September Konigsmark succumbed, which was a big blow for the Doge. A month later he ordered a last desperate attack with his remaining army of eight thousand, including volunteers from the fleet. After taking severe casualties of more than a thousand, the assault was called off and Morosini had to face the fact that he had not succeeded in his final endeavour. The capture of Negroponte would have given Venice full military control of Greece and the Aegean.

Despondently, Morosini ordered the evacuation of the army and Prince Maximilian of Hanover covered their embarkation for Thermisis on the Gulf of Hydra, where they landed a few days later. In early November the remaining regiments of Hanoverians and Hessians took ship to Venice, their services no longer required.

Before returning to Venice, Morosini had yet another target. That was to take the last remaining Ottoman fortress in the Morea, Monemvasia, or Malvasia as the Venetians called it, in the extreme south-east. The Venetian fleet arrived in early 1689. After many attempts on the ancient fortress, built by the Venetians themselves a hundred years before, Morosini, now not well, decided to give up his command to his successor, the *Provveditore Generale da Mar* Girolamo Cornaro, and left for Venice in January 1690. Later in the year the Ottomans surrendered. An exhausted Doge returned to Venice for the final time to acclaim that he was too ill to appreciate.

Extraordinarily, Francesco Morosini was summoned to the colours one more time. Cornaro had not only succeeded in taking Malvasia but on hearing of the approach of the Ottoman fleet had also sailed out and defeated them soundly. On his way home he made a surprise attack of the fortress of Valona on the Albanian coast, which was successful, but he too was brought low by disease and died there two days later. Now the experienced Domenico Mocenigo took command and in 1692 failed to recapture Canea on the northern coast of Candia. Hearing of an approaching Turkish fleet, he abandoned the attack and returned to home waters. It seemed as though the Ottomans were re-gathering their strength. Once again, the Venetian powers appealed to Morosini, now seventy-four years old, to take command. Of course he agreed.

On Wednesday 24 May 1693, dressed in his usual red but with formal gold embroidered robes as *Capitano Generale*, with his marshal's baton in his hand, he processed slowly into the dark Basilica of St Mark's, cheered all the way. Some republican purists may have considered it inappropriate that the Doge, freely elected by the Senate, should also carry the military baton, but this was soon forgotten when he emerged after the Mass to make a ceremonial tour of the whole Piazza, passing through a number of specially erected triumphal arches.

The next day, accompanied by his bodyguard of carabiniers and halberdiers, his standard bearers, military band and trumpeters, the Patriarch of Venice and all the clergy, the Signoria, the Procurators of St Mark, the Papal Nuncio and other foreign ambassadors, the Senate of Venice, his family and friends, proceeded in state from the Zecca on the corner of the Piazzetta along the Riva to the far end of the Castello, where he boarded the fabulously ornate decorated *Bucintoro*, the state galley of the Doges. From there, accompanied by dozens of brightly decorated gondolas, he was rowed across the lagoon, past that masterpiece of Palladio, the Chiesa of St Giorgio Maggiore, to the Lido where he went ashore briefly for a last blessing at the church of San Nicolo where lay the relics of St Nicholas the patron saint of sailors. It was the church where traditionally Doges celebrated the annual *Festa della Sensa*, the Marriage with the Sea. It was Ascension Day, the date for this tradition, and it is possible that Doge Morosini cast the golden ring of marriage into the sea as he departed.

As the skyline of Venice faded below the horizon beyond the stern of his flagship, the Doge could not have known that this would be the last time he would see those familiar landmarks of that ancient and beautiful city, and the great lagoon that had ensured its independence and safety since the time of the Romans.

There was work to be done to reinforce his achievements of previous years. Candia was no longer an option for re-conquest since the Ottomans had strengthened the defences of Canea, as they had also done at Negroponte. The third possibility was yet another attack on the Dardenelles against Constantinople, but the old man had never favoured this strategy, so why now?

Having joined up with the whole Venetian fleet at their new stronghold at Malvasia, he increased Venetian control of the Morea by reinforcing the garrisons at Corinth, Mithoni and Nauplia. He also occupied the Saronic islands of Salamis, Hydra and Spetses before retiring at the end of the summer to Nauplia. He was exhausted now and the summer heat of Greece must have taken its toll. As the cold winter winds set in, he suffered more and more from the agony of gallstones. On the Twelfth Night of Christmas, 6 January, he breathed his last. At the news the Venetian fleet fell silent and many a sailor and soldier mourned the loss of their captain.

A service was held at the church of St Antonio in Nauplia where his heart and entrails were buried with due ceremony and his body was transported to Venice, where a great funeral was held at the Basilica dei Santi Giovanni e Paolo. His body was laid to rest in the Gothic Santo Stephano. An ornately carved circular slab of stone marks his final resting place. But his greatest memorial stands in the Doge's Palace in the *Sala dello Scrutinio* where at one end of the gigantic and ornate room there is a marble triumphal arch reaching nearly to the gilded ceiling, with his name carved on it. It is a moving expression of gratitude from the people of Venice to their great commander, who for a few years had held back the inevitable decline of the Venetian Empire.

He was the last and the greatest of the warrior Doges, reminding us that wealth has to be shored up by political influence. And political influence has to be shored up by military might. Great generals ensure this. Franceso Morosini was clearly a great general, a great admiral and a great commander.

6

PRINCE EUGENE OF SAVOY-CARIGNANO

1663–1736

> Our enemies are not in the field. Yours are at Vienna and mine at Versailles!
>
> Claude Hector Villars, Marshal of France, to Prince Eugene at Rastatt, 1714

There is a giant equestrian statue in the middle of Vienna of a bewigged general astride a prancing horse. On one side it says, 'To the glorious conqueror of Austria's enemies' and on the other, 'To the wise counsellor of three Emperors'. The statue is of Prince Eugene of Savoy and it dominates the Helden Platz in Vienna in front of the curved Neue Burg Palace, a wing of the mighty Hofburg Palace, that symbolic seat of Hapsburg power. The soldier on the horse looks muscular and macho, Herculean, physically quite unlike the reality of the remarkable man who is immortalised there, who did indeed serve three Holy Roman Emperors – Leopold I, Joseph I and Charles VI – over a period of six decades.

Prince Eugene of Savoy was born on 18 October 1663 in the Hotel Soissons in Paris, the youngest son of Olympia, one of three young nieces of Cardinal Mazarin, known as the Mazzini girls. The ruler of France had brought to them Paris to be raised alongside the two Bourbon boys, Louis XIV and his younger brother, the Duc d'Orleans, at the Palais Royal. The charismatic Olympia was great friends with the young King from childhood. As he grew into manhood, she was certainly one of his favourites, and had great influence over the semi-literate King whose main interest was acting in elaborate tableaux and plays. When the chance of her marrying Louis diminished due to dynastic considerations, she was married off to the worthy Eugene Maurice, Prince of Savoy-Carignano and later, Count of Soissons, a descendant of the Emperor Charles V.

Their son was thus half Savoyard and half Italian, an interesting genetic mix. Eugene was the third son of this union and was destined for the priesthood, as was customary for a younger son. As soon as he was old enough, he was tonsured and dressed in a black cassock. With a large nose and bulbous lips, he was no cherub and the King mockingly called him 'my little Abbé'. He was raised rather apart in the hedonistic atmosphere of the Hotel de Soissons where his mother and her friends, some quite debauched in habit, enjoyed their dissolute lives secure in the knowledge that Olympia was under the protection of King Louis.

But once Mazarin was dead, the King moved on with his life, taking as his *maitresse-en-titre*, Madame de la Vallière, followed by the powerful Madame de Montespan, who, along with the King's minister the Marquis de Louvois, detested Olympia. After yet another shrill row in the corridors of Versailles, the King banished her to the country but, soon forgiven, she continued to cause trouble and was finally accused by her enemies at court of poisoning her husband who died prematurely in 1673, and then, far worse, of plotting to poison the King.

This was the final straw and Louis personally ordered her to leave the country. Eugene, just sixteen at the time, was now effectively an orphan, with his father's death when he was ten and abandoned by his mother fleeing to Brussels, the capital of the Spanish Netherlands, together with her fortune. The effect this shocking exit must have had on the young boy was clearly life-changing. He was left with no money and went to live with his paternal grandmother, Mary of Bourbon, Princess of Carignano.

Bored with matters ecclesiastical, he began to attend to the more rigorous training of a young man with an interest in things military. Though he was physically not very strong, he began to read military history and listen to stories about military campaigns from courtiers returning from war. He also rode regularly and even tried to become fitter and stronger with gymnastics. He was bored with the excesses of his mother's lifestyle and the dissolute goings-on at the Hotel de Soissons, not to speak of being mocked as a would-be man of the cloth. Eugene asked his friend Prince Louis Armand Conti, a nephew of the great Conde and a son-in-law to Louis XIV, to present him to the King so he could request to be made an officer in the army of France. Louis promptly refused his request. In later years, the King was asked why: 'The request was modest, but the applicant not. Nobody ever ventured to stare me in the face so insolently, like an angry sparrowhawk. Do you think that with his departure I have suffered a severe loss?'

On that fateful day King Louis did suffer the loss of a great general. Eugene's burning emotions were serious:

> Some historians in the future, good or bad, will perhaps take the trouble to enter into the details of my youth, of which, I scarcely recollect anything. They will certainly speak of my mother; somewhat too intriguing, driven from the court, exiled from Paris, and suspected, I believe, of sorcery, by people who were not, themselves, very great wizards. They will tell how I was born in France then left it, my heart swelling with enmity against Louis XIV who refused me a cavalry company, because, said he, I was of too delicate a constitution; that he refused me an abbey, because (based on I don't know what ill talks about me or what invented anecdotes from the gallery of Versailles) that I was more shaped for pleasure than for piety. There is not a Huguenot expelled by the revocation of the Edict of Nantes who hated Louis XIV more than I did. Therefore when Louvois heard of

> my departure saying: 'So much the better; he will never return into this country again,' I swore never to enter it but with arms in my hands. I have kept my word.

By chance, at this time one of his elder brothers had joined the Imperial service and had lost his life fighting the Turks. Prince Eugene of Savoy secretly left Paris on 26 July 1683 along with the Prince Conti to find employment with the Hapsburg Emperor. The King was furious, in particular with Conti, and they were pursued. They were caught in Frankfurt and Conti was persuaded to return, generously leaving Eugene a valuable ring and the last of his money to help the impoverished Prince.

In August the ascetic young Eugene first had an audience with Leopold I in his camp at Passau. Kneeling before the Holy Roman Emperor, he said:

> My mother's fate prevented me having a career in the French army although nothing could ever be proved against her or me. I assure you, most merciful Emperor, of my constant loyalty, that I will devote all my strength, all my courage, and if need be, my last drop of blood, to the service of your Imperial Majesty, and to the welfare and development of your Great House.

The young man had placed all his cards on the table and had changed his fate. Though French was Eugene's first language of course, he communicated with Leopold in Italian as the Emperor disliked French, though he spoke it fluently. Eugene also had a workable command of German, which was essential for him in dealings with the Austrian military establishment.

It should be remembered that anyone could serve the Hapsburg Empire regardless of race, religion or language in their endless wars with the Ottoman Empire in the Balkans. But Eugene was not just another soldier of fortune looking to seek fame and riches in campaigns against the dreaded Ottomans. After all he was a cousin to the strategically important Victor Amadeus, Duke of Savoy who controlled those border lands through the Alps which linked France to Northern Italy. And he was also a direct descendant of the two greatest Hapsburgs, Philip II of Spain and his father the Emperor Charles V. So he was politically potentially a useful ally for the Emperor. All he had to do was to prove himself as a soldier. The scene was set.

The Emperor Leopold I was safely in Passau where he had retreated from the enormous 200,000-man Ottoman army of the Sultan under the command of the sinister Grand Vizier, Kara Mustapha, known as 'the scourge of humanity'. Vienna, the capital of the Hapsburg Empire, was surrounded and in desperate straits with only an army of 10,000 to defend it. It would take time for the Hapsburg army to be assembled.

In the meantime, the Ottoman army was committing atrocities outside the city walls in the surrounding areas. In the village of Perchtoldsdorf the terrified villagers had taken refuge in the local church. A ransom was negotiated and paid and a young girl released, only for the villagers to be immediately set upon and massacred. Kara Mustapha was waiting for Vienna to surrender so he could capture the treasures of the city and fill his coffers, without destroying them in a drawn-out siege.

King John III Sobieski of Poland then arrived to lead the crusade against the Turks. Next to him were the Emperor's brother-in-law, the Duke of Lorraine, as well as the Margrave Louis of Baden, another cousin of Eugene. On Sunday 12 September the King of Poland addressed his officers, who included no fewer than thirty-two European princes, including of course Eugene, exhorting them to save Vienna, which would thus save Europe from the threat of Islam. The perennial threat of an Ottoman invasion of Europe in some ways ensured the position of the Hapsburgs as a bulwark against them. The Christian army fell upon the unprepared 90,000-strong Ottoman army, who had been waiting for the city to surrender, to the north-west of the city in the Vienna Woods. The Hapsburg army was motivated and well led. The Ottomans collapsed after a day of heavy fighting, Eugene's first experience of battle. He performed brilliantly as the enemy were put to the sword, and was personally awarded a pair of golden spurs by the Duke of Lorraine for his bravery. He was also rewarded by the Emperor, who made him Colonel of the Kufstein Dragoons. To be a Colonel of a cavalry regiment was an expensive exercise, so the impoverished young man sold the ring Prince Conti had given him and was lent further money by his cousin, Victor Amadeus, to cover his costs. The war against the Ottomans was to continue, the Hapsburg army led by the Duke of Lorraine.

The Holy League was formed in March 1684, an alliance between the Hapsburgs, John III Sobieski of Poland and the Republic of Venice. The hostilities continued into 1685 and at the tender age of twenty-two Eugene was made a Major General for his actions in a number of engagements with the enemy. The Margrave of Baden presented Eugene personally to the Emperor: 'Sir, this young Savoyard whom I have the honour to present to Your Imperial Majesty will in due course emulate all those whom the world regards as great generals.' These were prophetic words and in the next few years Eugene did much to ensure they were true.

In 1685, Buda was finally taken on 2 September. In fierce fighting Eugene had his horse shot from under him and was wounded twice. In 1687, Eugene attended the carnival in Venice and doubtless disapproved of some of the debauched activities taking place there before rejoining the army in Hungary. On 12 August, Eugene led the heroic cavalry charge into the heart of the Ottoman camp at Mohacs, which led to another victory for the Holy League, reversing the battle there of 1526, a victory for Suleiman the Magnificent that led to the Hapsburg loss of the Hungarian territories for 150 years. At Eugene's side during the charge was the French soldier and diplomat Claude Louis Hector de Villars, his friend and later opponent as Marshal General of France.

For his heroism Eugene was chosen to bring the news of the victory to the Emperor Leopold himself and was promoted again, this time to Lieutenant Field Marshal. The King of Spain made him a member of the Order of the Golden Fleece and the Duke of Savoy again lent him money to purchase the chain of office of that noble brotherhood.

In 1688 the Elector Max Emmanuel of Bavaria became the supreme commander of Imperial forces. Their next obvious target was Belgrade. This key city on the confluence of the Sava and Danube Rivers was besieged for three months in the summer and on 6 September the city walls were breached. Eugene was in the thick of the fighting and suffered a serious head wound.

During the following winter Eugene became ill with influenza, so his notorious mother invited him to Madrid. King Carlos II of Spain made him a Spanish Grandee of the First Order and gave him an income to match. He then approached the Duke of Savoy for permission to start a Spanish branch of the House of Savoy, but by then his mother was at the centre of yet another poisoning scandal, this time when the young Queen of Spain suddenly died, having been administered milk by Olympia. She immediately fled from Madrid and lived her later years out of the limelight in Brussels.

The following year Eugene was once again wounded, this time at Mainz where the French had waged a brutal campaign against the Empire in Germany. He was now posted to Northern Italy to ensure that Piedmont and Savoy were stabilised. He commanded the cavalry in the Duke of Savoy's army and despite a defeat at Staffarda he was able to retrieve the situation for the Savoyard army and continue what was effectively a guerilla campaign against a much larger French army. Critics have pointed out that some of his Balkan irregular units failed to behave according to the rules of war, and there are stories of a French unit being captured and castrated before their execution.

Inevitably, though, when Duke Victor Amadeus, defeated again at Marsaglia by the efficient Marshal Catinat, went over to the French side at the Treaty of Turin in 1696, Eugene was criticised and even suspected of treachery by his opponents at the Austrian court. He had already bought a large palazzo in the centre of Vienna, which was to become his Stadtpalais, or Winter Palace, and also bought the land for what was to be his masterpiece, the Belvedere Palace, just to the south of the city. He had now established himself at the heart of the Holy Roman Empire and the Hapsburg Empire.

The Ottomans had retaken Belgrade in 1697, and their threat loomed once again. After much discourse, Eugene was promoted Supreme Commander of Hapsburg forces at the remarkably young age of thirty-three. It was his first truly independent command and was a credit not only to his courage and judgement in battle but to his ability to persuade and advise the old Emperor. He was the man of the moment.

Soon he learned that the Ottoman army was once again advancing towards Buda and Vienna and was advised that his army only had 31,142 men against, probably, 100,000. On hearing this he replied, 'Thank you for the information. I am the 31,143rd and we will soon be more.'

On 11 September 1697 he was advised that the Sultan with a flotilla of boats had bridged the River Theiss at a place called Zenta and was planning to advance northwards into Transylvania. Eugene decided to face them and made a ten-hour march to Zenta. He arrived at the head of his army with just three hours of daylight left in the day. Seeing that the Ottomans had managed to cross with their cavalry while the infantry were only just getting off the bridge, he went straight into the attack, cornering the enemy near the bridge.

The Hapsburg army was ferocious, cutting down the enemy and forcing thousands into the river. Twenty thousand were killed and ten thousand drowned, while the Ottoman army on the other side of the river was unable to help their comrades. Those killed included the Grand Vizier, Elmas Mehmed Pasha, the Viziers of Adana, Anatolia, and Bosnia, plus more than thirty aghas of the Janissaries, spahis, and silihdars. The next day the Hapsburg army crossed the river and captured a vast amount of booty that had been left behind. Apart from prisoners, they took herds of cattle, camels, horses and carts, money and discarded weapons. Even the Great Seal of Office of the Grand Vizier was taken, which had never been captured before, as well as seven horsetails, symbols of high authority, 100 pieces of heavy artillery and 423 banners. Eugene's casualties amounted to only two thousand killed or wounded.

It was, without doubt, Eugene's greatest triumph to date and the Battle of Zenta proved to be the decisive victory in the long war against the Ottomans. Keen to follow up his victory, Eugene advanced south into Bosnia with a smaller army of seven thousand men. At Sarajevo they met with some opposition and a massacre ensued. Eugene's attitude to such conduct was, at times, laissez faire. He knew that most of his army was erratically paid and poorly equipped. He felt that booty was a fair benefit for the common soldier. In the autumn Eugene returned in triumph to Vienna, once again the saviour of the Hapsburgs. With Leopold I's Hapsburg interests now focused elsewhere and with the imminent death of Charles II of Spain, the Emperor terminated the conflict with the Ottomans a year later and the Holy League signed the Treaty of Karlowitz on 26 January 1699.

Austria regained most of Hungary while Venice gained the Peloponnese in Greece and control of the Dalmatian coast. Peter the Great of Russia had wanted the Holy League to continue the war with his traditional enemy the Ottoman Empire, but he did not succeed. Eugene was awarded land in Hungary on the Danube and he commissioned yet another Palace to be built on Czepel Island. Freed momentarily from the conduct of war, Eugene could now spend time indulging in his other two pastimes, the construction of fabulous palaces and the collection of antique books and works of art.

With the death of the infirm and childless Charles II of Spain on 1 November 1700, the succession of the Spanish throne and subsequent control over her Empire once again embroiled Europe in war – the War of the Spanish Succession. On his deathbed Charles II had bequeathed the entire Spanish inheritance to Louis XIV's grandson, Philip, Duke of Anjou. This threatened to unite the Spanish and French kingdoms under the House of Bourbon, something unacceptable to England, the Dutch Republic, and Leopold I, who himself had a claim to the Spanish throne. From the beginning of the crisis, the Emperor refused to accept the will of King Charles II and did not wait for England and the Dutch Republic to begin hostilities. Before a new Grand Alliance could be concluded, Leopold I prepared to send an expedition to seize Spanish lands in Italy. Once again Eugene was called to the colours. In 1703, at the age of thirty-nine, he was chosen as the President of the *Hofkriegsrat,* the Imperial War Council.

At first he was sent to Pressburg to face the increasing threats from the Hungarian rebels. But when the Elector of Bavaria joined with France and crossed the border into Austria, Eugene returned to Vienna. Initially, England and the United Provinces did not oppose the idea of Louis XIV's grandson, the Duke of Anjou, becoming King Philip V of Spain, nor did the Duke of Savoy. But since the Spanish Empire in Europe was now vulnerable, Eugene realised that the Italian Sates could be taken from Spain for the Hapsburgs. The French also saw this opportunity, and in early 1701 sent reinforcements for their army in Milan and the Quadrilateral, that quartet of fortresses Verona, Legnago, Peschiera and Mantua.

Eugene now led an army of 30,000 men south to cross the Alps into northern Italy. Under his command were three of his best generals, Graf Guido Starhemberg, Prince Commercy, and General Borner. The French general, Marshal Catinat, with an army larger by 10,000 men, blocked the exit routes from the mountain passes down onto the Italian plain. But the wily Eugene, advised by local village people, took another more difficult route via Monte Baldo and crossed down into Italy at Vicenza. He attacked the reluctant French at Carpi near Legnano and drove them off, though he was wounded yet again. During the next few weeks, the outnumbered Hapsburg army managed to out-manoeuvre the French and eventually Catinat was replaced by the less competent Marshal de Villeroi. But the French now outnumbered the Austrians by 50,000 to 30,000.

On 1 September the French attacked, and the well-prepared Eugene got the better of them once more. He had set up his defences well at Chiari, and when the French attacked they lost more than 2,000 men and 200 officers, while the Hapsburg losses were minimal. The French withdrew and Eugene took effective control of the Duchy of Mantua.

Within a week the maritime powers of England and Holland had thrown in their lot with the Hapsburgs and the Grand Alliance was formed. Troops to be supplied were agreed: Austrian Empire, 82,000, United Provinces, 82,000, England, 40,000, which included 18,000 British troops. Bavaria allied with France, which geographically gave France a good strategic position in central Europe. The Alliance only went into action of any sort in the spring of 1702. England, rich at that time, was to hire more than 20,000 mercenaries, but France often hired as many as 80,000.

War at that time was *de rigeur* for young men of the aristocracy and sometimes profitable for more modest men. It appears that nobody particularly cared which side they fought for, as long as they performed honourably. Loyalty tended to be towards either a particular regime or even a good general rather than along the lines of modern nationalism. The price to be paid for a private soldier's death was 20 *thalers*, a horse was 40 *thalers*.

In Italy, Eugene continued his campaign against the French in the winter of 1702. Based in the Duchy of Mantua, he heard from a priest that Marshal Villeroi was based in Cremona. He was advised that there was an unguarded canal that ran into the city, enabling a company of Imperial grenadiers to enter and take control of the St Margaret Gate. Eugene, at the head of 4,000 men charged into the city, taking Villeroi prisoner and the French by surprise. In fierce fighting the French fought back and retrieved the situation, but Eugene's plan had worked and the French commander was his prisoner. Prince Eugene was a general full of cunning, as all good generals should be. And he was one of those who considered that a victory not followed up is a victory thrown away. Exasperated by all this, Louis XIV now sent the formidable Vendôme to command the Italian theatre. But even he was nervous of the abilities and tactics of the enterprising Eugene, and though under orders from Versailles to attack without delay, he hesitated. Eugene, with the elderly and weak Emperor Joseph in charge, had more of a free hand, but still he was hugely outnumbered by the French with an army of 80,000 against the Hapsburg 28,000.

It was a case of a strong king with weak generals against a brilliant general with a weak king. The *Hofkriegsrat* in Vienna even had the effrontery to request Eugene to send 10,000 of his men to take Naples, which he refused.

In these critical days before the Grand Alliance, now led by the charismatic Duke of Marlborough following the death of William III, had moved into action, Eugene fell ill once again and was unable to prevent Vendôme retaking the Duchy of Mantua. On 10 June at Rivalta, he came near to kidnapping the corpulent French Marshal while he was conducting his lavatorial routines in full sight of those around him. One of Eugene's men gave them away, the French were alerted and the attempt failed.

Vendôme was now joined by King Philip V of Spain himself on campaign, and they attacked at Crostolo and on 15 August at Luzzana, where Eugene's great friend, Charles of Lorraine, Prince of Commercy, was killed, much to the distress of Eugene. But in fierce fighting the Empire troops held the line which became news throughout Europe. The Duke of Marlborough wrote congratulating him and the newly crowned Queen Anne of England was delighted, despite the fact that the battle was hardly a victory for either side. In 1703, Eugene was summoned back to Vienna where the situation was, as usual, dire.

At the age of 39 he was now made the President of the *Hofkriegsrat*, effectively Prime Minister, and during the next few years he and the Duke of Marlborough in England, who was in a similar position of both civil and military power, dominated European affairs for nearly a decade.

For the moment, Austria was under pressure. Max Emmanuel, the Elector of Bavaria, whom Eugene had fought alongside in former years, had sided with France and sent an army south into the Tyrol to join up with Vendome in Italy. To block this attempt, Eugene sent an army to attack their rear as they crossed the mountain passes alongside the Hapsburg local militias. He also had to deal with the Hungarian uprising led by Prince Fransis Rakoczi. In the Austrian Netherlands, pretty much controlled by a large French army, Marlborough had been prevented by the nervous States-General of the United Dutch Provinces from attacking the French. By 1704 Count Johann Wratislaw, the brilliant ambassador of the Empire to London, was pressing the Duke to move on the Danube against the French. The Dutch were now led by the more flexible Grand Pensionary, Antoine Heinsius, but still through the first three months of the year any aggressive military moves were thwarted. Then Wratislaw, quite possibly in cahoots with the Duke, wrote a memo to Queen Anne asking her

> ...to instruct Marlborough to concert with the States General the provision of effective help to the Emperor, or at least ensure that the troops which her Majesty maintained on the Continent would be used to protect Germany from a complete collapse.

You could argue that it was Wratislaw who orchestrated the whole triumphant Blenheim campaign. Marlborough, once back in the Low Countries, insisted that he only intended to advance to the Moselle and wrote to the Emperor urging him to send Eugene with an army to meet him. The French-Bavarian army under the Elector and Marshal Marsin were in a holding position near Ulm and Marshal Tallard was commanding an army in the Alsace, blocking the Margrave of Baden in the Black Forest from joining up with the Elector.

On 19 May 1704, the Duke of Marlborough began his epic march deep into the heart of Europe, further than any British army had ever been before. As he marched to who knows where he was joined by increasing numbers of Danes, Dutch and Empire troops. Marshal Tallard managed to get about 10,000 men through the Black Forest to join the Elector in Bavaria. The Margrave of Baden was criticised by many for this, but not by Eugene. Marlborough, accompanied by the ever-eager Wratislaw, marched south along the Rhine, then suddenly struck out south-east into Bavaria towards the Danube.

Marlborough and Eugene, the two most eminent commanders of the age, met at a village called Mundelsheim on 10 June. At this critical moment they both needed each other, and fortunately these two highly experienced soldiers were to forge a close friendship from there on. The stakes were high. As Clausewitz pointed out:

> If an army is completely destroyed it would be impossible to make another, so behind the army there is nothing. This calls for great prudence. Only when some decisive advantage is likely to be gained, can the risk be undertaken. It is in the creation of such chances that the art of the commander lies.

The Duke with the larger army wanted the Prince to fight alongside him, but initially, due to his seniority, the Margrave of Baden had that honour while Eugene was sent north to a crucial position on the Rhine. As the situation became urgent and Marlborough attempted to draw the French and Bavarians into open battle, it became clear that the Empire needed a decisive victory, given the dire situation in other theatres, with the Hungarian rebels on the move and Italy overrun by the French.

With a decoy march north to confuse the enemy, Eugene doubled back and made a forced march to join up with Marlborough on 12 August between Munster and Donauworth. The two generals then managed to persuade the Margrave to move off and lay siege to Ingolstadt. The scene was now set, with each army numbering a little over 50,000. Though the French had a slightly better position, the plan was for Eugene with 16,000 men against 23,000 to attack on the left against the Elector and Marsin, while Marlborough with 36,000 men versus the 33,000 of Tallard was to advance on the right near the banks of the Danube. At dawn on the 13th, the French in their positions across a four-mile front and with greater numbers doubted that these two such experienced generals would attack. But they calculated wrong.

Both Marlborough and Eugene had cavalry in greater numbers than their opponents and they were both cavalrymen. The Allies went straight into the attack, charging at the enemy repeatedly. It was late afternoon when Marlborough's famous final cavalry charge finally broke the French line and they were routed. Many were drowned trying to flee across the Danube. The Elector and Marshal Marsin had also failed against Eugene's units.

Frustrated by lack of progress towards the end of the day, Eugene was obliged to shoot two of his men who were retreating, then placed the command of the cavalry in other hands and personally took command of the infantry, leading them once more into the attack. His personal courage was extraordinary and on one occasion he was nearly shot at point-blank range by a Bavarian dragoon. He was only saved by one of his men cutting the man down. A Prussian officer, witness to the battle, reported: 'Eugene and Marlborough exposed their persons repeatedly. Eugene went so far that it is almost a miracle that he escaped with his life.'

The battle, as Sir Winston Churchill wrote, 'changed the political axis of the world'. France and her armies were no longer invincible, the Austro-Hungarian Empire was saved and even the Dutch Republic was to survive. Perhaps most important of all was the rise in international importance of Great Britain, who, apart from supplying a great general and significantly effective front-line troops, provided much of the campaign with mercenary troops and supplies.

Of course, the importance of Blenheim in English history is not forgotten. What is sometimes overlooked is that Eugene had made as big a contribution to the victory as had the great Duke; Hochstadt, not Blenheim, as it is called in continental Europe, is considered Eugene's victory there. And don't forget more Dutchmen than Englishmen died on that battlefield, where the French lost 30,000 and the Allies just 4,000.

Eugene did not rest on his laurels and with the Empire like a floundering galleon holed in different places, he turned his attention to northern Italy where he endured the following year, though outnumbered by Vendôme, and held the Imperial army together through his mystique and reputation. It's hard to put a finger on how exactly he achieved this. He lacked the personal charisma of the handsome and charming Marlborough, being quite short in stature and with unusual features, but he had other qualities. On campaign he wore a simple brown coat with brass buttons, continually took pinches of Spanish snuff, and had the appearance more of a man of the cloth than a soldier. But a soldier he was, and what a soldier. In combat, he changed character in seconds. He charged into the thick of the action, seemingly fearless, shouting at his enemy and urging on his men. If ever anyone led from the front, it was Eugene and there is much correspondence in existence in which the Emperors he served under exhort him to protect himself for the sake of the nation. But Roman blood coursed in his veins, not to speak of the mountain men of Savoy, so in times of battle these underlying qualities dictated his bearing.

On 23 May 23 1706, Marlborough won another spectacular victory over the French at Ramillies and Villeroi was replaced by Vendôme by Louis XIV. Vendôme had been bottling up Eugene in the mountain passes of the Alps since his victory at Calcinato in April, but Eugene, by feeding false information to the sedentary Vendome, managed to lead his army south, crossing the Adige beyond Verona on a 500-kilometre march in mid-summer due west to the south of the Po River. This epic march was brutal due to the extreme heat and lack of food, but once again Eugene's ingenuity triumphed when he devised a plan for his men to march in the cool of the night until they finally met up with the Duke of Savoy's army. Once again, Eugene was outnumbered with the French troops around Turin numbering about 60,000 to half that number commanded by Eugene and his cousin.

Marshal Marsin, who had been at Blenheim, was overawed by the reputation of Eugene. He had feared being posted to Italy and was full of foreboding. His nervousness permeated through to his subordinates, the Duke of Orleans and Louis de la Feuillade, yet another courtier masquerading as a soldier. Eugene, while reconnoitring with the Duke of Savoy could see that their preparations were hopeless and commented, 'It seems to me that those people are already half beaten.'

On 3 September 1707 he attacked at a weak point in the investment of the city and, after fierce fighting against the desperate French, he prevailed, as much by his strength of personality as anything else. In combat, even though Eugene had some tough German and Austrian regiments on his side, the French forces always outnumbered his. By midday, Marsin was mortally wounded and a prisoner. Eugene was in the thick of the fighting and had his horse shot from under him. Both sides lost about 3,000, but Eugene captured 6,000 prisoners and 3,000 horses.

The French army fled west towards the borders of France, and northern Italy remained under the control of the Hapsburgs for the following 150 years. For his triumph Eugene was given a diamond-studded sword by the Emperor and the Governorship of Milan. The Duke of Marlborough, delighted with Eugene's achievements, wrote to the Dutchman Antoine Heinsius, 'I am assured that the French take more to heart their misfortune in Italy than they did that of Ramillies.' On 4 January 1707, the Margrave Louis of Baden died and was replaced by Eugene as Imperial Field Marshal. He was even offered the crown of Poland but declined, citing his loyalty to the Imperial crown.

Otherwise, the year was not a good one for the Allies. Marlborough was once again hamstrung by the reluctant Dutch. Eugene was obsessed with the idea of marching west into the south of France and making an amphibious attack on Toulon alongside the English fleet under the command of Admiral Sir Cloudesley Shovell. Needless to say, the Toulon campaign never happened and the only positive that Eugene achieved was the capture of Susa in Piedmont in September, an important strategic town. The British admiral was drowned with many of his men when his flagship ran into rocks off the Isles of Scilly returning to England later in the year.

During the winter of 1707-8, Charles III of Spain, the Emperor's brother, was holding on in Catalonia, having been evicted from Madrid. This was during the often overlooked Iberian campaigns of the War of the Spanish Succession. It was generally agreed by the Duke of Marlborough, Queen Anne, who wrote to the Emperor making the request, and even Count Wratislaw, that only the presence of Prince Eugene could change things in Spain. Marlborough was probably only paying lip service to this idea, and Eugene was definitely against being posted to Spain without the guarantee of an army.

The Duke of Marlborough and Prince Eugene met again on 12 April 1708 at The Hague. Along with Heinsius, they planned their summer campaign against a vast French army of 110,000 led by Marshal Vendôme. Marlborough had only 80,000 men and was reliant on Eugene recruiting in the Palatinate during the early summer months. On 28 June Eugene began his march north from Coblenz with only 15,000 men under his command. Bad news came from the Low Countries that the French had taken Bruges and Ghent, thus cutting off England, so Eugene hurried ahead of his army to find Marlborough. The Duke was depressed and only cheered up when he saw Eugene. A Prussian general wrote: 'Our affairs improved through God's support and Prince Eugene's aid, whose timely arrival raised the spirits of the army again and consoled us.'

Though thirteen years younger than Marlborough, Eugene was often described as the 'old Italian Prince' due to his lugubrious manner, shortness of stature, his slumped shoulders, and his sagging cheeks accentuating the folds on either side of his bulbous nose. But what a soldier he was.

On 10 July the Allied army, after a forced march of over 70 kilometres, surprised Vendôme and the French army at Oudenarde, where Eugene commanded sixty battalions, including the whole British contingent, while the Duke was in charge of twenty. The battle next day, more a contact action than a set-piece engagement, ended in a resounding success for the Allies, helped by constant disagreements between Marshal Vendôme and the Duke of Burgundy. Dutch and German troops bore the brunt of the fighting, which started late in the afternoon and lasted into the darkness. It was really Eugene's victory. It was the first time the Prince had fought alongside Marlborough in Flanders. As the battle wore on with each side putting in attacks, Marlborough, sensing that Eugene was under pressure, at about 6 o'clock sent him reinforcements, returning the favour the Prince had done him at Blenheim when, though hard pressed, he had sent over his last regiment of cuirassiers to his corner of the battlefield. While Marlborough remained in overall command, Eugene had led the crucial right flank and centre. Once again the Allied commanders had co-operated remarkably well. 'Prince Eugene and I shall never differ about our share of the laurels,' wrote Marlborough.

After this success, Marlborough proposed an Allied advance along the coast of Flanders into France itself, avoiding the frontier fortresses, followed by an advance towards Paris. Prince Eugene liked the plan but insisted on capturing the formidable Vauban-designed fortress of Lille first. While the Duke commanded the covering force, Eugene oversaw the siege of the town, which finally surrendered on 22 October with Marshal Boufflers surrendering the citadel on 10 December. Yet for all the difficulties of the siege, during which Eugene was badly wounded above his left eye by a musket ball and survived an attempt to poison him, the campaign of 1708 had been a remarkable success. The French had been driven out of almost all the Spanish Netherlands.

The recent defeats, together with the severe winter of 1708-09, had caused famine and privation in France. *Le Roi Soleil,* Louis XIV was close to accepting Allied terms, but the demand of the leading Allied negotiators, Antonie Heinsius, Charles Townshend, Marlborough and Eugene, that Louis XIV should use his own troops to force Philip V off the Spanish throne, proved unacceptable to the French.

Neither Eugene nor Marlborough had objected to the Allied demands at the time, but neither wanted the war with France to continue and would have preferred further talks to deal with the Spanish issue. But the French King offered no proposals. Lamenting the collapse of the negotiations and aware of the vagaries of war, Eugene wrote to the Emperor in mid-June 1709: 'There can be no doubt that the next battle will be the biggest and bloodiest that has yet been fought.' He was not wrong.

Marshal Villars joined by the ageing Marshal Boufflers moved his army to defend Mons after Tournai had fallen to the Allies. Marlborough and Eugene had already decided to force a full engagement with the French but were delayed waiting for reinforcements, allowing Villars more time to prepare his positions, particularly defensive earthworks in the centre. Some say that the battle should have been fought on the 10th or not at all. In any event it turned out to be the Duke of Marlborough's last battle and so his last with Prince

Malplaquet turned out to be the bloodiest single day of fighting in the whole of the eighteenth century, with appalling bloodshed on both sides, the French losing 22,000 killed or wounded and the Allies 11,000 killed or wounded. The Dutch infantry lost more than 8,000, some say in half an hour of heroic fighting.

The great battle started at 7 am on the morning of 11 September with forays from both sides and artillery exchanges. The Allies had an army of 86,000 with 80 cannon and the French 75,000, also with 80 cannon. Marlborough and Eugene's plan was straightforward and as had prevailed at Blenheim, Ramillies and Oudenaarde: they would attack the French flanks, weakening the centre, then pour cavalry into the attack there. This time, however, Villars's centre held.

Furthermore, his two wings were anchored in woods, which made the Allied attacks more difficult. After two hours the Allies on the right led by Eugene were making little progress in Sars Wood and had taken heavy casualties including Eugene, who was wounded in the neck but refused to leave the engagement. On the left flank, the Prince of Orange led his Dutch infantry plus Swiss and Scots in desperate charges, only for them to be cut to pieces, mainly by the legendary fighting Irish Wild Geese. On the other flank, Eugene continued with his relentless attacks, putting more and more pressure on the valiant Villars who by midday had been forced to move 77 battalions to the centre. Now Marlborough made his attack in the centre and drove the French back. Villars was severely wounded. The elite French Maison du Roi regiment counter-attacked and the Allies were driven back. Amongst the French cavalry in the Gendarmes rode the remarkable Irish soldier of fortune, Colonel Peter Drake, who was taken prisoner and wrote a first-hand account of the fighting. He recorded that when he tried to surrender to a German soldier the man was going to shoot him on the spot and he only survived by killing him. An attack by the Dutch cavalry on the left constituted the largest cavalry encounter of the eighteenth century.

At around 3pm the sixty-five-year-old Marshal Boufflers, the stand-in commander, ordered the French to withdraw and Marlborough and Eugene were left on the field to claim a close-run victory, a Pyrrhic victory in truth, in the words of the Duke, 'a very murdering battle'.

In the ensuing weeks Villars was unable to save Mons, which subsequently capitulated on 21 October, but his and Boufflers' resolute defence at Malplaquet, inflicting such severe casualties on the Allies, gave the French army back its pride after so many defeats. In his report Boufflers wrote to the King: 'Misfortune compels me to announce the loss of another battle, but I can assure your Majesty that misfortune has never been accompanied by greater glory.' Once he had recovered, Villars wrote: 'Si Dieu nous fait la grace de perdre encore une pareille bataille, Votre Majeste peut compter que tous ses enemmis seront detruits.'

Prince Eugene's work was not done. In August 1709 his chief political opponent and critic in Vienna, Prince Salm, retired as court chamberlain. Eugene and Wratislaw were now the undisputed leaders of the Austrian government: all major departments of state were in their hands or those of their political allies. There was no alternative but to continue the war, and in June the Allied commanders capture Douai. This success was followed by a series of minor sieges, and by the close of 1710 the Allies had cleared much of France's protective ring of fortresses. Yet there had been no final flourish. Much changed in 1711.

The Emperor Joseph I died on 17 April and his brother, already King of Spain, succeeded him as Charles VI. The Hungarian revolt was settled with a peace agreement. In England a Tory government had deposed the Whigs and were determined to make peace. They gained Queen Anne's support following Sarah Churchill's fall from grace and her husband, the Duke, had been dismissed on charges of embezzlement. In a desperate attempt to keep his Allies on board, Eugene, in appalling weather, crossed the North Sea to England. He was wildly greeted by the people, but the Queen and government hardly acknowledged the great man. It was as though Blenheim, Oudenaarde and Malplaquet had been forgotten. The Duke managed to welcome him privately, but he could no longer influence political matters, and the Prince was finally compelled to leave having achieved little.

The following year, England and France had reached agreement and, to Eugene's dismay, Marlborough's successor, the Duke of Ormonde, received an order forbidding him from any military action against France. Despite some successes, Eugene's hands were tied with no cooperation from the other Allies and by the end of the summer, following the French victory at Denain, all the positions worked for on the borders of France during the previous decade were back under the control of Louis XIV. Realising his position was hopeless, Eugene tried to persuade the Emperor to join in the peace agreement at Utrecht in 1713, but he was ordered to persist and only after another bad year did the Emperor Charles VI finally agree to peace. His allies in Germany were reluctant to carry on and the finances in Vienna were exhausted.

Ironically, it was Prince Eugene and Marshal Villars, who had known and respected each other back in Vienna twenty-six years before in the Turkish campaigns where they had fought side by side, who were to negotiate the peace. Negotiations started at the end of November and the Treaty of Rastadt was signed on 7 March 1714. During those weeks Eugene and Villars dined alternately in each other's headquarters, cementing their friendship. In his memoirs Eugene describes how they played card games together late into the night on many occasions. The profession of soldiering brought these two very different characters together, the self-effacing, aristocratic aesthete and the ebullient, hard-drinking, self-made Frenchman, who had even served under the great Turenne. Eugene, due his experience of such matters, was the better negotiator and Villars was only too keen to enhance his reputation at Versailles. Due to his effective negotiations and despite the disastrous campaign of 1713, Eugene was able to write to his Emperor, 'In spite of the military superiority of our enemies and the defection of our Allies, the conditions of peace will be more advantageous and more glorious than those we would have obtained at Utrecht.'

The Hapsburgs' main reason for calling for peace in the west was the growing danger posed by the Turks in the east. The Ottomans were now reviving, and after success against the Russians in Wallachia and Moldavia they attacked the Venetians in the Peloponnese. Clearly, their next target would be Hungary and a dismantling of the 1699 Peace of Carlowitz. Emperor Charles VI despatched Prince Eugene to Hungary in June 1716 at the head of an army of between 80,000 and 90,000 men. By early August 1716, the Ottoman Turks, some 200,000 men under the Sultan's son-in-law, the Grand Vizier Damat Ali Pasha, were marching from Belgrade towards Eugene's position west of the fortress of Petrovaradin on the north bank of the Danube.

After resisting calls for caution and foregoing a council of war, the Prince decided to attack immediately, on the morning of 5 August. The Turkish army had some initial success, but after an Imperial cavalry attack on their flank Ali Pasha's forces fell into confusion. Although the Imperials lost almost 5,000 dead or wounded, the Turks, who retreated in disorder to Belgrade, seem to have lost double that amount, including the Grand Vizier himself who was mortally wounded. Eugene now advanced deeper into Hungary and in October 1716 took the fortress of Timisoara, which had been under Turkish control for more than 150 years.

The key to the Turkish occupation of Serbia and Hungary was the great fortress of Belgrade standing where the Danube and Sava Rivers met. It was occupied by a garrison of 30,000 men under the Vizier Mustapha Pasha when the Imperial troops began the siege in mid-June 1717. During the next few weeks Eugene bombarded the city with artillery. But in August a vast Turkish army, nearly 200,000 strong, led by the new Grand Vizier Halil Pasha appeared on the heights to the east of the city. Word spread to most of the capitals of Europe that Prince Eugene of Savoy was finally doomed. But once again, by force of character he was to achieve the unachievable.

The intractable Prince had no intention of abandoning the siege and at once resorted to his usual *modus operandi*. With many of his men suffering from starvation and disease, he realised that the only way out of the situation was to take the attack to the enemy. At about midnight on 15 August, the mist still hanging over the Danube, 40,000 Imperial troops climbed up through the heights through the fog and caught the Turks unaware. At dawn Halil Pasha's army was destroyed, largely due to a powerful cavalry charge led by Eugene himself, and where he was once again wounded, for the thirteenth time. A week later Belgrade surrendered, bringing the war to an end.

The victory was the crowning point of Eugene's military career and had confirmed him as the leading European general. His ability to snatch victory at the moment of defeat had shown the Prince at his best. The Hapsburg Empire had won the battle without allies, and the army had been led by Eugene alone. The principal objectives of the war had been achieved: the task Eugene had begun at Zenta was completed, and the Carlowitz settlement secured.

By the terms of the Treaty of Passarowitz, signed on 21 July 1718, the Turks surrendered the Banat of Temeswar, along with Belgrade and most of Serbia, although they regained the Morea, the Peloponnese, from the Venetians. The war had dispelled the immediate Turkish threat to Hungary and was a triumph for the Empire and for Eugene personally.

In June 1716 he had been named Governor General of the Austrian Netherlands, but he never went there and resigned the post in November 1724. The Emperor then made him Vicar-General of Italy, which yielded 140,000 gulden a year plus an estate in Siebenbrunn worth twice that. But the Prince was over sixty years old, getting sick in the cold and damp winters of Vienna.

During the ensuing years European politics flowed to and fro until finally the Second Treaty of Vienna, signed on 16 March 1731, secured the Anglo-Austrian alliance once again, providing security for the Empire against the constant threat from a Spanish-French alliance. In it, King George II agreed to guarantee the Pragmatic Sanction securing the right of the Emperor's daughter, Maria Theresa, to inherit the entire Hapsburg Empire. This was largely the achievement of Prince Eugene's political machinations and was a fitting end to his achievements as a diplomat.

Top: 'The Continence of Scipio' by Nicolas-Guy Brenet, 1788, Palais Rohan, Strasbourg. Scipio, known as a womaniser, was brought a girl prisoner after the capture of Cartagena. Being advised that she was betrothed to a local chief, Allucius, he honourably returned her to her fiancé, refused to accept the ransom offered and instead gave it to them for their nuptials. The story has been portrayed in paintings, opera and music many times. (Public domain)

Above right: This 1st-century AD bronze bust found at Herculaneum and held at the Museo Archeologico Nazionale, Naples, was understandably thought to be of Scipio Africanus. It is now thought to portray a priest of Isis.

Above left: Hannibal is as much associated with Scipio as he is with elephants. This fanciful c.1510 fresco of Hannibal crossing the Alps by Jacopo Ripanda is in the Palazzo dei Conservatori, Rome. (Courtesy José Luiz under creative commons 4.0)

6th-century mosaic portrait of Belisarius in Basilica San Vitale, Ravenna. (Courtesy Petar Milošević, creative commons 4.0)

Painting by François-André Vincent of the aged and blind Belisarius being given alms by one of his veterans. Musée Fabre, Montpellier. (Public domain)

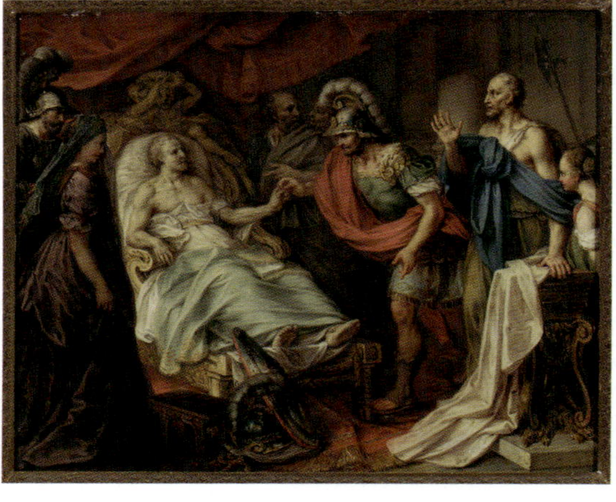

18th-century Bohemian painter Franz Xaver Wagenschon's Death of Belisarius. National Museum in Warsaw. (Public domain)

Above: An unfortunately wholly imaginary portrait of Bohemond I, Prince of Antioch, by Merry-Joseph Blondel (1781-1853) at Versailles. (Public domain)

Above right: The Siege of Antioch. Miniature painting from Sébastien Mamerot's Les Passages d'Outremer. Bibliothèque Nationale de France, Paris. (Public domain)

Right: Canosa di Puglia, Tomb of Bohemond, San Sabino Cathedral. (Courtesy Berthold Werner, creative commons 3.0)

Albrecht von Wallenstein portrait by Julius Schnorr von Carolsfeld, after a 1629 original by Anthony van Dyck, Bayerische Staatsgemäldesammlungen, Munich. (Public domain)

Above: Albrecht Wallenstein as Mars, God of War. Detail of a ceiling decoration in the main hall of the Wallenstein Palace, Prague, by Luigi Baccio del Bianco (1604-657). (Creative commons 4.0)

Left: Equestrian painting of Albrecht von Wallenstein in his familiar black armour. Wallenstein Palace, Prague. (Public domain)

Portrait of Morosini by an unknown artist, Museo Correr. (Public domain)

Doge Morosini by an anonymous artist, Museo Correr. (Public domain)

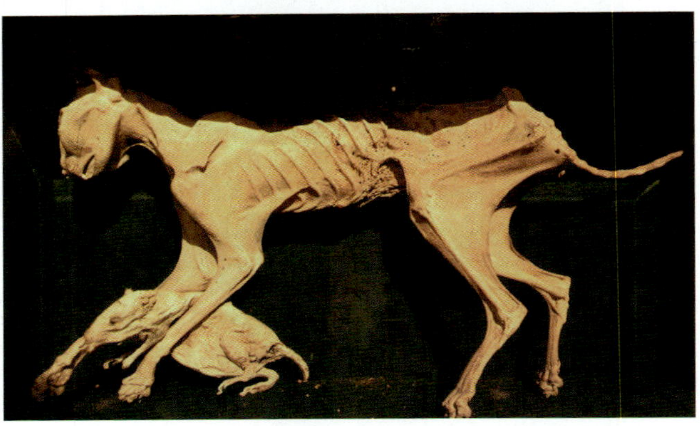

Above: Tomb of Francesco Morosini in the Chiesa di San Stefano, Venice. (Courtesy Giovanni Dall'Orto)

Left: Doge Morosini's embalmed cat, Nini, with a rat, Correr Museum, Venice.

Below left: The Arsenal of Venice, showing the Lion of Piraeus on the left, taken by Morosini in 1687 during the Great Turkish War. (Public domain)

Portrait of Prince Eugene of Savoy, 1718, by Jacob van Schuppen, court painter in Vienna, held at the Rijksmuseum, Amsterdam. Prince Eugene wears his familiar brown battle coat. (Public domain)

The Battle of Vienna, 12 September 1683, when the Ottoman army was driven back from the walls of the city after a two-month siege. This was Prince Eugene's first battle. (Public domain)

Equestrian portrait of Prince Eugene c.1700 attributed to the Flemish painter Jan van Huchtenburg. (Public domain)

The Battle of Blenheim, 1704, known in Europe as the Battle of Hochstadt, where Prince Eugene and the Duke of Marlborough teamed up for the first time. (Courtesy The Royal Collection)

Above left: King Charles XII of Sweden (1682-1718). 'I have resolved never to start an unjust war but never to end a legitimate one except by defeating my enemies.' (Public domain)

Above right: Equestrian portrait of the young King Charles XII by David von Krafft. (Public domain)

Below: Painting by Daniel Stawert, Battle for the crossing of the Duna, 18 July 1701, near Riga in modern Estonia, where the Swedish army defeated the Saxon-Russian forces under Adam von Steinau. (Public domain)

Left: Monument to Charles XII at Kungsträdgarden, Stockholm. He is pointing towards Russia where all his dreams of conquest were shattered. (courtesy I99pema, creative commons 4.0)

Below: Final journey of Charles XII. Bringing Home the Body of King Charles XII, a dramatic painting of the great hero by Gustaf Cederström, 1884. (Public domain)

Above left: Count Maurice of Saxony holding his marshal's baton by Swiss painter Jean-Etienne Liotard. (Public domain)

Above right: Portrait of Count Maurice of Saxony wearing the Polish Order of the White Eagle by Maurice Quentin de La Tour. (Public domain)

Right: Maurice of Saxony's magnificent tomb in L'Eglise de St Thomas, Strasbourg. (Courtesy Chabe01, creative commons 4.0)

Left: Suvorov and his army crossing the Alps by Vasily Surikov. (Public domain)

*Below:*The wounded Suvorov saved by Grenadier Novikov at the Battle of Kinburn by Alexander F. Petrushevsky. (Public domain)

Top: Battle of Kinburn Spit, by Christian von Mechel. Kinburn fortress was garrisoned by the Russians under the command of Alexander Suvorov. (Courtesy The Royal Collection)

Above: Fierce fighting on the Devil's Bridge 1799, part of Suvorov's Swiss campaign. (Courtesy Дмитрий Скляренко, 3.0 creative commons)

Below: Depiction of Suvorov's final departure from his village of Konchanskoye for the 1799 campaign by Nikolay Shabunin in the Suvorov Memorial Museum, St Petersburg. (Public domain)

Above left: Sir Hugh Gough, 1st Viscount Gough wearing his Order of the Bath and his Peninsular War medal.

Above right: Coat of Arms of Viscount Gough. (Courtesy MostEpic, creative commons 4.0)

Below: The Battle of Talavera 27-28 July 1809 by English cartoonist William Heath. At this battle Gough was severely wounded and nearly captured. Sir Arthur Wellesley was created Viscount Wellington after the battle. (Public domain)

In 1839, Lin Zexu was tasked with stopping the opium smuggling into China. He seized opium from foreign ships and introduced a system where traders would only be permitted to enter the country if they signed a bond stating that they had no illegal goods. In March of the same year, as the First Opium War began, Gough was appointed commander-in-chief of the British forces in China. (Public domain)

Col Edwardes was the British officer involved in the attempt to stem the Multan rebellion. In charge of the Derajat (trans-Indus) region, Edwardes secured the whole area. He would later cross the Indus and approach Multan with his own largely mercenary army and begin preparations for a siege of the city. He had served in Gough's personal staff at Mudki where he was wounded, and at Sobraon. Photograph by John McCosh c.1849. (Courtesy of the National Army Museum)

Sir Edward Hardinge, Peninsular War and Waterloo veteran who became Governor General of India. (Public domain)

The Chillianwala monument commemorates the battle fought in 1849 during the Second Anglo-Sikh War. (Courtesy Dr Sohaib ul Hassan under creative commons 2.0)

But now the Emperor planned for Maria Theresa to marry Francis Stephen of Lorraine, which would present an unacceptable threat on France's border. By the beginning of 1733 the French army was ready once again for war: all that was needed was the excuse. In 1733 Augustus the Strong, the Polish King and Elector of Saxony, died. There were two candidates to succeed him, his son Augustus, supported by Russia, Austria, and Prussia, or Stanislaw Leszczynski, the father-in-law of the twenty-three-year-old King of France, Louis XV. The Polish succession had afforded Louis XV's chief minister Cardinal Fleury the opportunity to attack Austria and take Lorraine from Duke Francis Stephen. Prince Eugene entered the War of the Polish Succession as President of the *Hofkriegsrat*, the Imperial War Council, and commander-in-chief of the army, but was severely handicapped by the quality of his troops and shortage of funds to pay them. More importantly, now in his seventies, he was also burdened by rapidly declining physical and mental powers.

France declared war on Austria on 10th October 1733, but without the funds from the maritime powers, Great Britain and the Netherlands, who, despite the Vienna treaty, remained neutral throughout the hostilities, Austria could not hire the necessary troops to wage an offensive campaign. 'The danger to the monarchy,' wrote Eugene to the Emperor, 'cannot be exaggerated.'

Despite all these factors, Prince Eugene once again took command on the Rhine in April 1734, but vastly outnumbered, was forced onto the defensive. In June he set out to relieve Philippsburg, a key fortress on the borders of the Empire. Accompanying the fast-fading Eugene was the young Frederick the Great, sent by his father to learn the art of war. Frederick gained considerable knowledge from Eugene, recalling in later life his great debt to his Austrian mentor, but the Prussian prince was also aghast at Eugene's condition, writing later, 'His body was still there but his soul had gone.'

Fortunately for the Emperor Charles VI, Cardinal Fleury, effectively the ruler of France, offered reasonable peace terms at the end of 1735. Prince Eugene returned to Vienna in October and during the winter months was too sick to attend the grand wedding of the Archduchess Maria Theresa to Duke Francis Stephen of Lorraine in February 1736. He apparently returned home alone to his Stadtpalais on the evening of 20 April 1736 after playing cards with his old friend the Grafin Eleonore Batthyany. When his servants arrived to wake him the next morning, they found the great man had passed away quietly during the night.

It has been said that on the same morning he was discovered dead, the great lion in his menagerie at the Belvedere Palais was also found dead. Prince Eugene's heart was buried with the ashes of his ancestors in Turin, in the mausoleum of the Superga. His remains were carried in a long procession to St Stephens Cathedral in Vienna where his embalmed body was buried in the Kreuzkapelle. It is said that the Emperor secretly witnessed this as a private mourner without anybody's knowledge.

In what has been interpreted as a sign that he considered himself French by birth, Italian by dynastic extraction, and German-Austrian by allegiance, Eugene of Savoy often signed himself using trilingual forms such as *Eugenio* or *Savoia* in Italian, *Von* in German, *Savoye* or *Eugène* in French. He often used 'EVS' as an abbreviation. During his years of triumph, the originally impoverished Prince accumulated an enormous fortune and became one the great European collectors of art. He surrounded himself with some of the great intellectuals of the age, the philosopher, mathematician and inventor of calculus Gottfried von Leibniz, the writer Jean Baptiste Rousseau and one of the great art connoisseurs of the time, Cardinal Alessandro Albani, in his legendary library. Rousseau wrote: 'It is hardly believable that a man who carries on his shoulders the burden of almost all the affairs of Europe should find as much time to read as though he had nothing else to do.'

Eugene's greatest contribution to baroque art was the building of three magnificent palaces in Vienna, the Stadtpalais, or Winter Palace, and the Upper and Lower Belvederes. The Stadtpalais built in the narrow streets of central Vienna has a remarkable central staircase reaching to the top of the building and a magnificent library. The Lower Belvedere merges seamlessly into the formal gardens, as though one piece of work. It once housed a menagerie of rare animals and an aviary in which was his favourite eagle, which he himself fed when he was at home. The Upper Belvedere is an even more exotic piece of architecture, with pavilions and cupolas decorated with frescoes, ceiling paintings, chandeliers and mirrors.

But perhaps Eugene's favourite palace was the more classical *Schlosshof* along the banks of the Danube where he hosted hunting parties, though he considered hunting a waste of time, and preferred to spend time enjoying the stillness of the countryside, as the poplars moved in the breeze and the rolling cornfields of Hungary changed colour according to the seasons. It was in this region on the banks of the Danube, the frontier of the Roman Empire, that Marcus Aurelius had died in 180.

Sadly, the *Schlosshof* has long since disappeared and only exists in paintings by Bernardo Bellotto made after Eugene had died and his country retreat was owned by the Empress Maria Theresa, whose inheritance and reign had been guaranteed by Prince Eugene and whose Empire had been served so loyally by this enigmatic and somewhat distant man for more than fifty years.

On the battlefield Eugene demanded inordinate courage in his subordinates and expected his men to fight where and when he wanted; his criteria for promotion were based primarily and rightly on obedience to orders and courage on the battlefield, rather than social position. His men responded because he was willing to push himself as hard as them. His thirteen wounds testify to that. He would say,'You should only be harsh when, as often happens, kindness proves useless.'

His position as President of the *Hofkriegsrat* proved less successful. Following the long period of peace after the Austro-Turkish War, the idea of creating a separate field army or providing garrison troops with effective training for them to be turned into such an army quickly was never considered by Eugene. By the time of the War of the Polish Succession, therefore, the Austrians were outclassed by a better prepared French force. In his opinion, unlike the drilling and manoeuvres carried out by the Prussians, which to him seemed irrelevant to real warfare, the time to create actual fighting men was when war came. To his responsibilities Eugene attached his own personal values: physical courage, loyalty to his sovereign, honesty, self-control in all things, and he expected these qualities in his commanders.

Eugene's approach to command was dictatorial, but he was willing to co-operate with someone he regarded as his equal, such as the Duke of Marlborough. Yet the contrast with his co-commander of the Spanish Succession war was clear. Marlborough was a family man working with his wife, Sarah, to build a dynasty. Prince Eugene was quite the opposite. Rarely seen in the company of the opposite sex, constantly working for the success of the dynasty he served, the Hapsburgs, he was more the austere soldier. The result was a figure inspiring respect and admiration rather than affection, essentially a lonely warrior.

The sheer range of his soldiery has few rivals. He not only campaigned in the Spanish Netherlands with Marlborough but extensively in Northern Italy and, of course, the Balkans. The range and variety of his leadership is surpassed by no general in history

7

KING CHARLES XII OF SWEDEN

1682–1718

> I have resolved never to start an unjust war but never to end a legitimate one, except by defeating my enemies.
>
> Charles XII quoted by Voltaire

On 27 April 1707 at the Schloss Alt-Ranstadt, near Leipzig, John Churchill, Duke of Marlborough, the victor of Blenheim and Ramillies, was ushered in to the presence of King Charles XII of Sweden, conqueror of Poland and Saxony. Their meeting, in which the Swedish Count Carl Piper was the interpreter, was formal.

The young King was a shy man in contrast to the suave and handsome fifty-seven-year-old Duke. Marlborough handed him a personal letter from Anne, the Queen of England. She sent her greetings saying he was a prince admired by the whole universe, to which Marlborough added in his well-practised courtly style, which in all probability irritated the twenty-four-year-old King, 'I am in this particular more happy than the Queen, and I wish I could serve some campaigns under so great a general as your Majesty, that I might learn what I yet want to know in the art of war.'

King Charles privately considered Marlborough looked more like a dandy than a soldier, while the Englishman thought that the young king dressed so simply through false modesty. Marlborough noticed nothing but maps of Russia on the desk. He also observed that whenever the Czar was mentioned, the King's eyes darted about and his cheeks flushed. He realised then and there that this was Charles's obsession, and he would never involve himself in the politics of Western Europe.

Charles XII, King of Sweden, is one of the most mysterious and extraordinary characters in European history and one of the most remarkable generals. In the century that followed his death such great and fiercely critical literary figures as Voltaire and Dr Johnson hero-worshipped him. He became almost a mythical character drawing comparisons with Alexander the Great, likewise a warrior who was to die young.

He was born into the House of Palatinate-Zweibrücken, a branch line of the House of Wittelsbach and was the only surviving son of the autocratic Charles XI and the genuinely charitable Ulrika Eleonora the Elder, a Danish princess. She died when he was only eleven years old and his father four years later, leaving him to inherit the throne aged fifteen on 17 June 1697.

Charles XI, was always seemingly under the influence of his formidable mother, Hedwig Leonora of Holstein-Gottorp, widow of Charles X. She had acted as regent during his childhood and was always referred to as 'the Queen' by her son, who had nominated her again as regent during his son's minority. This was not to last long, despite the wishes of the old Queen. One November afternoon while he was reviewing one of his regiments, he spoke to Carl Piper, one of his councillors: 'I am thinking that I feel worthy to command these brave men, and I wish that neither they nor I should receive orders from a woman.'

Three days later the States General handed over the government to him and after entering Stockholm on a chestnut horse shod with silver he was crowned on 24 December 1697. The Archbishop of Upsala, as was the custom, anointed the young King and, just as he was about to place the crown on his head, had it taken out of his hands by the young man, who crowned himself. The congregation applauded their new leader.

At first it was difficult to make a judgement of the young ruler and the only clue was that he was a great admirer of Alexander the Great, having read the Quintus Curtius biography of the man in the original Latin.

'I wish I could be like him,' said the boy king.

But he lived only thirty-two years,' his tutor replied.

'Is that not enough when one has conquered kingdoms?'

On another occasion in the palace, on a map of Riga, the capital of Livonia, he wrote: 'God gave it to me and the Devil shall not take it away.' He spoke Latin for political reasons and German for practicality in his territories, but he refused to speak French, considering it corrupted people and was too widely used in Europe.

In 1700, when he was eighteen years old, a triple alliance of Denmark, Saxony and Russia declared war on the Swedish Empire, which at that time included a number of territories around the Baltic Sea on the European mainland, and launched a threefold attack on the Swedish protectorate of Holstein-Gottorp and the provinces of Livonia and Ingria, aiming to take advantage as the Swedish Empire was now ruled by a child. This initiated the Great Northern War.

King Frederick IV of Denmark and Norway, Charles's cousin, made his first attack against Sweden's ally Holstein-Gottorp in March 1700 when a Danish army laid siege to Tönning. At the same time King Augustus II of Saxony's troops advanced into Swedish Livonia, captured the Swedish fortress of Dünamünde and laid siege to Riga. Due to reforms initiated by his father by which Swedish subjects were obliged to perform military service, Charles XII had control of an army of more than 75,000 men. Wisely, he decided to deal with each of his opponents separately.

First, he forged an alliance with the maritime powers England and the Netherlands, who both disliked the idea of Denmark controlling the straits into the Baltic Sea, which could adversely affect their prosperous trade there. On the 8 May 1700, the eighteen-year-old monarch set out at the head of a fleet of forty-three ships with 8,000 men aboard, applauded by a vast crowd. He was never to return to Stockholm.

The plan was to sail to Holstein to help their ally who had been attacked by Denmark, but then Charles came up with the idea of attacking Copenhagen directly. General Rehnskiold, his senior officer, was so impressed by the plan that he swiftly put it into action. An extra 5,000 troops were embarked off the coast of Sweden, and the fleet, evading enemy warships, managed to make a landing on the Danish coast just outside Copenhagen. They were protected in this action by the presence of English and Dutch naval forces who, together with the Swedish navy, bombarded Copenhagen from 20 to 26 July. As King Charles boarded his landing boat to lead his men ashore, he realised that the French Ambassador, the Count of Guiscard, was at his side. He told him that he had no argument with the Danes and that he need not go any further.

'Sire,' the diplomat replied, 'the King my master ordered me to reside at your majesty's court. I trust you will not drive me from it today when it has never been so brilliant.'

With that they both leapt into the landing boat followed by Count Piper. As they approached the shore, the King jumped into the sea and with his sword drawn waded ashore, closely followed by the Ambassador, Count Piper and officers and soldiers. As they came up the beach they came under fire and the King, who had never in his life heard the sound of enemy musket fire, asked what the whistling sound he could hear all around him was.

An officer replied, 'It is the noise of the bullets they are firing at you.'

'Good,' said the King, 'From now on that shall be my music.'

At that moment the officer was hit by a bullet in the shoulder and another man next to the King was killed.

Within days Charles sent a message to the King of Denmark that he should cease the siege of Tonning or Copenhagen and Zealand would be laid waste. Within a few weeks the two sides sat down at Travendal in August and a peace was agreed, in which Holstein would be recompensed.

Now Charles turned to face his more serious enemies, Saxony and Russia. A Saxon army led by King August II King of Saxony and King of Poland had already invaded Swedish Livonia, and on 22 February 1700 had laid siege to Riga, the most populous city of the Swedish Empire. Here the venerable 80-year-old Swedish Count Dahlberg led the defence of the city, the Saxon army was led by Count Fleming and the Livonian aristocrat, Johann Reinhold Patkul, who had turned against Sweden when the 'Great Reduction' of Charles XI in 1680 had stripped him and many others of the nobility of their lands and properties.

Charles XII was able to speedily deploy his army to the eastern part of the Baltic Sea and face his remaining enemies. He landed at Parnu on the Baltic coast in October, and aware that Riga was holding out with fresh Finnish troops, advanced eastwards. Besides the army of Augustus II in Livonia, there was the more serious threat of the Russian army led by the ambitious and capable young Czar, Peter I, who had already invaded Ingria and was laying siege to Narva. The commander of the garrison, Colonel Henning Horn, signalled the King: 'The cavalry has been fighting since this morning and it is still facing the enemy's advance units outside the city.'

On 29 November, the Swedish army approached the citadel. The Russians under the command of the newly promoted Charles Eugene de Croy numbered nearly 40,000 men while the Swedes had a force of 10,500 plus the 2,000 or so defenders of the city. As they were approaching the village of Pyhajoggi less than 20 miles from Narva, Russian cavalry suddenly appeared. Swedish dragoons held them off while the cannons were quickly deployed and opened fire on the clusters of Russian cavalry from close range.

The next day Charles positioned his army before the city. Seeing them, de Croy thought they were merely the vanguard of a much larger army. Charles very simply divided his infantry into two as they advanced to the north and south of a small hillock in front of the city. To the south were 11 battalions under the overall command of General Vellingk. To the north were 10 battalions under Major General Rehnskiöld, including two battalions under the command of the formidable Magnus Stenbock, where the King chose to position himself. Each unit was led by grenadiers carrying fascines, great bundles of branches, a common practise to ensure their advance was not impeded by ditches or entrenchments. The cavalry of about 4,000 advanced on the flanks of the infantry. The artillery, 37 guns positioned on higher ground, bombarded the places targeted for the attack.

In the early afternoon, just as a snowstorm was swirling about the walls of the fortress, the Swedes attacked. Soon the Russian infantry broke under the methodical firing of the highly trained Swedes and despite brave actions by the elite regiments, the Russians began to retreat, some blaming their foreign and inexperienced commanders, and Narva was captured. The night before the battle, Czar Peter and his senior general Golovin had departed, leaving the unfortunate de Croy in command.

The Battle of Narva was a severe setback for the Russian army. But though the Swedes had captured 10 generals, 10 colonels, and many regimental officers had died in battle, the Russians, with losses of about 10,000 men in all, not to speak of huge losses in armaments, would live to fight another day. If Charles had pushed on with the campaign, as General Vellingk suggested, there is every chance he might have ended the war there and then.

With the Russians driven back within their borders, Charles XII was now to turn south to meet Augustus II, Elector of Saxony,King of Poland and Grand Duke of Lithuania. But this could only occur when the weather improved, and in the meantime Charles, having placed the army in winter quarters around Dorpat, took up residence in the castle of Leis nearby and spent the winter hunting, sledging, skating on the frozen lakes with his dog Pompey and even, apparently, playing blind-man's-buff with his officers.

In seemingly faraway Western Europe, King Charles II of Spain died in November 1700, bequeathing his throne to the grandson of Louis XIV, which was to lead to the War of the Spanish Succession. There was a chance for the King of Sweden to become the arbiter and referee of all the complex political manoeuvrings which were inevitably to spring up, but the determined and single-minded young soldier had no interest in such matters. Russia is what concerned him. He did not even reply to letters sent to him from Stockholm by his advisers and in the late spring of 1701, 10,000 reinforcements arrived, which put him in a position to go on the offensive against the Saxons. On his birthday, 17 June, he led an army of 15,000 men towards Riga. On the far side of the river Duna were the Saxons, numbering 10,000, plus double that number of Russians sent by Czar Peter. They were commanded by General Adam von Steinau, who had been preparing for this moment since his arrival in early April.

On the night of 8 July, the Swedes, led inevitably by the fearless Charles, made the crossing in shallow boats and fought their way ashore. Though the Duke of Courland and the giant Patkul fought bravely, they were forced to retreat, and the Swedish King was now left in control of all of Courland. He established his winter quarters there at Wurgen from September until the end of the year.

In negotiations with Poland, really a dual state made up of the Kingdom of Poland with an elected king and the Grand Duchy of Lithuania, its borders stretching from the Baltic in the north to Moldova on the Black Sea in the south, Charles demanded the deposition of Augustus and threatened an invasion if nothing was done. He would never forgive the Saxon King for attacking Sweden without warning a year before.

Cardinal Radziejowski, the scheming spiritual and political leader of Poland, wrote to him reminding him that Sweden was not at war with Poland and offering to mediate between the two kings. Charles rejected this offer abruptly and refused to meet two emissaries from Augustus. The first was the legendary beauty and intellect Marie Aurora, Countess of Konigsmarck, the Swedish former mistress of Augustus, from an illustrious family of Swedish generals and the mother of the future Marshal of France, Maurice de Saxe. Legend has it that King Charles encountered her while he was out riding and having tipped his hat to her, turned swiftly away. The second emissary, Count Viszthum, who arrived with large cheques and high-quality horses with which to bribe the Swedish officers, was arrested and imprisoned in Riga.

In March 1702, Charles XII started his march to Warsaw in the knowledge that Augustus's position was tenuous at best and had only been secured by influence from France and his rejection of his Protestantism in favour of Catholicism. At the head of his army Charles marched into Warsaw on 14 May, and in the castle square a Te Deum of thanks was sung before his drawn-up soldiers. He then retired to modest quarters after his men had all been found suitable accommodation. Augustus meanwhile had fled to Kracow.

In the ensuing weeks, Cardinal Radziejowski was summoned to Warsaw repeatedly and finally attended after three requests. Charles made his predictable demands, but the Cardinal advised him that no Polish *Sejm*, the convocation of noble leaders, would tolerate the election of a new king while the incumbent still lived. Charles's senior officers were also advising him not to waste Sweden's energies on Poland when the real threat was from Russia. But Charles was adamant and within two weeks left Warsaw to hunt down Augustus.

On 2 July, the Saxon army of 19,000 left Kracow and took up positions at Klissow, where they were joined by a Polish contingent of 6,000. The Swedish army approached five days later and within hours were reinforced by Major General Morner and his division of 5,000 men, who had arrived by forced march from Vilnius in Lithuania. The King wanted to attack immediately but was persuaded by Piper to delay till 19 July, the anniversary of the Swedish victory at Dunamunde the year before.

At the Battle of Klissow the Swedish army of 10,000 now fought one of the epic battles of the eighteenth century and ended victorious with 2,000 losses, including the King's beloved brother-in-law, the Duke of Holstein, despite heroic opposition from the Saxons and Poles who lost more than 3,000 men killed or wounded.

Charles XII's tactics during the battle were impeccable and it was probably his greatest victory, placing him high in the pantheon of field commanders. He was still only twenty-one and, if you argue that others planned the invasion of Zealand or even the attacks at Narva and Dunamunde, Klissow was his masterpiece. It was fought by a Swedish army, outnumbered two to one, far from home in central Poland, exhausted by endless marches across hostile lands, yet led by brave and intelligent officers of the highest order.

Three weeks later, Charles XII stood before the walls of Kracow. With him was Stenbock and just three hundred men. Stenbock demanded to speak to the commandant to negotiate. After a few minutes the King became impatient and, on one of the few occasions where he deigned to speak French, ordered, 'Ouvrez la porte!' The commandant opened the gates to see who was making the demand and within seconds Stenbock, the King and their troopers had forced their way into the city. The King then rode alone around the city main square and surrounding streets, surveying this conquered ancient city, his thoughts his own as he clattered across the cobbles on his nervous war horse, surveying the ancient buildings as hidden eyes watched the pale rider whose reputation went before him.

Before rejoining his army, Charles appointed Stenbock as Governor of Kracow with a garrison of Swedish troops. He now controlled the two greatest cities of Poland. The Pomeranian division of 16,000 men arrived to reinforce the Swedish forces in late July, and for two months Charles could ponder the situation as the stand-off between him and Augustus continued. Poland was ravaged by both marauding armies looking for sustenance and taxes to sustain them.

In September, Charles had a bad fall from his horse, breaking his thigh bone, a serious matter, but within days he was being transported in a litter around his army, showing his men that all was well. Despite a memorandum from Piper at the end of August warning him of the consequence of his actions in Poland, the King ignored the advice. In January 1703, he went into winter quarters near Lublin. Matters remained the same until the spring, when the King set off on one of his raids at the head his cavalry and routed the Saxons led by the unfortunate Steinau once again, at Pultusk on 21 April.

He then, for some unknown reason, turned towards Thorn and laid siege to it, though it was defended by 6,000 of the best Saxon infantry. Sieges and the prospect of them bored the impetuous Charles, he was only ever involved in three: Thorn in 1703, Poltava in 1709 which led to his downfall, and Fredrikshald in 1719, which led to his death. The siege of Thorn lasted from May until early October, the whole summer, with the Swedes finally victorious and Charles magnanimous as always to his honourably defeated enemies.

But much time had been wasted and in the meantime the Russians had retaken a number of Swedish outposts on the Baltic. In September and October, Augustus had again invaded Poland but had been forced to retreat by Rehnskjold's army, who captured Pozen. Augustus was now joined by Patkul, who came as an emissary from the Czar and a treaty was signed whereby Russia paid an annual fee to Saxony and contributed 12,000 troops in exchange for a mutual defence agreement against Sweden.

Early in 1704, Charles sent Arvid Horn to negotiate with the Poles about a new king. After much bargaining, the young aristocrat Stanislaus Leszczynski, the Palatine of Pozen, was selected and crowned outside Warsaw by the Bishop of Pozen, watched over by Arvid Horn and a number of Swedish dragoons and infantry. Stanislaus was King Charles's choice, a puppet king imposed on the people of Poland by Sweden. He was subsequently to become the father-in-law of Louis XV.

There now occurred a strange event, stranger even than the siege of Thorn. Spurred on in the knowledge that the city of Lemberg, or Lvov, situated far to the south in the western Ukraine nearly 300 miles away, had never been captured, Charles headed southwards at the head of his dragoons, arriving before Lemberg on 27 August and captured it, rather pointlessly.

As a result of this mistake, there now followed a game of political musical chairs. While Charles was in Lemberg, Augustus had re-taken Warsaw, laid waste the city, destroyed the palace of the Cardinal who had fled to Danzig, captured Horn, evicted Stanislaus and sent the disgraced Bishop of Pozen to Rome.

Charles now advanced from the south, persuading the southern palatinates to support Stanislaus on the way, and re-took Warsaw. He then went off once more in pursuit of Augustus, travelling 360 miles in nine days before confronting and defeating the Saxon army commanded by General von Schulenburg at Punitz on 7 November. Schulenburg retreated into Silesia and Charles stayed on the border for the next 8 months into the summer of 1705 before Stanislaus was finally crowned king in Warsaw on 24 September. During this time, his reputation across Europe as a conqueror now legendary, Charles was approached by a number of European courts with proposals of alliance, but they were summarily rejected.

In hindsight, the proposal from the rising power of Brandenburg-Prussia offering a treaty and military support would have been well worth considering. Towards the end of the year the Swedish army set off once again northwards where the city of Grodno had been occupied by the Russians. In seventeen days, Charles and his men covered nearly two hundred miles through rugged terrain in the middle of winter before appearing in front of Grodno in January 1706. For two months the city was blockaded, before General Ogilvie managed to get away with half his troops and reach Czar Peter to the south in Kiev. Charles pursued them but failed to find them in the mud and marshes of western Russia, only reaching Pinsk.

In Poland on 2 February General Rehnskjold had won a decisive victory over von der Schulenberg and the Saxon army at Fraustadt in western Poland, driving the enemy finally from the borders of Poland. On 5 August 1706, Charles, in conjunction with the newly promoted Marshal Rehnskjold, invaded Saxony itself.

Europe, in the midst of the War of the Spanish Succession, was shocked and endeavoured to discover what master plan the young Swedish King had in mind. The truth was simple, a personal vendetta against Augustus, the Elector of Saxony, a man whom he personally distrusted and detested. He set up his headquarters in the castle of Alt-Ranstadt near Leipzig.

On 13 October 1706, Charles compelled the reluctant Elector Augustus to sign the Peace of Alt-Ranstadt, whereby he agreed to renounce his powers in Poland, return the Royal regalia, hand over prisoners including Patkul, and have the Treaty ratified by the maritime powers and the Emperor within six weeks. Though this was humiliating for Saxony, it brought no tangible benefit to Sweden and was really little more than a personal victory for Charles, though he had insisted on guarantees for the Protestants of Silesia from the Emperor in the tradition of his predecessor, King Gustavus Adolphus.

On 23 August 1707 he ordered his now grand army to evacuate Saxony. Charles had never commanded so effective an army, numbering 24,000 cavalry and 20,000 infantry, all fit, fed and watered after a year in Saxony with no combat. The Saxon people regretted seeing the immaculately behaved Swedes leave and drew unfavourable comparisons with their Elector sitting down at his banquets in attire encrusted with jewels and pearls, while his young conqueror dined more simply in plain dark blue cloth and mud-stained elk-skin boots.

It is rare that an invader takes away with him the good wishes of a conquered people, but Charles XII achieved this, largely by the iron discipline he enforced on his army and his own example of self-discipline and self-denial. He was indeed a remarkable man, striking fear into his opponents in battle and gaining respect from those with whom he had peaceful dealings. Now he was to meet his nemesis, Russia.

He had already indicated to the Imperial ambassador during his sojourn in Saxony that he intended to depose Czar Peter and perhaps replace him with James Sobieski, the son of the legendary Polish leader John Sobieski. Delayed waiting for further military aid from Pomerania, the Swedish army finally set out from central Poland in November and by Christmas Day had reached the Vistula, which they crossed, despite the thinness of the ice, by New Year's Day 1708, taking Grodno at the end of January. Now his generals advised him to turn north towards the Baltic states and cities, including Narva, which Czar Peter had re-taken during Charles's absence in Poland. Charles did not listen and ordered his troops southwards towards Minsk, beyond which lay Smolensk and then the tempting prospect of taking Moscow itself, a knife straight into the heart of Czar Peter and the Russian Empire. There was an inevitability about this and there is a pervading sense of doom when reading about the events that followed. In June, the Swedish army crossed the Berezina River without loss and advanced deeper into Russia in their blitzkrieg campaign. Like Napoleon in 1812 and Guderian in 1941, it seemed as though nothing could stop the inexorable march of the invaders.

On 1 July they arrived in front of the Russian stronghold of Holowczyn protected by the Wabis river. Early on the morning of the 4th, the Swedish king, having waited for more of his troops to arrive, crossed the river into the marshland beyond at the head of his troops. He seemed as always, fearless. His infantry behind him, sometimes up to their shoulders in water, carried their weapons above their heads to keep them dry before advancing into the enemy ranks. The Swedish dragoons led by Marshal Rehnskjold charged into the enemy, even though outnumbered. By evening, the Russians, under General Sheremetev, vacated the field having lost more than three thousand men, double the losses of the Swedes. It was a clear victory for Charles, but every one of his losses counted in his relatively small army, the Russians had access to a bottomless pit of new recruits.

For a month the Swedish army rested nearby, but it was a desolate land they were advancing into, the Russians carrying out a relentless policy of slash and burn. During the burning heat of August the Swedes marched on, the soldiers and animals suffering from the chronic lack of provisions. At Czerikow and Malatitze there were skirmishes with the Russians but no more than that, since Czar Peter did not want to risk an all-out battle with the ferocious King and his army.

One day that summer, Charles asked one of his officers which direction they should go. The officer replied that he could not advise him without knowing his plan. Charles answered, 'I have no plan!'

His officers then recommended that they abandon the march on Moscow and wait for General Levenhaupt to arrive with his army of 14,000 veterans, and it was finally decided to march south into the Ukraine in the hope of the unlikely possibility of a Cossack uprising in their support. Hindsight is an exact science, but thinking about those desperate days in the middle of the Russian steppe it must have crossed the King's mind that discretion might have been the better part of valour, and he should retrace his steps north. But he was a driven man and the alternative was a further advance deep into the Ukraine, far from home, and into who knows what issues that might lie ahead.

Charles XII feared no one and believed nothing was impossible. He was clearly the heir to the glory and tragedy of the great Macedonian, Alexander the Great, who two thousand years before him had gazed across distant horizons in pursuit of the unattainable. Suffering in the terrible heat of the summer, Charles and his men continued south and in early October were joined by Levenhaupt and his depleted army of six thousand, who had been severely mauled at Lesna by Czar Peter's army of thirty thousand men and had forfeited their cannons, stores and ammunition, all of which had been destined to reinforce the main army.

In early November they were joined by Ivan Mazeppa, the Hetman of the Cossacks, who arrived with his entourage bearing the silver staff before him and the horse-tailed standard behind him. He arrived with only one thousand five hundred horsemen, rather than the promised horde of thirty thousand.

Within days the combined force entered the Ukraine and fate intervened. The winter of 1708-9 was one of the coldest winters in history – in Scandinavia, elks froze to death in the forests, in Venice the canals froze over, as did the estuary of the Tagus in Lisbon and the Thames in London. In the vast open steppe of the Ukraine the temperatures were so severe that about four thousand men of Charles's army froze to death and many others were permanently mutilated by frostbite.

In May 1709, despite the flooding following the winter, Charles laid siege to Poltava with an army now only of eighteen thousand fighting men and carrying about two thousand walking wounded, having started out on the campaign with forty-one thousand.

They had no artillery, and they were running low on ammunition. The heat of summer now began to be oppressive again, and little progress was made in a campaign which favoured the defenders and where the superior tactics and quality of the Swedes could not be brought to bear.

Then disaster struck. On 17 June, the King's birthday, he was riding along the Worskla river with General Levenhaupt when he was hit in the foot by an enemy musket ball. The bullet passed through the length of his foot, which must have been agony. His servants thought his horse had been hit, there was so much blood coming from his boot. His boot had to be cut off and painful surgery carried out to remove some of the shattered smaller bones in his foot. Though he recovered, he was now *hors de combat*.

Hearing of this situation, Czar Peter, having been rightly nervous of the presence of the warrior king and realising that he could now no longer lead his men into battle, moved most of his army of eighty thousand men towards the Swedish camp.

On the morning of 27 June, the tiny Swedish army went into the attack against the eighty thousand Russians. It was a hopeless cause and despite incredible gallantry displayed by the Swedes they were cut to pieces. Charles, who had been carried around the whole day in a litter, was placed on a dying officer's horse and left the field. There are many stories of heroic deeds and if at the beginning of the day they had managed to capture all the Russian gun batteries, which they nearly did, it might have been a different story.

Count Piper and Marshal Rehnskjold had been captured. Czar Peter asked Rehnskjold why he had invaded the great Russian Empire with just a handful of men. Rehnskjold replied that the King had commanded it and he had obeyed. 'You are an honest man,' answered the Czar, 'and for your loyalty I return you your sword.'

Two days later, the remnants of the Swedish army led by Levenhaupt and carrying their wounded King reached Perewoloczna on the Dnieper River. Charles was persuaded to cross the river into Turkish territory with his entourage, including Mazeppa and 1,500 cavalry. A few days later Levenhaupt surrendered the ragged remains of the immaculate blue coated army that had invaded Russia less than a year before. Hearing the news, the King was furious, but the unfortunate general had no choice.

Poltava set the growing Asiatic power of Russia against the ebbing European power of Sweden, and it was hugely significant. By putting herself in a strong position in the Baltic, by occupying huge swathes of the Ukraine and by destroying the power base of Stanislaus in Poland, Russia, hitherto an Asiatic power, had placed herself on the European stage. Now, and for the next centuries, Europe always had to be aware of the dark spectre over the Eastern horizon of encroachment and invasion from the East. Though Czar Peter's European style modernisations were impressive and revolutionary, they were brought about by brutality. The Czar even had his own son, Alexis, flogged to death.

The wounded and lame King Charles XII was now trapped in a strange land, more than a thousand miles from home, with no army. There now followed a period of five years when Sweden had no King, and Charles's status in the Ottoman Empire changed from honoured guest to political prisoner, to political embarrassment. Effectively, the King was forgotten by those in power in Europe as he languished at Bender, deep in Moldavia, the back of beyond.

At midnight on 11 November 1714, after sixteen days of hard riding from dawn till dusk across more than one thousand miles from the Black Sea to the Baltic, two mysterious cloaked figures demanded entrance to the gates of the Swedish fortress of Stralsund in Pomerania, one of Sweden's last possessions on the mainland of Europe. They commanded the guards to open the gates on pain of death and demanded to be taken to the sleeping governor, General Carl Gustaf Ducker. On waking, he immediately recognised one of his visitors and fell to his knees. It was Charles XII.

As soon as the news reached Sweden there were outpourings of joy that their King had returned after fourteen years. He would save the nation. By now Sweden was besieged by her enemies, Russia, Saxony, Prussia, Denmark and England. Charles did not return to Sweden but remained in Pomerania defending his last possessions there.

On 12 December 1715, a year later, after a valiant defence against Great Britain, Hanover, Russia, Prussia, Saxony and Denmark, Stralsund fell to the enemy forces and the King escaped in a small boat and managed to reach landfall in Sweden. He never returned to Stockholm. The following year, to take the war to Denmark, the King led the Swedish army over the mountains into Norway. This invasion failed due to lack of provisions, but within two years the King attacked again and with an army of 60,000 men invaded Norway and laid siege to the fortress of Fredriksten. Trenches were dug very close to the defensive wall, which the King, fearless as always, inspected with his officers. A junior officer, Lieutenant Carlberg, later wrote:

> Now the unhappy hour had arrived that put an end to everything. For hardly half of a quarter of an hour, I and some other officers had stood at the feet of His Majesty, when a shot entered the left side of His Majesty's head, whereupon he made no movement apart from his hand falling from his left cheek and his head slowly drooping down on his jacket. His body lay as still as it had lain before. Without the slightest movement, as was to be expected after such an accurate shot, which causes instant, motionless, death. Adjutant Kaulbars, who was standing closest to him, struck me on the shoulder, shouting in complete despair, 'Lord Jesus, the King has been shot.'

The army slowly retreated back into Sweden in the most terrible winter conditions; many froze to death as they sat on their horses.

The Swedish Empire, that Baltic Empire, initially created by the great King Gustavus Adolphus, had lasted less than a hundred years and despite his brilliance as a general, it would be unwise not to lay some blame at the feet of the charismatic, impulsive King Charles XII. He fascinated many of his contemporaries. Only Alexander the Great, who also lit up the firmament briefly yet brilliantly, compares to him in their consummate belief in themselves, the loyalty of their comrades and men, their fearless bravery in the face of awesome odds and their relentless drive towards dangerous horizons.

In 1731, Voltaire wrote a biography of Charles XII in which he portrays the Swedish king in a positive light, in contrast to the brutal and cowardly nature of Peter the Great.

The great Englishman of letters Samuel Johnson wrote of Charles in a poem entitled, 'The Vanity of Human Wishes':

On what Foundation stands the warrior's pride,
How just his hopes let Swedish Charles decide;
A frame of adamant, a soul of fire,
No dangers fright him, and no labours tire;
O'er love, o'er fear, extends his wide domain,
Unconquered lord of pleasure and of pain;
No joys to him pacific sceptres yield;
War sounds the trump, he rushes to the field;
Behold surrounding kings their power to combine,
And one capitulate, and one resign;
Peace courts his hand, but spreads her charms in vain;
'Think nothing gained,' he cries, 'till nought remain,
On Moscow's walls till Gothic standards fly,
And all be mine beneath the polar sky.'...

...Hide, blushing Glory, hide Pultowa's day:
The vanquished hero leaves his broken bands,
And shows his miseries in distant lands;
Condemned a needy supplicant to wait,
While ladies interpose, and slaves debate.
But did not Chance at length her error mend?
Did no subverted empire mark his end?
Did rival monarchs give the fatal wound?
Or hostile millions press him to the ground?
His fall was destined to a barren strand,
A petty fortress, and a dubious hand;
He left the name, at which the world grew pale,
To point a moral or adorn a tale.

8

MAURICE OF SAXONY
1696–1750

> The starting point in all matters pertaining to warfare is in the human heart.
>
> *Mes Reveries*, Maurice de Saxe

Standing in the Rue de Sevigne in the 3rd arrondissement of Paris, just to the north of the Isle St Louis, is the immaculate Hotel Carnavalet, which houses the often overlooked Musee Carnavalet, an eclectic collection of paintings, sculptures, furniture and other objets d'art which pertain to the illustrious history of Paris. There is the wheeled chair in which Voltaire sat during his last hours, the death mask of Napoleon Bonaparte, a remarkable stone model of the Bastille, a painting of Madame Recamier. And there is a victor's *couronne de lauriers*, or laurel crown, made of metal. It is the victory wreath awarded to Count Maurice of Saxony, Marshal of France, favourite of King Louis XV, on his triumphant return to Paris on 18 March 1746 after his victory over the English at Fontenoy the previous year.

At the end of the summer of 1708 during the War of the Spanish Succession, the Grand Alliance led by the Duke of Marlborough and Prince Eugene of Savoy was besieging the mighty French fortress of Lille. They were joined by a contingent of four thousand five hundred Saxon troops, amongst whom was a twelve-year-old boy. On arrival in the camp, the precocious boy asked to see Count Missein and was ushered through by the redoubtable General Johann von der Schulenburg, who was commanding the Saxons in the trenches beneath Lille, defended by the obdurate Marechal de Boufflers.

Count Missein was, in fact, the incognito of the Elector Augustus Frederic II, known as the Strong, King of Poland and Elector of Saxony, the boy's father. Augustus was proud of the war-like boy who preferred military matters over matters intellectual and had, despite protests from his mother, been determined to campaign alongside his father during the disastrous Great Northern War where his father had been humiliated by the ruthless King Charles XII of Sweden. The King instructed Schulenburg to make Maurice his Aide-Major General and within a short time the boy was seated alongside those great captains Marlborough and Eugene of Savoy.

His mother was the beautiful Aurora von Konigsmarck, according to Voltaire 'the most famous woman of two centuries, celebrated throughout the world for her wit and beauty'. Her great-great-granddaughter, George Sand, described her as 'a woman of striking beauty. She was extremely dark, and her tresses, as black as ink, were caught up by ruby clips. Her smooth high forehead gave her a bold appearance.'

She had become the mistress of the charismatic Elector King at his glamorous and sophisticated court in Dresden and at his summer palace of the Castle of Moritzburg, like one of the fairy stories of Charles Perrault and Madame d'Aulnoy, so fashionable at the time. Maybe the boy born of this union was named after where he was conceived or maybe after one of the Elector's famous ancestors. Perhaps his warlike capabilities came through his mother's side. From her the boy christened Arminius-Maurice de Saxe, in German Moritz-Hermann, was descended from a line of great soldiers.

His great-grandfather, Hans Christoph, later celebrated as Old Konigsmarck, left the Catholic armies of the Emperor when still a young officer and joined the Lutheran cause of the young Swedish king, Gustavus Adolphus, fighting under his command at Lutzen in 1632 where the Swedes were victorious but lost their King. Konigsmarck managed to rally the dispirited Swedes and within a month had led the Protestants to victory over the Imperial troops at Wolfenbuttel. In 1648, in a daring attack, he led a raid on Prague and laid siege to the city. Its sack by the Swedes was only prevented by the signing of the Peace of Westphalia. Ninety years later his great-grandson was to achieve the same, the capture of Prague, with greater success. He died in 1663 a Count of Sweden and Field Marshal and is immortalised in stone as one of the generals that adorn the tomb of Gustavus Adolphus.

His eldest son Karl-Christoph, Maurice's grandfather, a commander of artillery, was killed at the siege of Bonn in 1673 leaving his young children to be raised by his brother Otto Wilhelm. He, in turn, fought with distinction under Turenne and was rewarded by Louis XIV himself. He then became the Generalissimo of the Venetian Army in their war against the Most Sublime Porte, the ruler of the Ottoman Empire, fighting in Greece under Doge Morosini and capturing Corinth and Athens before dying of disease outside the walls of Chalcis.

Two of Maurice's uncles, the last of the Konigsmarcks, lived dangerous lives. The eldest, Karl Johann, became a favourite of King Charles II of England but was tried at the Old Bailey for the murder of a love rival. His three accomplices were executed but he was saved by the King. Having to leave England he travelled to France but due to the Edict of Nantes, as a Protestant, he, like his father, offered his services to the Venetian Republic. He died of pleurisy in Greece. His younger brother, the equally dashing and handsome Philip Cristoph, became Colonel of the Hanoverian Guards at the Palace of Hanover due to the favour of the Elector's mistress, the Countess von Platen. He then embarked on a torrid affair with the Elector's daughter-in-law, Sophia Dorothea, the daughter of the Duke of Brunswick, which ended in the most brutal fashion when he was ambushed and murdered in the Hall of Knights at the Leine Schloss. As he lay dying, the rejected Countess von Platen stamped on his face. Sophia Dorothea, the wife of the future King George I who should have become the Queen of England, was cruelly punished for her unfaithfulness. She was held under close arrest for thirty-three years at the remote Schloss of Ahlden, her children taken away from her.

These dramatic events were to some extent mirrored in Maurice's turbulent life. Extraordinarily, his mother Aurora somehow contrived to be accepted by the Electress Christina Everhardina of Brandenburg-Bayreuth. She had given birth to an heir eleven days before Maurice arrived in the world, who was to become Augustus Frederic III on his father's death. The half-brothers co-existed happily in the ensuing years.

Shortly after these happy events, the Elector went on campaign as an officer in the Emperor's army at Belgrade and returned with yet another lover, whose dancing he had admired at a ball hosted by Joseph, King of the Romans.

Despite this set-back, Aurora was treated with the highest respect and was bequested the Protestant Abbey of Quedlinburg along with suitable revenues. The young Maurice was placed in the care of French tutors there. Despite the endeavours of these earnest men, Maurice's interests were not intellectual but martial. In this he was little different from many other members of royal and aristocratic families all across Europe, who for generations had found fame, power and wealth fighting for causes in which they had no personal or patriotic interest. The practice of bearing arms was a fashionable thing to do, particularly in the summer months, offering glory for the officers and possibly financial gain for the ordinary soldiers. Maurice, with no great inheritance to look forward to, was ideally suited to this style of life. Just like his father he was enormously physically attractive, very strong to the extent of being brutish and very ambitious. They say he could straighten a horseshoe with his bare hands. In the camp of two such dashing examples of the life and fame that he craved, John Churchill, Duke of Marlborough and Prince Eugene of Savoy, he was taught by the best.

The citadel of Lille was finally surrendered by the redoubtable old Boufflers and the year's campaigning now ended. The teenage

Maurice retired to Brussels in the company of a pretty young girl from Tournai, but after some weeks was recalled to Dresden by his father. In the spring of 1709 peace efforts failed and Maurice once more went on campaign with the Duke of Marlborough and Prince Eugene, who commanded the Hapsburg Imperial army, at the siege of Tournai, which surrendered on 28 July. The Allies then moved on Mons, which was defended by the French under Marechal Villars. Maurice was in the Saxon cavalry units commanded by the Prince of Hesse-Cassel.

Louis XIV, stung by the fact that the French armies had been humiliated the previous year, instructed Villars to ensure that Mons did not fall. As Marlborough advanced, the French army blocked his way. On 10 September the Allied army paused for 24 hours to wait for the heavy artillery to arrive. This gave Villars time to build earthworks and entrenchments across the lines, which were flanked by thick woods on either side. The two armies were finally brought to battle on 11 September in the valley of Malplaquet.

During a day's heavy fighting the slaughter on both sides was appalling, with about 50,000 casualties and 30,000 killed. Technically it was an Allied victory but at great cost, and the stubborn resistance of the French brought their nation pride and assurance that they were still a great power.

Prince Eugene and Villars were both wounded during the encounter and the youthful Maurice experienced his first major engagement between the great powers of Europe. The young man never forgot the scenes of slaughter he witnessed that day. Only the Battle of Borodino surpassed it in terms of casualties, as Napoleon approached Moscow in 1812.

Rejoining the Allies the following season, Maurice was admonished by Prince Eugene for displaying an excess of valour which he confused with rashness. Maurice, now elevated to the title of Count, campaigned alongside his father allied with the Russians under Peter the Great and in 1712 fought at the Battle of Gadebusch, where the Saxons were defeated by the Swedes in one of the last actions of the Great Northern War.

The following year, at the age of just 17, he was given command of his own regiment in the Royal Saxon Army. But Maurice was not a wealthy prince, so in March 1714 he was married to Johanna Tugendreich von Loeben, an heiress. The marriage was not a great success. The couple had no children and Maurice went through the money very quickly and was continually unfaithful. His marriage was annulled on 21 March 1721.

Bored with his genteel life at the Saxon Court, Maurice gained permission to join the Imperial army commanded by none other than Prince Eugene in their war against the Turks on the Danube. In the summer of 1717, Eugene led his army out to capture the great fortress of Belgrade. In an epic engagement the Imperial forces, hugely depleted by disease, finally overcame the Turks and the lands of the Empire in south-eastern Europe returned to Hapsburg control. The young Maurice had been part of this great enterprise and was to learn from it.

On his return from Serbia, his father invested him with the Order of the White Eagle of Poland, a rare honour.

Having finally achieved an agreement on his divorce, the restless Maurice set out for France, no longer ruled by the magnificent Louis XIV but by his great-grandson Louis XV, still a young boy. Within a year, Maurice was made a maréchal de camp or ADC, and on 1 March 1721 he took command of the famous Regiment Greder, which, of course, he renamed the Regiment Saxe. He drilled his men on the Champ de Mars and personally supervised these exercises. These were not the displays of a martinet but of a colonel who realised that by complex drill movements and the handling of firearms his men would be better prepared for the time when they would be tested in battle. He befriended the ageing Chevalier Folard, a famous French military theorist who thoroughly approved of his training methods. He wrote: 'The Comte de Saxe is one of the most promising commanders I have ever encountered and the next war will prove the correctness of my forecast.'

In 1725, a rather messy period of his life began, as once more his martial exploits clashed with his love life. Always looking for new opportunities both in love and war, Maurice attempted to be elected the Duke of Courland in modern-day Estonia. He entered negotiations for election at the insistence of another lover, the Duchess Anna Ivanovna, who had offered him her hand in marriage. He was chosen Duke in 1726 but declined marriage with the duchess, which naturally displeased her. He soon found it impossible to resist her opposition to his claims, but with the assistance of a huge loan of £30,000 from the French actress Adrienne Lecouvreur, another lover, he raised a force by which he maintained his authority until 1727, when he finally withdrew and took up residence in Paris once again.

His relationship with the beautiful Adrienne continued. She was dying of tuberculosis. He had first encountered her on the stage of the *Comedie-Francaise* where she had entranced him many years before. Lecouvreur was to die mysteriously soon afterwards and there is still controversy as to whether she was poisoned by her rival in love for Maurice, Maria Karolina Sobieska, Duchess of Bouillon.

Like many actresses of the period, she was denied a full Christian burial and was cast into a pit of quicklime. Voltaire, who was also in love with her, wrote her funeral oration in 1730, praising her as 'that inimitable actress who practically invented the art of speaking from the heart, and who put sentiment and truth where before there had been merely pomposity and rhetoric.'

Maurice, now in his mid-thirties and still a French officer, travelled to Dresden to visit his father and family during festivities arranged to entertain the visiting Frederick William I, King of Prussia. It was an eighteenth-century version of the Field of the Cloth of Gold engineered by Henry VIII of England some two hundred years before. Here Maurice became close to some of his half-siblings, the more than three hundred illegitimate children that Augustus had sired: George, the Chevalier of Saxony, Count Augustus Rutowski, Frederick Augustus, Count von Cosel and the glamorous Countess Orzelska. During the next three summers he became closer to his father, advising him on the Saxon army and in particular the use of light cavalry on which he wrote extensively and in some detail, and on the condition of the Polish army. On returning to Paris Maurice fell seriously ill and while recovering he wrote his remarkable *Mes Reveries*, a serious and detailed study of military tactics and military philosophy.

Tempted to return to Saxony where he would immediately be made a Lieutenant General by his father, he compared this with the fact that he had served France for twelve years without advancement and was still considered by those with influence in Court as a foreigner and a Protestant. Nevertheless, the French army created by Cardinal Louvois decades before was still the gold standard in terms of military prowess in Europe, even though its numbers had dwindled from over 400,000 to about 250,000. What greater glory could there be but to command a French army and follow in the steps of Turenne and Villars?

The death of Maurice's father at the age of 63 in 1733 led inevitably to yet another War of Succession, this time Poland. The King of France and the Bourbons in Spain, advised by Villars and the Duc de Belle-Isle, saw this as an opportunity to revive the alliance of France and Poland by restoring Stanislas Leczinski, the father of the Queen of France, to the Polish throne. The Saxons thought otherwise, invaded Poland and with the support of the Diet, made August III, Maurice's half-brother, King of Poland on 12 September 1733.

Once more, war broke out with France and the Austrian Empire as the main protagonists, the campaigning starting in 1734.

In October, three French armies moved towards the frontiers on the Rhine; the Duc de Belle-Isle, 49 years old, commanding in the north, the Duke of Berwick, the son of King James II and Arabella Churchill, the Duke of Marlborough's sister, aged 73, in the centre, and Marechal Villars, 80 years old, on the Italian front. The comparably aged Prince Eugene of Savoy, Maurice's hero and former commanding officer, was to command the depleted Imperial forces of 20,000 against the 100,000 the French had assembled. This was the campaign in which the burly Saxon was to make his mark.

In aggressive style, Maurice, serving under Berwick, crossed the Rhine at Strasbourg and captured the fortress of Kehl. Looking for action wherever he could find it, he then joined Belle-Isle as he advanced down the Moselle towards Koblenz. Trier was quickly taken before Maurice moved once again to join the Duc de Noailles's army at Ettlingen. Noailles, 55 years old, was both a general and a courtier who had acted as Controller of Finance for Louis XV. He was an admirer of the ebullient Maurice, but at the same time was essentially a cautious man. Maurice, of course, advised him that they should attack the Austrian defensive Lines of Ettlingen. Once breached, nothing could stop the French army from marching triumphantly across southern Germany towards Vienna, 400 miles away. Given permission, Maurice at once went into the attack and personally led his men, in appalling conditions, in a successful advance. But further action was denied by Noailles, who insisted on waiting for the arrival of the artillery, and by Prince Eugene, who cleverly mustered enough troops to slow the French advance by random counter-attacks that made the French believe they were up against a larger force than they were.

Berwick and Noailles tentatively decided to capture the formidable fortress of Philippsburg before advancing any further. Berwick mistakenly wanted to lay siege to the citadel when he could have just left enough troops around it to neutralise it and thus advance deep into southern Germany. Now the war, unlike most combat in the 18th century, became one of of attrition, with both sides dug into trenches in terrible weather conditions and countryside in which it was easier to defend than to advance. Two hundred French infantrymen were drowned in their trenches, but despite this Maurice continued to cajole his men not to retreat. When the Austrians attacked, Maurice personally led infantry units and drove them back.

The man we think of as a swashbuckling maverick was also a gutsy foot soldier who understood his men and fought alongside them. When he asked the Duke of Berwick for more troops, the Duke replied, 'Count, I had intended sending for three thousand of Monsieur de Noailles' men, but you alone are worth more than that to me.'

Maurice, desperate for recognition, wrote to his commanding officer, the Duc de Noailles:

> I have led and conquered at the head of your grenadiers. It is fourteen years, Monsieur, since I had the honour to enter the King's service as a maréchal de camp. I am now nearing forty and am anxious not to be thwarted by the usual rules of promotion. I do not want to remain a maréchal de camp forever. You will recall too that I am a foreigner, and you will understand that this makes me doubly eager to secure promotion. Will you please speak to the King on my behalf?

On 12 June 1734, Berwick was killed by a cannon ball when visiting the trenches and five days later the redoubtable Marechal Villars died of old age in Turin. The Duc de Noailles and the Marquis d'Asfeld were immediately made Marshals of France. Maurice's frustration at his lack of promotion was palpable.

While all these changes were being made in the upper echelons of the French army, Maurice continued to slug it out in the trenches, where he was visited by his old friend Voltaire.

Prince Eugene now advanced to Wiesenthal near Philippsburg, so Johann Wutgenau, who had already lost 2,000 men in the siege, repulsed Maurice's attacks on 14 July in the hope that the intrepid Eugene could save him. This was not to be, since Eugene could not risk his only army in an open battle and Philippsburg finally surrendered three days later, a triumph for Maurice.

Asfeld now sent 40,000 men north to join Belle-Isle at Worms with the idea of marching on Mainz. Maurice was at the head of part of the army and quickly captured the castle of Niederulm 7 miles south of Mainz. Maurice's worth was now finally noted by Louis XV who promoted him to Lieutenant General. He was on his way.

The war dragged on into the next year, with French successes in Italy and Austrian and French moves and counter-moves on the Rhine border. Maurice, wounded once again in the head, was frustrated by the lack of decisive action; while his superiors had reputations to lose, he still had a reputation to make. Opposed by his old commander, Prince Eugene, at Mannheim, he followed his wise words, 'not to confuse courage with recklessness', though later he narrowly avoided a trap near Trier.

Hostilities dragged until in November 1735 an armistice was declared on the Rhine and in the spring of the following year the war was over. Stanislas had abdicated at Konisburg and Maurice's half-brother Augustus III was triumphant. The War of the Austrian Succession had ended and that remarkable man Prince Eugene of Savoy reported one last time to the Schonbrunn Palace before passing away peacefully in the spring. Maurice had not had the chance to fight him in battle or meet him during that dour campaign. The deaths of Villars and Eugene of Savoy marked the end of a style of warfare inherited from Turenne, Conde and Marlborough. Warfare was destined gradually to become more fluid and technical, and Maurice de Saxe would make some of those innovations, as he was now assured of a senior command.

During the next few months Maurice returned to visit his family in Dresden where his half-brother Augustus was secure as Elector of Saxony and King of Poland and, despite a chance of the Dukedom of Courland once more becoming available, he returned to France in the autumn of 1739, meeting up with Voltaire once again who, on this occasion, presented him with his poem, *Défense du Mondain ou l'apologie du luxe*, promoting the pursuit of worldly pleasure as a social benefit, an idea the Saxon Count could certainly warm to.

Now, once again, Maurice was waiting for war but nothing happened. Generals without wars do not appear in history books. Maurice was the wrong side of forty now and time was running out. Once more he spent time travelling between Paris and his beloved Dresden. He badly damaged his knee in a riding accident while pursuing prey in his childhood hunting grounds. But from bad comes good and he ended up convalescing in southern France and even dined off Toulon with the formidable Admiral Matthews of King George II's Royal Navy.

On 20 October 1740 the Hapsburg Emperor Charles VI died, leaving his throne to the eldest of his two daughters Maria Theresa, then only twenty-three years old. Maria Theresa automatically became Queen of Hungary, but many in Europe baulked at the idea of her becoming Empress of Austria. Twenty-seven years earlier in 1713 the old Emperor had drawn up the so-called Pragmatic Sanction, the *Pragamtische Sanktion*, stating that the hereditary possessions of the Hapsburgs which included the Archduchy of Austria and the Austrian Netherlands, the Kingdoms of Hungary, Croatia, and Bohemia, the Duchy of Milan, the Kingdom of Naples, and the Kingdom of Sardinia could be inherited by his daughter, contrary to ancient Salic Law.

Britain had agreed to the proposed arrangement in 1731 and France in 1735, but France had now changed her mind. Allied with Prussia, Spain and Bavaria, the French saw it as a chance to challenge the power of the Hapsburgs yet again in central Europe. The Austrians were supported by Britain, Holland and Hanover, known as the Pragmatic Allies, after the edict.

In December 1740 Frederick the Great seized Silesia and in August 1741 the War of the Austrian Succession broke out two months after Maria Teresa had been crowned in Pressburg. France and Bavaria were now intent on placing the Elector of Bavaria on the Austrian throne. The French army commanded by the Duc de Belle-Isle, alongside Maurice de Saxe, now advanced deep into Southern Germany to Ulm and St Polen, only 30 miles from Vienna itself.

At this moment the French army could have taken Vienna, of that there is no doubt, but instead, in October they veered northwards into Bohemia. It appears the Elector of Bavaria was somehow reluctant to depose the Hapsburgs. Anyway, there were easier pickings elsewhere and by November the French and Bavarians were at the gates of Prague. If they couldn't have the capital of Austria just yet, they could take the capital of Bohemia in the meantime.

It was now winter and the defences of Prague were formidable, but the ever confident Maurice was not to be deterred. Within days, Prague had fallen following a night attack of great cunning. The French army was on one side of the city and in the north the defenders were hemmed in by the advancing Saxon army officered by a number of Maurice's half-brothers. On 25 November 1741, Maurice sent in a small unit of infantry who climbed into the city at a point where the walls were not defended and within hours Prague had surrendered as Maurice's cavalry entered the open gates. Maurice's losses were, extraordinarily, only 14 killed and 22 wounded. With this daring exploit Maurice became the talk of the salons of Europe. He had repeated the exploit in 1648 of his maternal great-grandfather, Hans Christoff von Königsmarck, just over one hundred years before.

After capturing the fortress of Eger on 19 April 1742, where Wallenstein had met his bloody end, Maurice received a leave of absence and journeyed to Russia to once again push his claims for the Duchy of Courland, but returned to his command after getting nowhere.

In the meantime an epic struggle for survival had occurred in the forests of western Bohemia outside the walls of Prague and Eger. The French army, commanded by Broglie and Belle-Isle, had been trapped in Prague for nearly a year by now and winter was setting in. Broglie attempted to break out at the head of twelve thousand men but failed to link up with a column sent by Marshal Maillebois. He escaped to safety leaving his men to make their way back to Prague as best they could. Many were picked off by the pursuing Austrian mounted units, in particular the sinister Croat freebooters notorious for their cruelty.

On 16 December 1742, the Duc de Belle-Isle, with little alternative, also decided to break out. The writer, philosopher and aphorist, the Marquis de Vauvenargues, a friend of Voltaire, was a young officer in the French army at this time and during those desperate weeks marooned inside the bleak walls of Prague formed a close friendship with another young aristocrat, Hippolyte de Seytres, to whom he was later to dedicate his writings. Two columns, a total of fifteen thousand men, with provisions for just twelve days came out of the city gates secretly at night, stealing a march on the surrounding Imperial army and headed due west into the primeval Bohemian forest avoiding the roads. Those in extreme medical condition were left behind to die, while the remaining eighteen hundred sick or wounded inside the city were ordered to hold out as long as possible. The dying Hippolyte was amongst them.

During the next days, in heavy snow and arctic conditions, the French held off their pursuers through the quick positioning of horse-drawn artillery under the command of Joseph Florent de Valliere, one of the first recorded uses of horse artillery.

To say it was a portent of the retreat from Moscow would not be an exaggeration, as hundreds died of cold or famine. The Duc de Biron heroically commanded the rearguard as they trudged through the hostile country, finally reaching safety within the walls of Eger on 26 December. Vauvenargue, though suffering frostbite, survived this terrible ordeal, but he was never the same again. He was later to fight at Dettingen under the command of Maurice and died of tuberculosis two years later.

Maurice, now recognised by the French high command, was charged with defending the Rhine crossings near Breisach planned by Prince Charles of Lorraine. As soon as the danger passed, Maurice handed over command to yet another ageing general, Marshal Coigny. Maurice returned the hero to Paris, feted by the King whose interests in hunting and matters of the bedroom exactly coincided with those of the Saxon. Maurice, who was now forty-seven years old and had been soldiering for more than thirty years, was admired by all of the senior Marshals he had served under. Even Frederick the Great of Prussia wrote to Louis XV telling him Maurice should be given supreme command. This Saxon student of Prince Eugene of Savoy and the redoubtable Schulenburg had the blood of the Konigsmarcks flowing in his veins.

Maurice was aware that the constant threat of an Austrian advance across the Rhine had to be dealt with before he could concentrate on the Austrian Netherlands. Following the defeat of France in the summer of 1743 at Dettingen, where the French army had been commanded by de Noailles, Maurice's strategy was to separate Britain from her European allies, Hanover and Prussia. He travelled north from Paris having been appointed to support Prince Charles Edward Stuart's vain attempts to invade Britain, depose King George II, and install his father on the throne as King James III.

On 26 March 1744 Maurice was promoted to Marshal of France. At this moment there were just 11 other full Marshals, most of them aged or retired. As a full Marshal, he had joined his illustrious family members Old Konigsmarck, who had been a Marshal of Sweden, and his great uncle, Otto Wilhelm, who had been a Marshal of the Venetian Republic.

The Duc de Noailles, always a supporter of Maurice, was still senior to him and together they had to endure the presence in the war zone of King Louis XV, his mistress, the Duchesse de Chateauroux, and the whole court entourage who were greeted wherever they went by wildly cheering crowds. Louis had become 'le bien-aimé', which is hard to fathom.

As the weeks passed, Maurice, with a smaller army, was able to deftly out-manoeuvre his opponent, the unimaginative and ageing Field Marshal Wade. Just as Maurice was planning the coup de grace, danger once again threatened on the Rhine where the Austrians invaded Lorraine. The King and Marshal Noailles immediately headed for the east of France, leaving Maurice with a much-depleted army facing the Pragmatic Army of the Allies, who had double the number of men, more than 75,000 under arms. Maurice, as he had pointed out in *Mes Reveries,* realised this could be an advantage and without having been able to force a decisive engagement, he held Flanders for France despite the fact that once again, the Austrians had been allowed to escape back across the Rhine.

Though no major victories had been achieved, the King and Maurice returned to Paris triumphant and began to prepare for the next year of campaigning. That winter, Maurice became very sick with what was known as the dropsy, in modern terms, oedema, which is caused by a malfunctioning of the kidneys causing very uncomfortable swelling in the legs and abdomen. The cures at that time were barbaric and included the awful procedure of 'tapping' whereby the patient suffered cuts into the flesh to release the liquid which was causing the swelling. In his poor state, Maurice was visited by his friend Voltaire to whom he lamented, 'Il ne s'agit plus de vivre mais de partir.'

On 31 March 1745, just a year after he has been appointed a Marshal of France, Maurice took a coach out of Paris once more to the front. He was accompanied by his personal physician, Senac de Meilham. He claimed that he was in better health than he had been in the preceding weeks. That a man in this physical pain and discomfort was once more to command in the field says much about his character.

Despite his chronic medical condition, the same or similar uremia which had finished off Peter the Great of Russia, he was not to be denied what fate had in store for him. During the next three summers of campaigning Maurice stamped his name indelibly on the history of France with three successive victories over the Allies.

On 10 May 1745, his time had come. At Fontenoy, a village on the Scheldt, two great armies met face to face and the English infantry made a heroically disciplined advance into the heart of the French army. For a few minutes it seemed as though the young Duke of Cumberland, the second and favourite son of King George II of England, was about to claim a great victory as his infantry stood on the crest of the slope they had climbed and were about to put the French to flight. Maurice was observing all this as his officer, Ulrich von Lowendahl, galloped up to him asking permission to bring the Regiment de Normandie into the attack along with his cannons and the reserve cavalry.

Maurice agreed. 'Now for the coup de collier!' The final heave.

The French army went into all-out attack led by the Regiment de Normandie and the Regiment de Dillon along with other Irish 'Wild Geese' units yelling their battle cry of "'Remember Limerick!' The fighting was hand-to-hand and brutal with enormous casualties on both sides, including Colonel, the Chevalier Dillon. Slowly the British retreated, pausing every few yards to turn and deliver another lethal volley into their opponents, supported by constant charges by the British cavalry, the Blues to the fore.

By two o'clock, the two armies had fought each other to a standstill after nine hours of combat and Maurice took the victory with the words, 'Nous en avons assez.' He did not ask his army to go in pursuit. Maurice detested the notion of 'l'attaque a l'outrance'. He had seen too much brutality over the years of his campaigning to allow the carnage to continue.

By now he had collapsed to the ground in his agonies and was being treated by his doctor when the King and all his courtiers rushed up to congratulate him. The Allied losses had amounted to 10,000 and the French to 7,000. With tears in his eyes the kneeling Maurice said to the King, 'Sire, now you see what war really means.' Whether the vapid Louis really did is doubtful.

Maurice had won his first great pitched battle commanding large units of infantry, artillery and cavalry. Though the battle was close-fought, it was Maurice's long-term thinking that had prepared the French army to display great bravery in the face of an equally brave but less well commanded Allied army.At Fontenoy, the power of French organisation under Maurice de Saxe had prevailed over English bravery.

Louis XV wrote thanking Maurice: 'I owe this triumph to the valour of my troops and particularly to those of Ma Maison and my Regiment of Carabiniers, you also contributed to it no less by your steadfast daring, by your sage counsel and by your remarkable foresight.'

In the next few days, Maurice, while continuing the siege of Tournai, visited many of his wounded men and displayed great sympathy with their suffering, a rare quality. He valued his men as individual human beings, not as cannon fodder: 'the starting point in all matters pertaining to warfare is in the human heart.' In other words, the morale of a single soldier was what made a great army. He might also have said that it was all about preparation. With this and with the good individual morale that would come from it, and commanders with the quick-wittedness to exploit a changing battlefield, any army was formidable.

During the ensuing months Maurice was to take Tournai and once again march into the city as a conqueror, as he had done more than thirty-five years before riding behind the Duke of Marlborough and Prince Eugene of Savoy. Oudenaarde, Bruges, Ghent, Ostend and, finally in the winter, Brussels, the capital of the Austrian Netherlands fell to Maurice and the triumphant French army. In Brussels they took back fifty-two captured flags including the legendary *oriflamme*, or royal standard, of Francis I, which had been lost to the Austrian Empire at Pavia in 1525.

With spring approaching the ailing Maurice had been on campaign for nearly a year, and he returned to Paris in triumph. His reasons for returning were three-fold: first to consult with Argenson, the King's minister, on the further conduct of the war against the Allies; second to counter the constant court criticism he was suffering, in particular from the ambitious Prince de Conti; and finally to enjoy his triumph.

In recognition of his brilliant achievement, Louis XV conferred on him ownership of the Château de Chambord for life, and in April 1746 he was naturalised as a French subject. On 18 March 1746 at the Opera there was a gala performance of Lully's *Armide*, an opera originally written to celebrate the military triumphs of Louis XIV, where Maurice was presented with a specially made laurel wreath placed on his head by his friend the Duc de Biron.

Once back in court, Maurice became entranced by the glamorous new mistress of the King, La Marquise de Pompadour, who quickly forged an alliance with the ageing general. They were both outsiders, she due to her modest background, he as a Saxon and born on the wrong side of the blanket.

Despite his success, Maurice was humiliated by the King who was persuaded to appoint the Prince de Conti and his cousin, the Comte de Clermont, as commanders of armies independent from Maurice. So France's outstanding general was forced to return northwards, debilitated by not having full command. He wrote to his old mentor Folard: 'This is a courtier's army, with all the drawbacks implied thereby. Politics, I refuse to discuss them. I leave them to those more clever than myself.'

Frederick the Great agreed with this view and later wrote:

> The presence of the king and his ministers was extremely embarrassing for Count Saxe and a strain on the resources of the army. The courtiers filled the camp with intrigues and generally thwarted the Marshal's intentions. So numerous a court required ten thousand daily rations of fodder for their horses.

For the first few months of 1746 Maurice had to deal with the political realities of serving at the whim of Louis XV, a sorry lot for a soldier with the vision and experience of the Saxon. Nevertheless, within weeks he had managed to master these Princes whose ambitions were in excess of their abilities. In October Maurice bore down on Liège, a city and area that he considered would be a good place for his armies to winter.

On 10 October, the main units of the King's army were approaching Liège. In a small town named Tongres, a public theatre was to hold a performance for the assembled troops. Unbeknownst to them, Maurice himself approached the producer Charles-Simon Favart and his wife Justine, who later became Maurice's mistress, with a plan. He asked them to include in their lyrics the words that tomorrow would be the day of a great battle – a novel way to reveal a secret plan. At the conclusion of the performance Justine Favart sang the words,

> Demain bataille, jour de gloire
> Que dans les fastes de l'Histoire
> Triomphe encore le nom francais
> Digne d'eternelle memoire!

The watching soldiers began to sing 'Demain bataille!' and the following morning took up their positions near the village of Roucoux. By the early afternoon of 11 October, Maurice's army had forced the Allied army consisting of British regiments under General Ligonier, the Austrians and the Dutch, into a retreat.

At the end of the day Maurice rode back through his men to the shouts of 'Vive le roi et Le Marechal de Saxe!' Each brigade offered him nine captured flags and sixty cannons. He estimated the enemy casualties at about five thousand with about three thousand taken prisoner: it was a victory indeed.

If any criticism can be laid against Maurice it would be that he had not finally finished off his enemies in either of his great victories. But the boy who had witnessed the bloodshed at Malplaquet was more the soldier than the brutal politician, who would have massacred thousands to reinforce not just a military victory but a political victory too.

Maurice returned to France in mid-November and attended at the Palace of Fontainebleau. Though it was late, the King was roused from his bed and gave him supper and handed him another brevet bestowing on him six cannons, three marked with the arms of England and three with the arms of Hesse. These trophies of war would be placed at Chambord. Not only was Maurice the supreme military commander in France but he also became hugely influential thanks to his political connections.

On 9 February 1747, his niece Maria Josepha of Saxony married Louis the Dauphin. His influence in the court had never been greater and it had been further consolidated at the end of January when the King conferred on him the title Marshal General of the Camps and Armies of France, 'to follow in every way the example of Monsieur de Turenne'. The great Turenne had converted to Catholicism on his appointment and had also died in battle. Maurice intended to do neither. He politely accepted his new promotion but refused to convert from his Lutheranism: 'It only remains for me, Sire, to die like Monsieur de Turenne.'

With regard to matters familial, little did Maurice know that one day he would be the great uncle of three Kings of France. During that winter of 1746-1747 you could say, to plagiarise Louis XIV, of Maurice de Saxe, 'La France en ce moment c'est lui.'

He had perpetuated the myth that France was as great as it had been in the time of Le Roi Soleil, but it was not. Nobody at that time could have predicted that the decades that lay ahead would bring national bankruptcy, revolution and dictatorship. Though some years before Voltaire had confided to Frederick the Great: 'I think the French are living in Europe on credit, like some rich man who is growing unconsciously poorer. Our nation needs a master to encourage it.'

Within ten years, India and Canada would fall to England and worse was to follow at home. Who knows what might have happened in the Seven Years War if Maurice had been fit and healthy enough to command the armies of France?

Despite Tolstoy's thoughts on the matter, there is no doubt that history can be changed by a single man. But Maurice, military genius as he was, could not change the tide of history. As the French 18th century, the *siècle francais* had taken over the Spanish 17th century, the *siglo espanol*, so now the 19th century was to be the century of the British.

During the spring of 1747 Maurice returned north and played cat and mouse with the Allied armies led once more by the youthful, indecisive and inexperienced Duke of Cumberland. The France now had the Spanish Netherlands and was threatening the United Provinces. If French armies were to take the strategic town of Maastricht, they would be in a very strong position to advance into what is now Holland. Cumberland was lured into battle at Laufeldt two miles west of Maastricht. On 2 July 1747, in pouring rain, the brutal struggle began with the Allies bravely holding back repeated French assaults on their lines for more than five desperate hours. Regiment after French regiment threw themselves into the enemy fire. The Allies suffered 8,500 casualties, the French 14,000.

When Maurice was about to unleash his cavalry onto the enemy lines, General Ligonier, that fine Gascon fighting for the Hanoverian monarchs of Great Britain, ordered the British cavalry to attack their French counterparts. In two desperate charges he did not turn the battle in the Allies' favour, since the battle had already been won and lost, but prevented the aftermath turning into a mass slaughter. Ligonier was taken prisoner and brought before Louis. Maurice is reported as saying, 'Sire, I have the honour of presenting to your majesty the man who has defeated all my plans of a single glorious action.'

In the days that followed, Maurice's army remained before the walls of Maastricht while, in search of new victories, he sent his loyal Dane General Ulrich von Lowendahl off to besiege Bergen-op-Zoom. Two months later the city fell to the French army, which resulted in a massacre largely caused by Breton irregulars.

Maurice was now made Commandant-General of the Low Countries by the departing King, which was confirmed officially in January 1748 when he was also awarded the nominal title of Governor of Alsace. He appears to have been a little disappointed he was not created Viceroy of the Spanish Netherlands as his hero, Eugene of Savoy, had been fifty years before. But Maurice's plans were not at an end. Just as negotiations to end the War of the Austrian Succession were taking place at Aix-la-Chapelle, he obliged Maastricht to capitulate to the French army. On 10 May 1748, he took the salute as the Austrian garrison filed past him in surrender. He made the newly promoted Marshal von Lowendahl its Governor. This was Maurice's final victory.

He had been a soldier for nigh on forty years. Starting out as a junior officer in the Saxon Army he had fought in the Great Northern War, the Ottoman wars and the Wars of the Spanish Succession, the Polish Succession and the Austrian Succession. A scion of the royal house of Wettin in Saxony and the remarkable Swedish family the Konigsmarcks, he had learned his profession under the tutelage of such great men as Schulenburg, Marlborough and Eugene of Savoy. He had been the victor is three major European battles and had captured numerous cities. When the Peace of Aix-la-Chapelle was ratified on 18 October 1748 and the Austrian Netherlands were returned to the Hapsburgs, Maurice could never understand why this had been agreed. His victories had been in vain.

On their return to Paris, the King and his family reviewed the troops and in particular Maurice's personal regiment of Uhlans, the Volontaires de Saxe, on their arrival from Flanders. The crowds who witnessed that day cannot have been aware that this was the end of an era, when these exotically uniformed soldiers, led by the last of the great *Ancien Regime* commanders, left the Champ de Mars and marched away towards Chambord far away on the Loire.

The Chateau de Chambord is vast. It was the nearest thing to a kingdom that the victor of Fontenoy, Roucoux, and Laufeldt could obtain. The superb château was neglected and uncomfortable, as Stanislas Leczinski, the former King of Poland, to his cost had found, but Maurice received permission from Louis XV to improve the place at royal expense. He proceeded to turn the fortified castle of the Middle Ages, a hunting palace of the Renaissance, into the pompous mansion that was the eighteenth-century idea of a royal residence. There was something in the regal size of the place, the vast squat towers, the huge parade ground, the soaring pinnacles and massive gargoyles, the great staircases and multitude of enormous chambers, that pleased the extravagant taste of Count Maurice of Saxony. If he could not have a kingdom, at least he had a king's palace, if not an army, at least a regiment and a barracks.

It had originally been built by Francois I during the early sixteenth century as a hunting lodge. What a hunting lodge! With its spires, its towers, its exterior staircases, its colonnades, it was a palace built in a dream. The King had denied Maurice his crazed request for a kingdom in Madagascar peopled by impoverished Saxons and other madcap schemes. But at Chambord he could give free rein to his Baron Munchhausen tendencies. He built barracks there for his personal regiment and sentries patrolled the corridors of the *cour d'honneur* at the heart of the great edifice. These Saxon Uhlans with their distinctive head dress consisted of a thousand men, Hungarians, Turks, Poles, Saxons, Silesians and Tartars, with French officers. There was also a 'Colonial Brigade' formed by Africans from the Congo and Guinea and Indians from Pondicherry led by an African officer in an exotic uniform resplendent on a white horse on parade. It was this private army that had so impressed the people of Paris on the Champ de Mars who continued their rather pointless drill practises on the lonely parade ground on the banks of the Loire. The gigantic stables looked after eight hundred horses, and in the park wild Ukrainian horses ran free. The cannons presented to him after Roucoux were on display at the grand entrance and in the ante-rooms were hung the regimental colours that had been surrendered to him after his victories.

Maurice spent much of his time enforcing strict military discipline on his soldiers, summarily executing some for particular crimes, but continually drilling them for future formal parades which would never take place. He even built a thirty-kilometre wall around the estate, which must have merely reminded him of the limitations of his land when he had dreamed of vast acreages who knows where. Apart from those pointless military drills his days were spent in the chase in the great parkland, followed by evenings at plays, operas and enjoying the delights of the flesh.

On 20 November 1750, despite the desperate ministrations of Senac de Meilan, the charade ceased when Maurice of Saxony died in his vast bed in his vast bed chamber in the vast palace that was Chambord. It was reported he died of 'a putrid fever'.

He was a Count of Saxony, Maréchal Général de France, Governor of Alsace, Duke Elect of Courland and Semigallia, and a Knight of the Orders of Poland and Saxony. Perhaps his regiments had been trained for this moment when they marched gloomily behind his enormous black draped coffin across the muddy roads of France to his burial place in the cathedral of Strasbourg.

Maurice's legacy was not only military. During the last years of his life, Maurice had yet another affair, this time with a French girl, Marie Rinteau, who at that time was only eighteen years old. In 1748 she gave birth to a daughter, the last of Maurice's several illegitimate children. The child was named Marie Aurore after her grandmother. She bore the surname de la Rivière until 1766 when the Parlement of Paris formally recognized her parentage and she could assume the surname of von Sachsen or de Saxe. Through her second marriage with Louis Claude Dupin de Francueil in 1777, she was the grandmother of Amandine Lucile Aurore Dupin, the writer George Sand. Maria Aurore died on 25 December 1821 when her granddaughter George Sand was seventeen. Sand included details of her grandmother's parentage in her memoirs.

Far from being just a swashbuckling man of action, Maurice de Saxe revealed himself as a serious student of things military with his strangely titled military text book, *Mes Reveries*, which probably translates better as 'My Thoughts' than 'My Dreams'. The opinionated Thomas Carlyle described it as 'a strange military farrago dictated, as I should think, under opium'. Clearly Carlyle, the sage of Ecclefechan, was not a soldier.

The work, which goes into great detail on battlefield tactics as well as the treatment of the ordinary foot soldier, was admired by Frederick the Great, who always believed in the abilities of Maurice and had met him as a young man. General Montgomery, a man never afraid to express his own opinions, described it two centuries later as 'a remarkable work on the art of war'. The Duke of Wellington took a copy with him on campaign in India.

Maurice can be clearly seen as an innovator in tactics and he was one of the first military thinkers to entertain the idea of avoiding frontal attacks in favour of more evasive action for infantry when faced with ranks of defensive fire or artillery bombardment.

In the rather sinister Walhalla Memorial building overlooking the Danube at Donaustauf in Bavaria, a monument to Germanic achievers, Count Moritz of Saxony is Bust no.115 to the right of Ludwig I of Bavaria. Despite his trappings as a French 18th-century aristocrat, he was at heart a stout Saxon soldier with a soft heart.

9

ALEXANDER VASILYEVICH SUVOROV

1729–1800

Train hard, fight easy.

High in the Lepontine Alps on the forbidding St Gotthard Pass, nearly 7,000 feet above sea level, a gigantic memorial decorated with an Orthodox Christian cross is carved into the glowering granite face. Beneath it are letters in Cyrillic commemorating the Russian victory there as they crossed into Switzerland from the Plains of Lombardy. The name of Alexander Suvorov stands out clearly. He was the commander of that Russian-Austrian army which, against terrible odds, fought their way through into Switzerland against the armies of Republican France.

A little further up the Pass there is a plateau and on a rocky outcrop silhouetted against the sky there is a strange sight, a statue of the thin and ageing Marshal Suvorov astride a tired horse being led across the Pass by his guide Antonio Gamba. It could be Don Quixote and Sancho Panza.

Few commanders in history have led armies across the Alps. Everybody knows about Hannibal, some about Hasdrubal, his brother, many about Napoleon Bonaparte, few about Suvorov, who made the crossing northwards in the face of constant enemy fire.

Interestingly Suvorov considered Hannibal, Alexander the Great, Julius Caesar, and Napoleon Bonaparte to be the greatest military commanders of all time, though he never fought a battle against the Corsican and never lived to see his great triumph at Austerlitz and could only have read about Napoleon's campaigns in Northern Italy, which he so swiftly reversed.

Suvorov is considered one of the greatest military commanders in Russian history, though the half-blinded Kutuzov, the general in the victorious 1812 campaign against Napoleon, and in more recent history, Zhukov, are more familiar names. From a Western perspective, he is certainly a forgotten general.

Suvorov's brief appearances on the battlefields of Western Europe were to take place in the last year of the 18th century and in the last months of his life. As a result, he was dismissed by some, ignorant of his momentous track record against the Ottoman Empire. They underestimated him and his unique ability to lead his armies.

In 1799, Russia was persuaded to intervene in the French Revolutionary Wars as part of the Second Coalition with Britain and Austria. It was one of two unprecedented Russian interventions in that year, the other being the disastrous Anglo-Russian invasion of Holland from August to November 1799. Suvorov's expedition was planned by British and Russian politicians and diplomats. Russia would provide troops that Britain would subsidise, and together they sought to encourage Austria to do most of the fighting since they were providing three-quarters of the army, and to pay for its own troops as well as supply the entire allied army, but while still maintaining Anglo-Russian strategic control over the campaign.

Russia and Britain distrusted Austria because they were cautious of the Habsburgs' territorial greed and hoped to persuade Austria to make war with their traditional enemy out of self-defence and to help ensure the pre-Revolutionary order in Europe. The monarchies of Europe were terrified of the prospect of the growing power and threat of Revolutionary France. Though Britain were still owed reparations by Austria after the War of the First Coalition, which had ended in 1797, and would not directly pay for the Austrian army, Britain and Russia exploited the rivalry between Prussia and Austria to persuade both to join the Second Coalition.

The man selected to command this coalition army was Alexander Vasilyevich Suvorov, Russia's most distinguished soldier, recently retired, after struggling in his dealings with the petulant and dangerous Czar Paul I. In 1799, he was nearly seventy years of age but was still one of the most competent generals of the age. He had won no fewer than sixty-three battles in the course of his long military career and had first been appointed Field Marshal during the reign of Catherine the Great, Czar Paul's mother. By now he was living in retirement having been dismissed by the monarch after criticizing the new Imperial Infantry Code.

His appointment, insisted upon by the Austrians, who had successfully fought alongside him earlier, was to command the Austro-Russian army to fight the Revolutionary French armies in Italy. It was to result in some of the most spectacular victories of his career.

The diminutive but wiry Suvorov was born into a noble family in the Moscow mansion of his maternal grandfather, Fedosey Manukov, on 24 November 1729. His father, Vasili Suvorov, was a general and a senator in the Governing Senate, and had translated Marshal Vauban's works on military engineering from the original French into Russian. Suvurov in relating his family history to his military aide, Colonel Anthing, always insisted that his family originated from Swedish nobility of the seventeenth century fighting against Tartars and Poles. The Empress Catherine II wrote in a letter in 1790, 'It is beyond doubt that the name of the Suvorovs has long been noble, is Russian from time immemorial and resides in Russia.' Perhaps the young Suvurov had heard about the legendary King Charles XII of Sweden in his childhood and admired his military exploits.

Suvorov was a sickly child and his father always assumed he would work in government administration when he grew up. However, he proved to be an excellent student in mathematics, literature, philosophy and geography and learning to read French,

German, Polish and Italian. In his father's great library he was an avid reader of military history from classical times, particularly Plutarch and Quintus Curtius, and from more recent times the diaries of Charles XII. This enabled him at an early age to develop a grasp of military engineering, siege warfare, use of artillery, and fortification techniques. Like Eugene of Savoy, he tried to overcome his physical limitations through rigorous exercise and exposure to hardship, but he was always a small, wiry man who appeared in later life much older than he was. He was never a man to indulge in the pleasures of the flesh, quite the contrary, he was puritanical in his daily life both on campaign and in the capitals of Europe.

His father insisted that he was not suitable for a career as a soldier until a significant event which was to change the young man's life. When Alexander was twelve, he came under the influence of a fabulously named neighbour, General Abram Petrovich Hannibal.

The story of this Hannibal is extraordinary. Whether he was born in Southern Sudan or Cameroon is debated, but certainly he was from sub-Saharan Africa, had been taken prisoner by the Ottomans and transported to Constantinople where he was put in the service of the Sultan. The Russian Ambassador then persuaded officials to give him to the Czar and he was transported to Russia, where he was baptised in Vilnius in 1705 with Peter the Great as his godfather. He became close to the royal family and went on campaign as a boy with Czar Peter. Fluent in several languages, he was sent to France to train in military engineering. While there he was described by Voltaire as the 'dark star of the Enlightenment' and took the name Hannibal in honour of the great African general.

When he returned to Russia, he taught some of Czar Peter's Imperial Guard mathematics and engineering. But when Peter died he was treated with suspicion by Prince Menshikov, who exiled him to Siberia in 1727. During his time there as a master engineer, he completed a number of military construction projects.

When Elizabeth the Great became monarch, Hannibal, now a general, became a senior member of her court and superintendent of Tallin for ten years. After that post he became chief military engineer of the Russian army, then a general-in-chief, before retiring to the enormous Mikhailovskoye estate near Pskov, which had been awarded to him by the Empress. His great grandson was Alexander Pushkin, who spent many summers on the estate, which remained in the family for many decades. When Abram petitioned for a coat of arms, he requested that the family crest include the emblem of an African elephant.

The young Suvurov, fascinated by the general's stories, fell under his spell and it was General Hannibal who persuaded his father, General Suvorov, to let his sickly child follow his dream of becoming a soldier. Suvorov entered the army in 1748 at nineteen and served in the elite Semyonovsky Life Guard Regiment for six years. The red-stockinged Semyonovskys had originated in 1683 as part of the so-called 'toy army' assembled by Czar Peter the Great when he was a boy. They took their name from a village just outside Moscow where they were based from 1700 until they moved quarters to the new capital, St Petersburg, in 1723. They had been one of the back-bone regiments of the Russian army during the Great Northern War and had performed heroically in the Battle of Narva in 1700. In that desperate defence of the fortress, they had lost 17 officers including their colonel and more than 450 soldiers. In honour of their bravery Charles XII of Sweden allowed them to leave the battlefield carrying their weapons, with standards unfurled and drums playing. Their red stockings were said to be worn in memory of their predecessors, men who had fought knee-deep in blood. The Swedish King encountered them once again when they took part in his final defeat at Poltava in 1709.

In June 1749, the young Alexander was made an under officer and was commissioned at the age of twenty-four in 1754; many of his richer and more flamboyant contemporaries had advanced further due to their connections. From this time as he continued his studies at the Cadet Corps of Land Forces, two incidents stand out. Firstly, when one day he was on sentry duty and presented arms for the Empress Elizabeth outside the Peterhof

Palace. Noticing the young boy, the Empress tossed him a silver rouble, which he could not accept while on duty. She told him to pick it up when relieved of his duty, which he did. He kept the coin all his life and proudly showed it to guests as a symbol of his loyalty to the Crown.The second episode of interest is in 1752 when the callow youth was sent alone to the Courts of Saxony in Dresden and Austria in Vienna to deliver despatches before returning to St Petersburg after seven months. His gruelling journey across the open plains of Europe and into the sophisticated capital cities must have opened his eyes. It is said that during this time he learned to speak German.

Suvorov gained his first combat experience fighting against the Prussians during the so-called 3rd Silesian War, part of the Seven Years' War, 1756-1763, fighting in frequent actions both with cavalry and infantry. That worldwide conflagration is largely known as a conflict between France and the United Kingdom, but Russia, allied with Austria, was at war with Frederick the Great's Prussia and much of the fighting took place in Prussia, particularly in East Prussia, Saxony and Silesia.

Shortly after the Battle of Sulechow, where the Russians commanded by General Saltykov had defeated the Prussian army trying to block them from joining up with Austrian forces, on 25 July 1759, with a squadron of dragoons, Suvorov attacked and routed Prussian dragoons. A few weeks later, he took part in the final victory of the war where the Russian and Austrian armies combined to defeat Frederick the Great at the Battle of Kunersdorf in the extreme east of Brandenburg province. More than 100,000 combatants were involved the Russians commanded by General Saltykov and the Austrians by General von Laudon. It was undoubtedly Frederick's worst defeat, fought over very difficult ground. There was savagery about the conflict, particularly on the part of the Cossacks, not familiar with the norms of European rules of engagement. The Prussians suffered severe casualties of about 20,000 with more than 6,000 killed, including eight colonels. The Prussian monarch, more familiar with the trumpets of victory than the ignominy of defeat, had vastly underestimated the fighting qualities of the Russian and Austrian soldier.

That evening, quartered in a peasant's home, Frederick wrote a despairing letter in French to his old tutor, Count von Finckenstein:

> This morning at 11 o'clock I attacked the enemy. All my troops have worked wonders, but at a cost of innumerable losses. Our men got into confusion. I assembled them three times. In the end I was in danger of getting captured and had to retreat. My coat is perforated by bullets and two horses of mine have been shot dead under me. My misfortune is that I am still living. Our defeat is very considerable. To me remains 3,000 men from an army of 48,000 men. At the moment in which I report all this, everyone is on the run; I am master of my troops no more. Thinking of the safety of anybody in Berlin is a good activity. It is a cruel failure that I will not survive. The consequences of the battle will be worse than the battle itself. I do not have any more resources, and, frankly confessed, I believe that everything is lost. I will not survive the doom of my fatherland. Farewell forever!

The thirty-year-old Russian officer Alexander Suvorov had witnessed many of these cataclysmic events. There followed the 'Miracle of the House of Brandenburg', so called by Frederick the Great, as the combined armies of Russia and Austria did not march on Berlin, only a few miles away, in a final triumph. Instead, they withdrew, thereby saving the House of Brandenburg.

The following year in October 1760 Suvorov took part in the Raid on Berlin as part of Major General Zakhar Chernyshev's army when a largely cavalry unit, led by the swashbuckling Saxon Count Heinrich Tottleben, detached themselves and struck north towards the Prussian capital. They were soon followed by an Austrian force under Count von Lacy. An attempt to take the city was held back by General von Seydlitz on 5 October, but after four days of negotiation the defenders agreed to terms with the Russian army rather than the hated Austrians. A large fine was extracted from the Prussians, and the Russian and Austrian troops wandered the streets taking caches of arms as well as captured regimental flags. But due to good discipline, the Russians did not destroy the city and, on hearing of Frederick's approach, departed.

They also took a number of hostages, particularly young military cadets, and Suvorov's Cossacks captured a boy he took care of personally, writing to his widowed mother: 'Dear mother, your young son is safe with me. If you want to leave him with me, he will not lack for anything and I will take care of him as if he were my own son. If you wish to keep him, you can have him here, or write to me where to send him.' The mother wrote asking to have her son back and he was allowed to go home.

In July 1761, Suvorov served under General Major Maxim Berg, successfully defending his position at Reichenbach and at Schweidnitz in Silesia and in desperate fighting managed to capture the high ground occupied by a force of Prussian Hussars. Near Landsberg on 15 September 1761, after wading across the river with his horses, his Cossack cavalry unit defeated three squadrons of Prussian Hussars. When told by his men how they were outnumbered, he replied, 'We came here to beat them, not to count them.'

On leaving the Friedberg Forest, he attacked General von Platen's flanking units and took a number of prisoners. He also was involved in rapid cavalry raids at Bunzelwitz, Birstein, Weisentine, Költsch, and this time leading an infantry unit, captured the fortress town of Golnau despite being wounded in the chest. In all these actions Suvorov had shown himself to be an extremely capable officer, working with speed and self-confidence despite fighting against a more than capable enemy. General Berg wrote that he was 'swift in reconnaissance, daring in battle and cold-blooded in danger'. Suvurov was promoted to colonel in 1762 when he was only thirty-three and given command of the Tver Dragoon Regiment, while their colonel recovered from his wounds.

Prussian observation detachments had now spread out from Kolberg in Pomerania and Berg moved there in two columns, the left led by himself, and the right led by Suvorov, which consisted of three Hussar, two Cossack, and the Tver Dragoon regiments. At Naugard the young Colonel attacked a Prussian unit of two battalions of infantry and a dragoon regiment. Forming his men in two lines, he drove off the enemy cavalry and overwhelmed one of the infantry battalions, taking more than a hundred prisoners before the other battalion retreated into the village buildings and stopped the Russian advance with heavy fire.

He now moved his unit twenty miles south to Stargard where he attacked the rearguard of von Platen, but without success, since the action took place on frozen marshland on which the Prussian infantry could move fast, whereas the Russian cavalry were too heavy and got bogged down. Despite this set-back, Suvorov managed to extricate his men without heavy losses.

Like all good officers should, he always paid attention to the well-being of his men. But he was different. Due to his lack of social self-confidence amongst his brother officers, he concentrated instead on the well-being and qualities of his men, many of whom were from the very lowest ranks of society. Wily peasants often avoided military service by bribing more lowly colleagues to take their place. The young officer, himself an outsider, admired the sterling courage and endurance of the simple Russian soldiers, understood them, and determined to improve their discipline and ingenuity. The young man had now experienced the trauma of battle. He had witnessed many deaths and seen badly wounded men from both sides being carried from the battlefield. He had become a veteran overnight.

With the war now ended, in late 1762 Suvurov was promoted to Colonel of the Suzdal regiment based at Lagoda, and he began to mould them into an impressive fighting force of nearly 2,000 men. It is said that on one occasion they were practising a route march past the great walls of a monastery. Instead of continuing their march an idea came into his head. Suddenly, their Colonel ordered them to attack and, sure enough, with their disciplined training, they scaled the high walls and 'captured' the monastery, much to the surprise of the monks within, none of whom were harmed. Certainly, Suvorov was an unusual officer.

Meanwhile in St Petersburg political intrigues were at work. Catherine II, the widow of the eccentric and hopeless Holsteiner, Peter III, who had reigned for only six months and had died in mysterious circumstances in July 1762, had been crowned Empress in Moscow on 22 September. Things were going to change. It is significant that Suvorov's father was one of her supporters. One of her first political moves was to nominate a former lover, Stanislaus Poniatowski, as King of Poland, which finally came about at the election *Sejm* of July 1764.

Many of the leaders in Poland were unhappy with this and wary of Russian control. In 1768, the Confederation of Bar was formed at a fortress named Bar in Podolia, an alliance of Polish and Lithuanian nobles claiming independence and declaring war on Russia. They had not only become suspicious of Russia but also of the attempted reforms of Stanislaus, such as freedom of worship for non-Catholics, which threatened their traditional powers.

In November 1768, the Russian commander in Poland, a General Nummers, requested the help of Colonel Suvorov and his Suzdal regiment. Expecting them to arrive in January, he was astonished when Suvorov and his disciplined men arrived at Smolensk on 15 December, exactly one month after they had set out. They had marched 600 miles and on arrival were in fighting condition. The following summer he marched 350 miles with his regiment and other reinforcements towards Warsaw, in the meantime seeing off a body of confederates.

As the Polish forces led by Casimir and Francis Pulawski advanced from the south, Suvorov moved to Brest-Litovsk and from there made a surprise attack on the enemy at Orekhovo. Francis Pulawski was killed and the Polish forces scattered. In 1769, France now entered the equation sending General Dumouriez to command the rebels who now numbered more than 15,000 men. The Russian forces in Poland only numbered 12,000 and Suvorov had just 4,000 to deal with the threat from the south. Having failed to take the stronghold of Tyniec, Suvorov attacked

Lanckorona at two o'clock in the morning and put Dunouriez and his men to flight. Operations against the Poles finally ended when the defenders of Wawel Castle, the citadel of Krakow, surrendered on 12 April 1772 after Suvorov had driven off the Polish army at Smerdionzce in early March. During this engagement he was very nearly killed when a Lithuanian hussar by the name of Reich singled him out and charged him. It became single combat and the wiry and small Suvorov was no match for the burly hussar. He was only saved when a Russian cuirassier stepped in and shot the Lithuanian dead.

The uprising now dwindled away and in May Poland was divided into three areas of control by Russia, Prussia and Austria. Though Suvorov had been promoted to major-general, he was not informed of these political plans and spent time back in St Petersburg.

Interestingly, Pulawski, known as the 'father of American cavalry', later travelled to America from France, where he was living in exile, and fought under George Washington in the American War of Independence, to whom he wrote: 'I came here where freedom is being defended, to serve it, and to live or die for it.' He did indeed die for the American cause, mortally wounded by grapeshot leading a cavalry charge in Savannah, Georgia.

It was in the Russo-Turkish War of 1768-1774 that Suvorov was to emerge as one of the outstanding commanders of his time. At Kozludzha in what is now Bulgaria, on 20 June 1774 he laid the foundations of his reputation. The Ottoman forces there consisted of about 40,000, the Russians fewer than half that number. Suvorov used only 8,000 in the battle itself. When he was advised by scouts of the presence of Abdul Rezak Pasha's forces, he immediately ordered an attack after artillery had devastated the Ottoman infantry. The Russians advanced in four squares, their defence against the Ottoman light cavalry. The Russian cavalry attacked from the rear of the Ottomans and they capitulated. They had 3,000 casualties while the Russians only suffered just over 200. The entire Ottoman artillery and supply camp was captured.

Kozludzha was subsequently named Suvorova, which it is called to this day, and the Ottomans abandoned the town. Suvorov was also victorious at Turtukaya where he stormed the Ottoman defences and at Hirsovo where he defended the castle before counter-attacking. On 21 July the Ottomans signed the humiliating Treaty of Kucuk Kaynarca, and Suvorov was promoted to Lieutenant General.

Campaigning in far-off places and often with bad communications, Suvorov naturally acted on his own initiative, as any general would. It was rumoured that he was censured by his commander in chief for 'unauthorized actions against the Turks', and at one point was sentenced to death. Apparently the Tsarina Catherine rejected the verdict, commenting 'Winners can't be judged.' The story seems most unlikely, since Field Marshal Pyotr Rumyantsev, his overall commander, was a stalwart supporter of Suvorov.

Late in the summer of 1774 Suvorov was suddenly ordered to take military action against the so-called Pugachev Rebellion led by the disgruntled Cossack former Russian army officer, Yemelvan Pugachev. He made the absurd claim that he was the assassinated husband of Catherine the Great, Peter III, who had been dead since 1763. Count Nikita Panin had been appointed by Catherine to deal with the situation and requested that Suvorov leave Field Marshal Rumyantsev's campaign and take military action against the rebels.

As Pugachev, at the head of a rebel Cossack and Tartar army, crossed the Volga hundreds of miles away from Moldavia, Suvorov was ordered to hurry back to Moscow to receive his orders. On reaching Moscow and briefly meeting up with his wife and his father, he immediately raced off south again, this time towards Ukholovo more than two hundred miles away. With a modest escort of fifty men he arrived there on 3 September 1774, where Panin authorised him to take charge.

He now moved swiftly to Saratov, another 250 miles along the great Volga River upstream from Tsaritsyn, later Stalingrad. Panin, a close associate of the Empress Catherine, told her of Suvorov's remarkable speed of travel. As a result, she sent a message of thanks and two thousand gold ingots to pay his men.

On reaching Saratov, Suvorov learned that the Estonian General Ivan Michelsohnen had already been tracking Pugachev and his rebel army and had inflicted a number of defeats on him. Building up his force, Suvorov headed south again towards Tsaritsyn, now by river on the Volga since there was a lack of available horses. With his slow but sure progress down the majestic waters of the enormous river, by the time he reached Tsaritsyn Pugachev had long gone, slipping across the two-mile-wide river with his fellow Cossacks and disappearing into the vast steppe. Undeterred, Suvorov continued his pursuit of the pretender after assembling two squadrons of Cossacks, two *sotnias* of mounted infantry, amounting to about three hundred men, plus two light artillery pieces.

He crossed the Volga and moved up-river, raiding a village and taking fifty cattle. Now he ventured into the endless wastes of the steppe, navigating with the sun by day and the stars by night. In the day it was hot, in the nights very cold, but still his small detachment kept going across difficult ground under foot, even harder for the horses. It was desolate country with few trees, without shade or water. They slaughtered some of the cattle to subsist and kept moving, enduring violent electrical storms and blistering heat.

From time to time they were joined by other army units who were also pursuing Pugachev. On 23 September, by which date there was already a distinct chill in the air when the sun went down, they came to the Uzen River in Kazakhstan, and Suvorov, aware they were closing in on the rebels, divided his small army into four groups and spread out to widen their chances of capturing Pugachev.

Finally Pugachev's own men, only a few miles ahead of their relentless pursuers, lost hope and turned on their leader. Pugachev was arrested and taken to Yaitsk where Suvorov, after interrogating him, formally took him prisoner and despatched him to Moscow where he was ultimately beheaded. Though Suvorov had desperately wanted to defeat the rebels in battle, he had been relentless in his pursuit of what the rulers in Moscow considered a serious threat to the stability of Mother Russia and as a result was much admired for his determined pursuit.

The distances the general had covered on horseback were astonishing, they approximate the vast distances the German *Wehrmacht* advanced two hundred years later in their mechanised vehicles. The Pugachev rebellion tells us much about Suvorov's character: his sense of duty, his obedience to his superiors, his determination and his courage, physical and mental, in a hostile and unfamiliar environment.

For the next decade the indispensable Suvorov was engaged largely in that vast no man's land between the northern borders of the Ottoman Empire and the expanding southern Russian borders of Catherine the Great's Empire. He served in the Kaban region against the Tatars to the east of the Sea of Azov, then moved south to the Crimea, commanding Russian troops there between 1782 and 1784 and preventing Ottoman landings. In 1783, he returned to the Kaban to crush a Nogai uprising.

In1787, the inevitable second Russo-Turkish War broke out and soon Suvorov was once more under enemy fire when he commanded an outlying Russian fortress named Kinburnska, badly exposed on a sandspit on the gigantic Dnieper River delta, which the Turks attempted to storm on 12 October 1787. The Turks wanted to take it since it covered the approaches to Kherson and Ochakov. Suvorov had more than three hundred old-fashioned artillery pieces and 1,500 infantry, though he could call on the support of a further 2,500 infantry, about 30 field guns and units of Cossack cavalry on the mainland. The Ottomans had about 400 guns in their fleet of warships, frigates, floating batteries and gunboats.

During September and October, the fortress was bombarded a number of times by the Ottoman fleet and on 12 October 6,000 Ottoman troops landed on the sandspit and another beach supported by naval fire and immediately began to dig in. The Pasha of Ochakov ordered the ships to leave to ensure the landing force could not retreat. Since that day was a Holy day in the Orthodox Church, Suvorov issued orders from the local church, including an urgent request for the reinforcements.

At first the Turkish attackers advanced towards the fort, but under the command of Major General Ivan von Reck, the commander of the garrison, the Oriol infantry and Schlisselburg Grenadier regiments drove them back in fierce fighting, taking most of the newly dug trenches. But von Reck was seriously wounded and they were forced to retreat back into the fortress. Now Suvorov himself led another Russian attack into even fiercer fighting. He was soon wounded in the side and the left hand, and was saved only through the courage of Stepan Novikov, a grenadier of the Schlisselburg Grenadier Regiment.

In the afternoon, the Russian reinforcements arrived and the wounded Suvorov again led his men into the attack. He ordered the Cossacks to ride round and attack the flank of the enemy in a dramatic gallop through the shallow waters. This was successful, and the Turks were forced back onto the beaches. Their naval guns could not fire any more due to the risk of hitting their own men. As the fighting continued, Suvorov had two horses shot underneath him until grapeshot fire from the Russian guns decimated the Ottoman troops. As night fell, some of the survivors were picked up by small boats and the remainder who had hidden in the coastal reeds were finished off by the Cossacks the following morning. The Russians had lost about twenty officers and more than three hundred men. The Turkish losses were estimated at about four thousand.

Suvorov in his report singled out the Schlisselburg Grenadiers for praise and he was awarded the Order of St Andrew by the delight Empress with the words, 'You deserved it by faith and by faithfulness.'

In the spring of 1788, the Russian army under Prince Grigory Potemkin, Catherine the Great's great favourite, general, adviser, lover and, possibly even husband, and General Alexander Suvorov made preparations for the siege of Ochakov, held by Ottoman troops commanded by Hasan Pasha.

Suvorov, as always, wanted to attack immediately, but Potemkin wisely preferred to surround the city, bombard it continually and cut off the garrison from food and ammunition. By not committing his men straight into combat, Potemkin saved many lives, though this was frowned upon by a number of his more aggressive officers.

After a naval engagement in May, the Russians began their assault on the city on 9 July and on the 18th they captured the strategic island of Pirzin on the Dnieper. Shortly after, a force of Turkish Janissaries broke out of the Ochakov city gates and successfully drove off a unit of Cossacks investing the walls. It was Suvorov who personally led a counter-attack, and though wounded again, forced the Turks back behind the city walls. As the year wore on through the baking hot summer and into the freezing winter, both armies suffered from disease and lack of supplies.

Suvorov finally had his way and on the night of 6 December 1788 the city was stormed. Hasan Pasha's palace was captured and it is estimated that the Turks lost more than 20,000 killed in vicious street fighting, with 4,000 taken prisoner including the 74-year-old Georgian Hasan Pasha, along with his beloved pet lion. The Russian army lost fewer than 1,000 killed and double that wounded.

In the summer of 1789 Alexander Suvorov found himself again deep in Moldavia at the head of a Russian army of 7,000 men, alongside the Austro-Hungarian army of 18,000 led by Prince Josias of Saxe-Coburg, the great-great-grandfather of Queen Victoria.

On the morning of 1 August 1789, the combined army faced an Ottoman army numbering 30,000 men led by Osman Pasha at Focsani, in what is now Romania. The battle began with Russian and Austrian artillery opening fire on the Turkish lines. The Turks had fortified their lines with ditches and earthen mounds as well as wooden palisades and emerged from these defence lines to attack. Russian and Austrian artillery and musket fire drove them back before Suvorov, the senior general on the field, advanced against the Turkish right flank. By this time in his career he had re-thought Russian linear infantry attacks, finding them wasteful, and had changed the battle formations into squares that could repel Ottoman cavalry and then advance. These squares were made up of individual regiments and battalions laid out on the battlefield like a chess board. This ensured strength in defence but flexibility and speed in attack.

Saxe-Coburg followed Suvorov's tactics and soon the Turks were driven back by the Russian infantry advance, which was followed by an Austrian infantry attack on their left flank. By mid-afternoon they had fled the field. Allied casualties were fewer than one thousand, while the Turks lost more than four thousand killed or wounded.

Now the Grand Vizier of the Ottoman Empire, Cenaze Hasan Pasha, swore revenge for the humiliation of Focsani. At the head of an army of more than 100,000 men he set out on a difficult night march towards the 18,000-strong Austrian army encamped on the flat lands near the Danube delta and began to close in on the enemy. Suvorov, over sixty miles away, was advised of the danger and set out on a forced march in the blazing heat of the day to join up with the Austrians, a distance he covered in two and a half days. He arrived on the eve of the battle.

On the morning of 22 September 1789, he divided the armies into two columns and having crossed the River Rymnik went straight into the attack using his infantry square formations to repel the Turkish cavalry attacks, then overran their defences and pursued them vigorously as they retreated. While the Austrians held the Turks down with musket fire, the Russian light cavalry surrounded the enemy and attacked from behind. The broken Turks fled, many drowning in the Rymnik River as they tried to escape. For his great victory Alexander Suvorov was made Count Rymniksky by the Empress Catherine, and the Austrian Emperor Joseph II created him a Count of the Holy Roman Empire.

He was now summoned by Potemkin to undertake the siege of Izmail, a Turkish fortress to the west of Odessa also on the delta of the River Danube. Suvorov arrived there in mid-December and immediately began to make preparations for an assault. Russian troops were already positioned around the walls and the Russian

Black Sea flotilla, commanded by the Spanish-born admiral Jose de Ribas, was policing the river side of the defences. After inspecting the situation, Suvorov had ladders and fascines prepared while a ditch was dug with ramparts some distance away, where the general himself demonstrated to his men how to scale the ladders and fight hand-to-hand. Two ten-gun batteries were positioned on each side of the city.

On 18 December 1791, just five days after he had arrived, the now 60-year-old general sent an unequivocal ultimatum to the Ottoman commander of the garrison:

> To the Serasker, elders and all your people, I have arrived here with the army. I will give you 24 hours to think about surrender, so 24 hours of freedom. My first cannonade of shots will mean that your freedom has gone, and my attack will mean death. This is what I leave you for your consideration.

The Turkish Seraskier Mehmed Pasha replied requesting some days to make his decision. On 20 December Suvorov said he could not agree to the Serasker's request and gave a deadline of the 21st.

No reply came, so Suvorov took action, despite the fact his troops were suffering from a shortage of supplies and ammunition and only had forty field guns. He was aware the Turks had fewer guns, many of which had to be trained on the Russian fleet and decided to pressure the defenders from all sides. An artillery duel began, including flanking fire from a Russian unit on Catal Island, and the Russian flotilla. The Turkish artillery scored a direct hit on the ammunition on board the Russian frigate *Konstantin*, which was blown out of the water. This did not deter the determined Suvorov. When he set his mind on an objective, nothing would stop him.

The Russian bombardment continued late into the night, but still the walls could not be breached. Then at 5am on the morning of 22 December the Russians began their ground assault, using light infantry for the initial assault then scaling ladders for the main army to breach the walls. The armies were evenly matched in numbers, with about 15,000 regular troops on each side supplemented by an equal number of irregulars and volunteers.

Lieutenant General Potemkin, cousin of the Field Marshal, commanded Suvorov's right to attack the eastern walls and General Samoylov to attack the western walls, with de Ribas commanding the fleet whose heavy guns were key in the battle. This was truly a combined operation. Ribas also commanded a detachment of 9,000 marines ready to land on the river side of the Ottoman defences. One of Samoylov's senior officers was Michael Kutuzov, famous twenty years later for commanding the Russians against Napoleon at Borodino and during the catastrophic French retreat from Moscow. Strong-points in Izmail such as the New Fortress and the Old Fortress were to be assaulted by different units, many of them ruthless Cossacks. The fleet was to approach in two lines with 145 five river boats carrying the landing troops, closing in first and the 58 naval ships behind, bombarding the city with their heavy naval guns.

This was largely to be an infantry encounter, with the cavalry held in reserve and guarding the different gates of the citadel as they were overrun. The fighting was fierce and unrelenting in most areas of the city, and the Cossacks were particularly savage and successful.

Later Western European criticism and suspicion of Suvorov, with allegations of barbarity being brought against him, were largely due to the behaviour of his Cossacks troops at Kinburn, Ochakov and Izmail. But Russian armies are notoriously difficult to discipline in combat, particularly where revenge is sought. At 7 am the beach landing was successful, despite fierce opposition from a large force of Turks and Crimean Tatars, and within an hour the Russian army was in the centre of the city. Then desperate house-to-house fighting broke out as the garrison of Crimean Tatars, with a fearsome reputation and commanded by Quaplan Giray, their tribal leader, led a counter-attack with 3,000 men. They quickly put the Black Sea Cossacks to flight, but then the disciplined regular Russian infantry regiments drove them back. Five of Quaplan's sons were killed, as well as Maqsud Giray, a direct descendant of Genghis Khan. By mid-afternoon Izmail was in Russian hands. The Ottomans had suffered more than 25,000 casualties with most of the garrison killed. Suvorov's army suffered more than 4,000 casualties with half of that number killed. These cold figures on a page hardly touch on the suffering and loss on both sides. Many of the innocent civilians of the unfortunate city were also massacred.

Suvorov is said to have wept on returning to his campaign tent, whether for the losses amongst his own loyal troops or for the victims of urban close-quarter combat, the collateral damage to the innocent onlookers. It is often said that some of Suvorov's methods were barbaric. That may be so in some of the actions of Cossacks and Tatars under his command as different times, but these were his troops, some of the best in desperate moments. They gave no quarter and expected no quarter themselves.

Kutuzov was made commandant of Izmail and Suvorov was created an honorary Lieutenant Colonel of the Preobrazhensky Life Guard Regiment, a great honour since the Empress herself was the Colonel. The first Russian national anthem, *Let the thunder of victory sound!* was written after the victory on 22 December, which later became the Day of Military Honour in Russia.

In military terms the storming, which was effectively a combined operation, was one of most organised and effective engagements of Suvorov's career. He had organised and executed the whole complicated plan himself. So often in history, battle plans do not come to fruition. This battle went entirely to plan. It was his masterpiece.

The siege of Izmail is dramatised in Cantos 7 and 8 of Lord Byron's, *Don Juan*. The poet says in the preface that he was inspired by Gabriel de Castelnau's eye-witness account of the siege in his *Essai sur l'histoire ancienne et moderne de la Nouvelle Russie*.

Two months earlier, on 16 October 1791, the great Prince Grigory Potemkin died out on the open steppe of Bessarabia, about a day's journey from the city of Iași where he was negotiating with the Ottomans. On 9 January1792, the peace treaty was signed by the Grand Vizier Koca Yusuf Pasha and Prince Bezborodko, who had replaced Potemkin as chief negotiator. The treaty transferred the flat marshy lands of the great river deltas, the Yedisan, the territory between the Dniester and Bug Rivers, to Russia, making the Dniester River the Russo-Turkish frontier in Europe. The sixty-five-year-old Suvorov's Ottoman campaigning was at an end, but his career as a soldier was far from over.

The Polish Uprising in 1794 was yet another attempt by the Polish-Lithuanian Commonwealth to shrug off the political and military domination of Poland by the powers of Russia and Prussia, a theme which had continued for centuries and was to persist well into the 20th century. On 24 March, Tadeusz Kosciuszko, already famous for his actions in the American War of Independence, declared the uprising in the main square of Krakow and was proclaimed Commander in Chief of all Polish forces. As the rising gathered momentum, Russian garrisons over Easter were attacked by mobs in Warsaw and Vilnius, resulting in many casualties.

The Russians equipped a new corps commanded by Suvorov who joined up with a second corps under Ivan Fersen near Warsaw. After two engagements with the rebels at Krupczyce, on 17 September and Terespol two days later, the combined army marched towards Warsaw. Trying to prevent the Russian armies from joining up, Kościuszko mobilised two regiments from Warsaw and with General Sierakowski's 5,000 troops engaged Fersen's force of 14,000 on 10 October in the Battle of Maciejowice, east of Warsaw. The fight was a victory for the Russians and Kościuszko himself was wounded in the battle by Cossacks who stripped him and left him for dead. He was later identified, taken prisoner and sent to Saint Petersburg.

The Russian army now closed on Warsaw and on 4 November advanced into the city, before being held up on the east bank of the Vistula River in the suburb of Praga where the Poles fought bravely, but after four hours of hand-to-hand fighting they were overwhelmed by the more than 20,000 Russian troops. The Russians, and particularly the Cossacks, who were enraged by the killings of their fellow soldiers earlier in the year and were out for revenge, lost their discipline in Praga and mayhem broke out as rebels and civilians were massacred. Suvorov, in spite of destroying the bridge across the Vistula, could not prevent it. He later rode into Warsaw in a simple officer's uniform and formally took the keys of the city. He reported to Catherine, Hurrah, Warsaw's ours!' The Empress replied, 'Hurrah, Field Marshal!'

'Thus the assignment entrusted to me was fulfilled in forty-four days from the entry of the forces with me into Poland,' he wrote proudly in his diary.

But yet again the reputation that had gone before him was now nourished by the bloody bodies lying in the streets of Praga, though he had done his best to hold his angry troops back, and the salons of Europe fed on that nourishment. He later responded angrily:

> It is very difficult to do one's duty. I was considered a barbarian because at the storming of Praga seven thousand people were killed. Europe says that I am a monster. I myself have read this in the papers, but I would have liked to talk to people about this and ask them, is it not better to finish a war with the death of seven thousand people rather than drag it on and kill one hundred thousand?

Suvorov's argument brings to mind the debate about Hiroshima.

Tadeusz Kosciuszko was pardoned in 1796 and emigrated to the United States where he formed a friendship with Thomas Jefferson and wrote a will dedicating his assets in America to the education and freedom of slaves. He eventually returned to Europe and died in Switzerland in 1817. His wishes for the benefit of slaves were never carried out.

The newly ranked Suvorov remained in Poland until 1795, when he returned to Saint Petersburg. But his sovereign and great supporter, the Empress Catherine, died of a stroke on 17 November 1796, and her petulant son and successor, Paul I, once crowned Emperor, brought back the old style of Prussian uniforms for the Russian army, which Suvorov disliked as impractical and promptly refused to use. He was dismissed and exiled to his estate at Konchanskoye near Borovichi, about two hundred miles from St Petersburg and was kept under surveillance. It is recorded that on Sundays he tolled the bell for church and sang among the rustics in the village choir. On week days he worked among them in a smock, in the Tolstoyan manner.

The heir to Catherine the Great, who had ruled Russia for thirty-five years, had constantly clashed with the Field Marshal since he was only interested in the flashy but impractical uniforms, parades, drills, and brutal corporal punishments of the Prussian Army. He even had his own regiment of Russian soldiers he dressed up in Prussian-style uniforms.

Earlier in 1796, on 6 March, a relatively unknown French officer had been selected as commander in chief for the campaign in Northern Italy, some saying that the appointment was only made because his wife had slept with the First Secretary. His name was Napoleon Bonaparte.

On 27 March 1796, when he joined his armies in Lombardy, Bonaparte immediately embarked on a hugely successful campaign, winning numerous memorable victories over the Austrians and Sardinians that ended with the Treaty of Campo Formio in the autumn of 1797. Across Europe he was now a hero or villain, and in May 1798, Napoleon, at the behest of the ruling Directory of the Republic of France and with the support of Talleyrand, sailed with the French fleet carrying his Army of Egypt from Toulon via Malta to invade Egypt.

The sovereigns of Europe had to take action, and in 1799 the Second Coalition was formed of Great Britain, Prussia, Austria and Russia to oppose Revolutionary France and its huge armies. In February, Czar Paul I, also concerned at the French successes, was compelled by his peers to reinstate Suvorov as Field Marshal and Commander in Chief of an Austro-Russian army to invade Northern Italy, traditionally Hapsburg lands, and drive the French out. This is exactly what happened. In a few months Suvorov erased practically all of the gains Napoleon had made for France during 1796 and 1797, defeating some of the republic's top generals in three bloody engagements. Though the Russian and Austrian forces under Suvorov suffered losses, they shocked the normally victorious republican French forces with their stubborn and relentless fighting.

The old Russian general set out early in the year and arrived in Vienna in mid-March, having visited the exiled King Louis XVIII at Mittau. He was greeted wildly in Vienna as the saviour of Europe who was going to drive out "the godless, flighty, madcap French'. The Austrian government was more suspicious of this uncivilised general who had only defeated the Ottomans and never been up against the French armies. When Johann Amadeus Thugut, the notoriously devious Austrian diplomat and chief of the *Hofkriegsrat*, asked him what his plans were, he took a piece of paper out of his tunic and unfolded it before the war council. It was blank. 'I have never made any other plan of campaign' he told them, and walked out of the meeting.

Suvorov would only make plans when he could see what he was up against. He knew already that he was to face the formidable French army, led by young adventurous commanders, united in a common spirit of nationalism and hope for a new world. But he also knew of the qualities of his Russian soldiers and believed deeply in their loyalty and determination.

Arriving in Verona, having travelled by coach from Vienna, he was given a liberator's welcome and there met his Russian and Austrian subordinate generals. He briefed them: 'It is not enough for the senior commanders alone to be informed of the plan of battle. It is essential that the junior commanders too, always have it in mind to lead their forces in accordance with them.'

He also outlined in detail how the infantry should attack. Once within a thousand yards of the enemy the troops were to form two lines and then advance at the ordinary slow step until within three hundred paces, this being the maximum range of the excellent French musketry. Then, when the order to advance was given, the troops should proceed at the usual rate, but after a hundred paces they should double their speed, and a hundred yards short of the French line, they must rush at it at full speed with bayonets levelled. The second line was to follow through as the first line regrouped.

At Cassano d'Adda, General Jean Victor Moreau was defeated on 27 and 28 April with losses of 2,500 plus more than 5,000 taken prisoner, while the Russians and Austrians lost the same number in the brutal fighting. 'The Adda is a Rubicon and we crossed it over the bodies of our enemies' Suvorov wrote after the battle.

Europe was amazed, Lombardy had been taken back for the Austrians and the way to Milan was open. Suvorov, who had often been despised in the West for the brutalities of his Cossacks in Poland and Bessarabia, as well as mocked as a fool and a clown by a number of self-important diplomats who had met him, for his drinking habits and eccentricities, was now the hero. *The Times* of London wrote, 'The progress of the Field Marshal has been brilliant beyond the most sanguine expectation.'

The captured French general Jean-Mathieu-Philibert Serrurier, at dinner with Suvorov, was allowed to keep his sword for his bravery. He politely commented to the wily old Russian that his attacks were too brazen. Suvorov responded casually, 'What can we do? We Russians have no rules or tactics, but I'm still one of the best!'

The Russian-Austrian army now occupied Milan at Easter 1799 with much rejoicing, then Suvorov moved west taking Turin on 14 May. A month later the 30,000-man French army of General Jacques Macdonald advanced from the south and Suvorov hurried to oppose him. Between the 7 and 9 June, about forty miles south east of Milan on the River Trebbia near Piacenza, the French suffered 6,500 men killed against Russian and Austrian losses of 5,000. 12,000 French soldiers were captured. During the three days of brutal and attritional engagement, the 70-year-old Suvorov hardly dismounted, constantly encouraging his men and urging them on. It is said the white shingle on the riverbed of the Trebbia was stained red with the blood of the French. The revolutionary armies of France had never come up against anything like this before. It was a portent of what would happen against the Russians in 1812.

Despite his victories, Suvorov now had to deal with the increasingly obstructive and hidebound Austrian *Hofkriegsrat*, who were only interested in repossessing previously held Austrian territory rather than the defeat of France. The Archduke Charles, the younger brother of the Austrian Emperor Joseph II, at the head of an army of 100,000 remained inert in Switzerland, much to Suvorov's frustration. Suvorov wrote to Czar Paul threatening his resignation:

> The timidity of the Vienna cabinet, the jealousy of me as a foreigner, the intrigues of individual two-faced commanders responsible only to the *Hofkriegsrat* and the requirement to negotiate everything at a distance of 700 miles, makes my position impossible.

Though the Czar did protest on his general's behalf, nothing much changed until on 18 July Mantua, which had held down thousands of Austrian troops in the siege, finally fell, so General Paul Kray with nearly 20,000 men was released to operate with Suvorov. On 15 Augus 1799 Suvorov again attacked the French, this time at Novi Ligure just north of Genoa. On the eve of the battle, in his usual fearless fashion, he rode out to inspect enemy positions and was nearly captured by French *voltigeurs* operating in front of their lines.

On the morning of the battle, as the Austrians under Kray advanced the thirty-year-old French commander, Barthelemy Joubert, was shot and killed in the first hour of the day by Russian infantry as he rode forward to encourage his *tirailleurs*. He was replaced by General Moreau. The long day's brutal and unrelenting fighting caused the French casualties in the region of 11,500 killed or captured, with another 9,000 fleeing or wounded, while the Allies sustained 6,000 killed or wounded.

Moreau who had been defeated twice by the resolute, almost fanatical, energy of the old Russian said, 'What can you say of a general so resolute to a superhuman degree, and who would perish himself and let his army perish to the last man rather than retreat a single pace.'

Suvorov had been welcomed in Milan in the spring like a conquering hero and the revolutionary French seemed to have been stopped in their tracks by the end of the summer. French troops were effectively driven out of Italy after his triumph at Novi Ligure in August, save for a handful in the Maritime Alps and around Genoa. Suvorov was awarded the title of Prince of the House of Savoy by the King of Sardinia.

After these spectacular victories, which mirrored those of the young Bonaparte two years before, there was some thought that Suvorov could march straight into France and to Paris, but this was not Suvorov's idea. Though the French had been roundly defeated, the old general was fully aware of their threat. The French levee en masse was instigated by Carnot in 1793 exactly six years before, and by the following year France could boast 1.5 million men under arms. No wonder Suvorov complained, 'At Cassano we beat 20,000, on the Trebbia 30,000, at Novi, 40,000. Now, we'll doubtless by confronted by 50,000.'

Unbeknownst to Suvorov, the armchair warriors William Pitt in London and Johann Thugut in Vienna decided that Lombardy should stay under the control of Austria while Suvorov should move north into Switzerland with his Russian army. Archduke Charles should move towards Alsace on the French border with General Rimsky-Korsakov replacing his army. Suvorov was to drive General Massena out of Switzerland with his army of 20,000 men plus the Austrian army of 22,000 under General Friedrich von Hotze and Rimsky-Korsakov's division of 30,000. It was a tall order against Massena's 84,000. It was never Suvorov's idea to cross the Alps.

The passes from the Lombard plains of Italy over the Alps are few and far between. The best known are, of course, the Grand St Bernard where Napoleon crossed and the St Gotthard, which Suvorov chose as the most direct way into central Switzerland. To the extreme west are a few passes such as the Col de la Traversette where Hannibal had crossed, and to the east is the Brenner leading up into Austria. The St Gotthard was a difficult, narrow and dangerous road with precipitous gorges dropping away from the main track. There was even a tunnel in one place and a rickety bridge crossing near the so-called Devil's Gorge. The fact that Suvorov had been asked to cross into Switzerland at the wrong time of the year when the weather was already deteriorating seemed of no interest to the Austrian *Hofkriegsrat*, or war cabinet, in Vienna.

Furthermore, it turned out to be pointless since, unbeknownst to the old general, now with grey and thinning hair, the Russian army under General Rimsky-Korsakov, more of a courtier than a general, was to be defeated by Masséna at Zürich on 25 September as Suvorov was still fighting his way across the Alps. The reliable von Hotze had been killed in a skirmish.

Suvorov arrived in Taverne at the foot of the Pass on 4 September and by the 12th had arrived at Airolo, where the French under General Lecourbe were waiting. Though no mules, promised by the Austrians, were there, Suvorov did meet Antonio Gamba who was to guide him across the mountains. It was only after some days that mules were arranged and in the meantime the Cossack ponies were used for transport of supplies. Captain Gryazen who kept a diary during the whole expedition recorded: 'Climbing still further, we suddenly realised that the enemy advance guard had taken up positions on inaccessible heights.' They were now 5,000 feet up and began to climb the last 2,000 feet to the Pass. Now the French snipers rained fire down on them and many fell. When Suvorov himself came up they pleaded with him to let them return into Italy. The old man ordered them to dig a hole in the ground where they stood. When they had done this he stood next to it and declared, 'Bury me in the ground here! Leave your commander here. You're not my children, I'm not your father anymore. Nothing is left for me but to die.' At once the mood of despair left thee soldiers and they launched themselves into the attack, and though losing more than a thousand comrades, drove the French back.

At the Hospenthal they bivouacked for the night before advancing the next day to Andermatt. But worse was to follow as they fought their way along the precipitous sides of the Reuss River. They forced their way, with huge losses, through the Urnerloch tunnel before taking the ramshackle Devil's Bridge across a raging torrent, again with heavy losses. Somehow, they fought their way through in one of the most remarkable advances in military history against a capable and determined enemy.

When Suvorov and his army finally arrived in Altdorf on the shores of Lake Lucerne, they received the news that Massena had defeated Rimsky-Korsakov at the Battle of Zurich. They were faced by Massena's formidable army occupying Switzerland and numbering 80,000 while Suvorov only commanded about 22,000 men. The Russian-Austrian army was trapped in hostile country with few routes of withdrawal. This is a position Suvorov would never have chosen himself.

Gathering his commanders, it was decided they should fight their way over the Pragel Pass to Glarus, then descend over the very high snow-bound Panixer Pass across the Bundner Oberland to Chur on the Rhine, and thence into Austrian Vorarlberg. Of the men who had journeyed from Taverne in Italy to Chur in Switzerland, three-quarters of them survived. They even brought with them 1,400 French prisoners. It was altogether a great achievement. They had conquered the elements, had fought their way through the most difficult terrain, achieved the objective of escaping the enemy, and had even taken many prisoners. The fact they arrived too late to support Rimsky-Korsakov at Zurich was no fault of theirs, since the five days' delay at Taverne was caused by the Austrian failure to give them supplies. Many years later, Marshal Massena was to say that he would have exchanged all his victories for Suvorov's crossing of the Alps. High praise indeed.

As Suvorov battled his way through the snow-covered Alps his army was checked but never defeated. Suvorov refused to call it a retreat, rather a tactical withdrawal, as he trekked through the treacherous Panixer Pass, where hundreds of his men either fell from the vertical sides of the Pass or died of cold. Here Gryazev described him: 'He was sitting on a Cossack pony. I could hear him trying to break away from the grasp of two sturdy Cossacks walking on either side of him, holding him in the saddle and leading his pony.'

Miraculously, he arrived in Chur at the head of 16,000 men which, considering the task they had endured, was a marvel, earning him the nickname of the Russian Hannibal. He would have been amused by this, remembering his original mentor.

Hannibal and Napoleon had not faced opposition as they crossed the Alps, so Suvorov's achievement, though flawed as a strategy, was remarkable. It was his last and most brutal campaign. He had been asked to achieve the impossible by taking his army across the highest mountains in Europe while fighting off an implacable enemy. On his return he was officially promised a military triumph, but soon the Emperor cancelled the ceremony and recalled all Russian armies from Europe.

Early in 1800, Suvorov returned to Saint Petersburg for the last time. Czar Paul I refused to give him an audience. Worn out and ill, the old veteran died a few weeks later on 18 May 1800.

Lord Whitworth, the British ambassador, and the Russian poet Gavrila Derzhavin were the only persons of distinction present at the funeral service in the Church of the Annunciation in the Alexander Nevsky Monastery. He lies buried there under the simple inscription: 'Here lies Suvorov'.

His titles merited a grander funeral than he was given: Aleksandr Vasiliyevich Suvorov, Prince of Italy, Count of Rymnik, Count of the Holy Roman Empire, Prince of Sardinia, Generalissimo of Russia's Ground and Naval forces, Field Marshal of the Austrian and Sardinian armies. Seriously wounded six times in battle, he was the recipient of the Order of St. Andrew, the Apostle First Called, Order of St. George the Bringer of Victory First Class, Order of St Vladimir First Class, Order of St Alexander Nevsky, Order of St Anna First Class, Grand Cross of the Order of St John of Jerusalem, the Austrian Order of Maria Theresa First Class, the Order of the Black Eagle, the Order of the Red Eagle, the Prussian Pour le Mérite, the Sardinian Order of the Revered Saints Maurice and Lazarus, and the Order of St Gubert, the Golden Lioness from the United Provinces, the United Orders of the Carmelite Virgin Mary and St Lazarus and the Polish Order of the White Eagle and the Order of Saint Stanislaus. (Perhaps that's why the inscription was so short.)

Within a year of Suvorov's death, Czar Paul I was murdered in his bedroom for his disastrous leadership by a band of army officers. His son and successor, Czar Alexander I, erected a statue of the great Russian general on the Field of Mars.

Suvorov's son Arkadi also became an officer in the Russian Imperial army, fighting in the Turkish and Napoleonic wars before drowning trying to save another man at the tender age of 27 in that same Rymnik River where his father had won such glory.

Russians have long cherished the memory of Suvorov as a great general. While on a campaign, he lived as a private soldier, sleeping on straw and contenting himself with the humblest fare. Suvorov considered victory as dependent on the morale, training, and initiative of the front-line soldier. In battle, he emphasized speed and mobility, accuracy of gunfire and the use of the bayonet, as well as detailed planning and careful strategy. He abandoned traditional drills and communicated with his troops in clear and understandable ways. Suvorov took great care of his army's supplies and living conditions, reducing cases of illness among his soldiers dramatically, and earning their loyalty and affection.

As a tactician his guiding principle was to detect the weakest point of an enemy and attack in that area. He believed in small units arriving on a battlefield to ensure speed and advantage. He preferred targeted fire instead of repeated volleys of line infantry and used light infantry as skirmishers and sharpshooters, as did the British and French armies of the time. He was in favour of varying his tactics depending on the opponent. He used squares against the Turks, lines against the Poles, and columns against the French.

He wrote often dramatic reports and orders of the day in staccato sentences and someone once said, 'His writings are as different from the common run of classical prose as his tactics were from those of Frederick the Great or Marlborough.'

Suvorov is also remembered for his military writings, the most well-known being *The Science of Victory*. His many sayings are memorable, 'What is difficult in training will become easy in a battle... The bullet is a mad thing, only the bayonet knows what it is about... Perish yourself but rescue your comrade!'

In Tolstoy's *War and Peace*, old Prince Volkonski observes: 'Suvorov couldn't manage them, so what chance has Michael Kutuzov?'

10

FIELD MARSHAL VISCOUNT GOUGH 1779–1869

> He has himself afforded the brightest example of the highest qualities of the British soldier in the attainment of the glorious successes which have attended the British Army under his command.
>
> Duke of Wellington

The cool of the Church of St James in Sialkot, in Punjab Province, Pakistan, is a sanctuary of peace and quiet from the busy streets outside. On one of the faded white stucco walls you will find a plaque:

> To the memory of Brigadier John Pennycuick, C.B. K.H., Lieutenant Colonel in HM 24th regiment who entered the army as Ensign in the 78th regiment, fought in fifteen general engagements and, after a service of forty-three years, fell at the head of his Brigade in the Battle of Chillianwalla, 13th January 1849 and of Alexander, his son, Ensign in 24th regiment, who fell in the same engagement while defending the body of his father, aged 17 years.
>
> Sarah Pennycuick, widow has erected this tablet.

It would be a hard heart that would not be moved on reading this.

The commander of the British Indian army that day at Chillianwalla was the Anglo-Irishman General Sir Hugh Gough. It was to be his last battle. After all, he was seventy years old and photographs of him at the time reveal a rather splendid looking white-whiskered gentleman, every bit the Victorian hero.

The Anglo-Irish are a special caste, a breed apart who over the centuries have excelled in many fields, both military and artistic. Whether they arrived with the Normans or later with Oliver Cromwell or William of Orange, they are sometimes compared to the Junker families of East Prussia, though not as sinister. They were high achievers too, Jonathan Swift, Oscar Wilde, W. B. Yeats, the Iron Duke himself, Field Marshal Montgomery, Field Marshal Alexander being amongst their number. But the most quintessential of them all must surely be the remarkable Hugh Gough.

Born the son of Lieutenant Colonel George Gough and Letitia Bunbury of Lisnavagh, County Limerick, he was to become famous ultimately as an early Victorian general. And before that he served as a young Regency army officer during the campaigns against revolutionary France in South Africa, the West Indies and South America before fighting in the Peninsula War against Napoleonic France under the Duke of Wellington. After a hiatus of a number of years, he was recalled to command the army off the China coast and finally in India, where he conquered the Punjab.

Not only was he a brave man himself, he also was the forerunner of three members of the Gough family who successively won the highest award for bravery in battle, the Victoria Cross. Bravery under fire seemed to be ingrained in their DNA.

Hugh Gough was commissioned into the Limerick Militia on 7 August 1793 when militias were being raised all over the United Kingdom against the threat of Revolutionary France. A year later, he transferred to a local regiment and became a lieutenant on 11 October 1794 in the 119th Regiment of Foot at the tender age of fifteen, then transferred once again to the 78th (Highlanders) Regiment of Foot in 1795. In April that year he sailed to South Africa in a fleet of seven warships commanded by Rear Admiral

Sir George Elphinstone, later Lord Keith, and Commodore John Blankett, carrying 515 officers and men of the 78th Foot under the command of Major General Sir James Craig, a veteran of the American War of Independence who had been badly wounded at Bunker Hill. The Cape Colony was controlled by the Dutch United East India Company, which since the revolutionary French takeover of Holland, and with the name changed to the Batavian Republic, had become an enemy of the United Kingdom.

Cape Town was a vital stopping off point for any trading ships going to and from British India, so it would have been disastrous to allow it to fall into enemy hands. The Cape Colony was administered from two towns, the larger Cape Town on the wide Table Bay facing west and the smaller Simon's Town on False Bay facing south. Neither bay was sheltered from Atlantic storms, which were particularly bad at that time of year, mid-winter, and both were notoriously dangerous, with winds, currents and rocks posing considerable threats to shipping.

Elphinstone's fleet arrived off Cape Town in June, and after negotiations broke down with the Dutch governor, on 7 August an amphibious landing was made on the beach at Muizenberg by the 78th and an equal number of sailors from the fleet. The settlement was quickly taken with the help of naval fire from some of the fleet, but it was clear that it would be difficult to dislodge a determined enemy from the heights above the shore. After the arrival of reinforcements and numerous skirmishes the Colony finally surrendered on 15 September.

The youthful Gough now transferred to the 87th (Royal Irish Fusiliers) Regiment of Foot in December, before being deployed with his new regiment to the West Indies in the forces under the command of General Ralph Abercromby, taking part in the capture of Trinidad in February and the failed invasion of Spanish Puerto Rico in April, when after two weeks of fierce fighting the British withdrew. Gough also took part in the military acquisition of further Dutch Colonies off the coast of South America, Demerara, Esseqibo and Berbice.

Returning to England Gough was promoted to captain in the 2nd Battalion of the 87th regiment on 25 June 1803 and major soon after. After all these perilous sea journeys, fighting against determined enemies and the constant threat of disease, he was still only twenty-three years old. Colonel Charles Doyle, the commanding officer of the battalion, was now promoted to Lieutenant General and posted to Spain.

In England Gough met and soon married Frances Maria Stephens. She was the daughter of a general, so fitted in with his military life, and was to accompany him to India when the time came. Theirs was a long and happy marriage with six children.

The youthful Major Gough now commanded the battalion when they embarked for the Peninsula from Ramsgate on 28 December 1808. The initial orders were to join up with the army of Lieutenant General Sir John Moore in north-west Spain but, after stormy weather made them put in at Cork, they were diverted to Lisbon to join the army of Lieutenant General Sir Arthur Wellesley, arriving on 12 March 1809.

Having taken part in operations to drive the French out of Portugal, the regiment marched some 300 miles into central Spain to take part in the Battle of Talavera on 27/28 July. Gough and his men were in the 2nd Brigade under Colonel Donkin, alongside the 60th and the 88th in the 3rd Division commanded by Lieutenant General Randoll Mackenzie. His battalion took frightful casualties during a surprise French attack on the evening of the 27th when the enemy appeared through the smoke of burning farm buildings. All through the night into the next morning they fought, and finally drove the French infantry back. The 87th lost 354 officers and men as casualties, with 111 killed, and Gough was severely wounded when hit in the right side by a cannon ball. Some of the wounded were to die in the fires that spread across the dry ground.

Despite his injuries Gough continued to command his battalion bravely, confirmed in a letter written by Colonel Donkin later: 'Let me repeat the assurances of the high sense I entertain of your personal exertions and gallantry at Talavera until the moment when I was deprived of your assistance by your being wounded and taken off the field.'

In the days after the battle, Wellesley, followed by the Spanish, withdrew from the area, leaving many of the wounded, including Gough, behind. Though technically missing in action, the young battalion commander, along with an officer of the 88th, Captain James Oates who had been badly wounded in the head, managed to walk or crawl away from the battlefield and hide in a nearby farmhouse. Oates later reported that they survived like this, fearful of capture, for nearly two weeks before joining up with their regiments at Almaraz. Whether Talavera was a victory is open to question, but Joseph Bonaparte had withdrawn and Wellesley, despite some criticism for his losses, was raised to the peerage as Viscount Wellington.

Gough and the 87th wintered in Lisbon and in February 1810 they sailed round from Lisbon to Cadiz to reinforce the besieged city. A year later they sailed further along the coast to Gibraltar before disembarking and joining the Spanish and British army under Lieutenant General Graham, later Lord Lynedoch, and taking part in the Battle of Barrosa on 5 March 1811, during the attempt to break the siege of Cadiz, an important British supply port and the seat of the Spanish government.

It was at Barrosa that the 87th, under the command of the now fully recovered Major Gough, gained yet another battle honour. Emerging from a wood they took withering fire from the French infantry before returning fire and charging with bayonets fixed. With their Irish battle cry of *Faugh a Ballagh*, meaning 'Clear the Way', Gough and his men prevailed. Ensign Edward Keogh and Sergeant Patrick Masterson captured the Imperial Eagle of the French 8eme Regiment. Keogh had only managed to get a hand on the staff when he was killed, so Masterson took over and wrenched the Eagle from the dying hands of its bearer. In 'the most terrible bayonet fight I have ever seen' this Irish regiment led by Gough defeated the formidable French infantry of the line who up to then had been the terror of Europe. General Graham, at the head of the Coldstream Guards, witnessed Gough and his men in action and personally congratulated him on the bravery of his battalion.

Hugh Gough was now promoted to Lieutenant Colonel and was awarded the Barrosa Medal. At the end of that same year the battalion heroically defended the walls of Tarifa.After leaving Seville in September 1812, they fought their way through Spain, enduring a terrible winter, to join the now Marquis of Wellington near Salamanca. They advanced the following summer to Vitoria where on 21 June 1813, as part of the 3rd Division they took part in arguably Wellington's greatest victory in Spain. Again, the 87th and their commander covered themselves in glory. Bugler Paddy Shannon of the 2nd Battalion captured Marshal Jourdan's baton, later presented to the Prince Regent, who promoted Wellington to Field Marshal.

As the British pursued the French out of Spain, Gough was severely wounded on the Nivelle on 10 November 1813 and was once more separated from his beloved regiment. His wound was in the hip and he took many months to recover. The journey back across France was painful. He finally joined up with them in England at the end of 1814, walking with the aid of a stick. In the meantime, his battalion had won further hard-earned battle honours at Orthez and Toulouse.

Gough was promoted to the substantive rank of Lieutenant Colonel on 25th May 1815, appointed a Companion of the Order of the Bath on 4 June 1815 and created a Knight Bachelor on 16 March 1816. He was now a battle-scarred and much decorated veteran of the Peninsula War with considerable combat experience for such a young officer. He had fought under Wellington, General 'Papa' Hill and General Graham, and he was still only thirty-five years old.

Most eminent soldiers accelerate at this stage of their career, but this was certainly not the case for the young officer. There was now to follow a twenty-year 'sabbatical' for Hugh Gough.

It seems as though he was almost forgotten. He must have thought this himself, during this time but he much enjoyed the company of his growing family and seemed to accept his lot. After all, by normal standards, he had experienced a distinguished career ending with due honours and a knighthood. Hugh Gough was, when all is said and done, a typical loyal and efficient British army officer, not politically motivated, modest about his own exploits, caring for his men, preparing them for the trials ahead and leading them by example. Not for him the vanity of leading armies in great victories. Not for him great victories. That was for other men. But fate had more, much more, in store for him.

On 25 January 1817, when his battalion had returned from the Peninsula War and been stationed in Ireland and England for some months, there was a reduction in the army and Lieutenant Colonel Sir Hugh Gough wrote the following order to his regiment, dated 24 January:

> It is with the most painful feeling of regret Lieutenant Colonel Sir Hugh Gough is necessitated to announce to the 2nd battalion, Prince's Own Irish, that their services as a corps are no longer required in consequence of the military arrangements it has been found necessary to adopt. In making this distressing though necessary communication, and in taking leave of those brave officers and men, at whose head it has been Sir Hugh Gough's good fortune.

He had sailed with these men across stormy seas, had landed on foreign shores with them, he had marched with them across the baking heat of summer in Spain, he had shared the fear of battle with them, had watched them die, had been severely wounded with them, had defended ancient walls and fought on steep mountain sides and crossed fast-flowing rivers with them. He loved those men and he had earned their respect and affection as he had suffered and triumphed with them. He had been a fine regimental officer.

For the next eighteen years Colonel Sir Hugh Gough was resident in Ireland where he was much respected as a Regency senior officer who, amongst a number of foreign engagements, had fought at Talavera. It seemed as though these years would be the prelude to his retirement in the land he loved.

Promoted to full Colonel on 12 August 1819, Gough now became the commanding officer of the 22nd Regiment of Foot in

County Tipperary, where he also served as a local magistrate. Here he set a fine example of keeping law and order in a fair and effective fashion. When he was nearing the end of his tenure he was sent this message from the local magistrates: 'We gratefully acknowledge that chiefly through your Prudence, Zeal, Activity and Example have we been enabled hitherto to avert those evils which were impending over us.'

In August 1826, his command of the regiment came to an end when certain companies were posted to the West Indies and for the next eleven years he lived a semi-retired life, his army career now seemingly over. He was promoted to Major General on 22 July 1830 and became a Knight Commander of the Order of the Bath on 18 September, 1831, automatic honours. Now a different chapter in his remarkable life was to begin.

In 1837, more than twenty years after his exploits in the Peninsula War and having lived pretty much the life of a privileged country gentleman, Sir Hugh was appointed the General Officer Commanding the Mysore division of the Madras Army in 1837. As all good officers do, he obeyed orders.

In October, three months after the coronation of Queen Victoria, he landed at Madras with his beloved family and proceeded inland to Mysore, where he spent the next three years enjoying his exotic posting and getting accustomed again to military matters.

On 30 November 1840, Sir Hugh was approached by Lord Auckland, Governor General of India, to take command of British forces in China, which came under the authority of India. His appointment as Commander in Chief was to involve complicated military and naval combined operations as well as political dealings of which he had no experience. He was sixty-two years old now and had last witnessed shots fired in anger twenty-eight years before, in the Pyrenees. He arrived on HMS *Cruizer* off the South China coast on the newly occupied island of Hong Kong at the mouth of the Pearl River on 2 March 1841, bringing with him reinforcements of just 700 men.

This was the so-called Opium War, that terrible episode in British history where the East India Company forced trade into

China, insisting that the key trading port of Canton remained open and that opium, grown in India, was exported into China. Other trading posts along the Chinese coast up to Shanghai and beyond were also up for grabs. Sir Hugh was a soldier through and through; it was not for him to question political decisions or the intentions of renegade traders on that lawless coast.

On arrival, Sir Hugh was immediately involved in the attack on the Whampoa dockyards near Canton. The British Superintendent Charles Elliot, with whom Gough had to cooperate, along with the Chinese Governor General of Canton, swiftly declared a three-day truce on 3 March. Elliot was a former naval officer and was now working for the Foreign Office. It is clear that Sir Hugh had some difficulty dealing with him, though he was experienced in the Far East, he lacked the authority to establish a clear and effective policy during this complicated time. During the next three days the British units that had evacuated Chusan, as per the Convention of Chuenpi, arrived on the Pearl River. The Chinese military was likewise being reinforced and by 16 March General Yang Fang commanded 30,000 men in the area surrounding Canton. Three British warships succeeded in closing in on Canton along a shallow tributary of the Pearl River.

Though reluctant to renew hostilities when the truce ran out on 6 March, Elliot authorised an attack on Canton on the 18th. This was successful and Canton retaken for the merchants, quickly followed by another truce on 20 March. Then Elliot ordered the withdrawal of the British navy warships. As a result, the next night, all along the Pearl River, British positions were attacked. Sir Hugh now took action and ordered his forces to attack Canton again, and the remaining four defensive forts around the city were captured, from where they began to bombard the city with artillery. The Chinese army fled and were pursued into the surrounding countryside. Gough had won a hard-earned victory.

On 30 May, yet another truce was agreed, with the British in full control of Canton and its surroundings but agreeing to evacuate their positions further down the river. This was agreed much to Sir Hugh's displeasure. As a military man he considered that his combined forces had the upper hand and should dictate terms. Elliot on the other hand, a diplomat, considered that in the long term the best way to sort out the Anglo-Chinese trade was by negotiation.

From the beginning he had been morally troubled by the intentions of this war and had written to Lord Palmerston the British Foreign Secretary two years before:

> No man entertains a deeper detestation of the disgrace and sin of this forced traffic on the coast of China. I have steadily discountenanced it by all the lawful means in my power, and at the total sacrifice of my private comfort in the society in which I have lived for some years past.

Now Yishan, the chief Chinese representative in Canton, misinformed the Emperor Dao Guang, hundreds of miles away in Peking, that the British had been defeated. The defence of Canton was declared a diplomatic success by Yishan. In a letter to the Emperor, he wrote that the barbarians had begged

> ...the chief general that he would implore the great Emperor in their behalf, that he would have mercy upon them, and cause their debts to be repaid them, and graciously permit them to carry on their commerce, when they would immediately withdraw their ships from the Bocca Tigris, and never dare again to raise any disturbance.

The now confident Imperial Court then demanded that Hong Kong be retaken.

Following their reluctant and unnecessary withdrawal from Canton, the British regrouped the expeditionary force on the island of Hong Kong and Sir Hugh was promoted to Lieutenant General in India and China on 18 June 1841.

Within a month, the unfortunate and well-meaning Elliot was replaced as Superintendent by Henry Pottinger, who ceased negotiating with the Chinese about Canton and gave permission for the combined military force commanded by Admiral Sir William Parker and General Sir Hugh Gough to expand their operations along the Chinese coast to Amoy and northwards. The belief was that the closer the actions approached the Chinese seat of government, the more they would realise the seriousness of the situation and the more they would be prepared to negotiate.

On 21 August the fleet sailed for Amoy, opposite the island of Formosa. Four days later they entered the Jiulong River estuary and the next day Gough ordered a combined naval and infantry attack on the city defences.With covering barrages from the Royal Navy, the Chinese batteries were overwhelmed. The city of Amoy was abandoned on 27 August, and British soldiers entered the inner town where they blew up the citadel's powder magazine. Twenty-six Chinese junks and more than a hundred guns were captured, which were thrown into the river.

Lord Palmerston had demanded that Amoy become another international trading port and Gough ordered that no looting on pain of death. The army now garrisoned a nearby island, blockading the Jiulong River. Many Chinese merchants had rejected British protection for fear of reprisals and with the city deserted chaos ensued, but the Chinese army re-entered and took control, the Governor advising the Emperor that he had won a victory over the British which, again, was far from the truth.

On 30 August, Palmerston was replaced as Foreign Secretary by Lord Melbourne who, though a supporter of the war, did not follow such an aggressive China policy. Charles Elliot might well have fared better under him.

In September 1841, the British transport ship *Nerbudda* bringing much needed supplies for Gough's force was shipwrecked on a reef off the northern coast of Formosa. Six months later, another British ship, the *Ann*, also sank in Formosan waters. The survivors of both ships were captured and marched as prisoners to southern Formosa. 87 died from ill treatment and on 10 August, 197 were executed. This shocking killing of innocent merchant sailors became notorious as the '*Nerbudda* Incident' and changed the tenor of the war.

Meanwhile, though Chusan, captured by the British previously, had been exchanged for Hong Kong in January 1841 and had been re-occupied by the Chinese army, on 1 October the British, fearing the Chinese would make the island into a fortress commanding the south of the great Qiantang River estuary, made a dramatic seaborne landing and retook Dinhai, re-establishing control over the Chusan islands. Casualties of only two killed and less than thirty wounded and more than a thousand Chinese casualties made it a stunning victory.

It was an aggressive and shrewd military manoeuvre much credit for which must go to Gough. Maybe the landings by the 55th Regiment of Foot reminded him of the landing he had taken part in off Cape Town so many years before.

He became a Knight Grand Cross of the Order of the Bath on 14 October 1841 and was promoted to Lieutenant General on 23 November. After the capture of the Chusan Islands, the city of Ningbo, fifty miles inland, was evacuated by the Chinese and after a few days British units marched into the deserted city where a cannon factory was discovered. Control of this imperial armoury would greatly reduce the Chinese ability to replace lost armaments.

The British commanders, Admiral Parker, General Gough and Superintendent Pottinger discussed the matter. It was decided that ten percent of everything captured would be seized as booty of war in retaliation for the *Nerbudda* Incident. The ever honourable Gough was against this, saying it would ignite public opinion in China against the invaders and would oblige his troops to 'punish one set of robbers for the benefit of another'. As always, he considered the career of the soldier was a patriotic and honourable duty, not for the financial benefit of others. The British and European traders were of a different opinion.

Now the war was to expand. No longer was it to be just British raids along the coast. In the spring of 1842, the Emperor Dao Guang, at last aware of the untruths he had been told about what was going on in southern China, ordered his cousin Yi Jing to retake the strategically important city of Ningbo.

In the Battle of Ningbo on 10 March the British garrison repelled the assault when they lured the Chinese army into the city streets before opening fire, resulting in heavy Chinese casualties. As they retreated the British infantry pursued them, capturing the nearby town of Cixi five days later. Gough was now commanding British infantry in battle order on the Chinese mainland.

The important harbour of Zhapu on the northern side of Hangzhou Bay was captured on 18 May after the British fleet had bombarded the town. It was here that 300 Chinese soldiers of the Eight Banners held back the advance of British troops for several hours, an act of bravery that was applauded by Gough.

With many Chinese ports now blockaded or under British occupation, Gough planned to strike deep into the heartlands of China by sailing up the giant Yangtze River. A force of ten thousand men was assembled at Ningbo and Zhapu on either side of the Yangtze estuary, and twenty five warships sailed up river in late May. By chance, they captured the Emperor's tax barges on the river, further crippling the Chinese war effort. During June, towns near Shanghai were captured including Wusong and Baoshan and Shanghai itself was looted both by British and Chinese soldiery.

Up river, the city of Nanjing, the former capital of China during the Ming dynasty, was now vulnerable, and the Chinese government raised an army of more than fifty thousand Manchu warriors. The Chinese commander in Liangjiang Province released sixteen British prisoners in the hope that a ceasefire could be agreed, but poor communications led both the Chinese and the British to reject any overtures toward peace. In secret, Emperor Dao Guang considered signing a peace treaty with the British that would make the Yangtze River out of bounds to the British.

On 14 July 1842, the British fleet on the Yangtze began to sail further up river, arriving a week later opposite the key city of Zhenjiang, where the defending forts were destroyed by British naval fire. The Chinese defenders at first retreated into the surrounding hills, causing a premature British landing, and the real battle started when large numbers of Chinese soldiers emerged from the city, beginning the Battle of Zhenjiang. British engineers blew open the western gate, enabling the infantry to storm into the city, where fierce street fighting ensued. Zhenjiang was devastated by the battle, with many Chinese soldiers and their families committing suicide rather than be taken prisoner. The British, with their superior weapons, tactics and discipline, lost thirty-six men killed. After Zhenjiang was taken, the British fleet cut the vital Grand Canal, paralysing the Caoyun system and severely disrupting the Chinese distribution of grain throughout their Empire.

On 9 August the British fleet arrived at Nanjing and two days later, as they prepared to attack, Chinese officials inside the city finally agreed to a British request to negotiate. On 14 August a Chinese delegation led by the Manchu high court official Ki Ying arrived on board HMS *Cornwallis*, a 74-gun ship of the line built in Regency days. Negotiations, in which Gough did not take part, lasted for several weeks, as the British delegation insisted the treaty be accepted by the Emperor Dao Guang himself. Back in Peking his officials advised him to accept the treaty and he authorised them accordingly.

The Treaty of Nanjing was signed on 21 August 1842 and was formally called *The Treaty of Peace, Friendship and Commerce between Her Majesty the Queen of Great Britain and Ireland and the Emperor of China*. The Imperial government was to pay England twenty one million dollars, to cede Hong Kong, to recognise her representatives as equals, and to throw open the foreign trade markets of Canton, Amoy, Foochow, Ningbo and Shanghai. The First Opium War officially ended on 29 August 1842. The conflict had lasted two years.

Where clearly Britain was morally in the wrong, the amphibious operations, carried out in relatively unknown waters by General Gough and Admiral Parker, were brilliantly executed. The ageing Duke of Wellington was the first to remark on this achievement, and though the Chinese government was remiss in underestimating the British, ill-informed by their representatives as to what was going on along their southern coasts, and slow to improve their decades-old military training and weaponry, it was a singular success, much of it due to Gough's military acumen and ability to cooperate with the Royal Navy, whose captains and navigators were the forgotten architects of the campaign. In a speech to the House of Lords the Duke of Wellington remarked:

> There is no individual, however sanguine, who could have expected such success as has been produced by the cordial cooperation of the admiral commanding the fleet and the general commanding the army and, following their example, of the officers and men of both services.

Sir Hugh left Nanking at the end of September and after visiting Chusan and Kulansu arrived in Hong Kong in November, where his promotion to a baronetcy was confirmed. On 20 December 1842 he sailed from Hong Kong to Singapore in a small and uncomfortable schooner since he had generously left his own steamer, the *Proserpine*, to police the Pearl River and protect the avaricious merchants of Hong Kong who were the main beneficiaries of all his efforts.

From Singapore Sir Hugh proceeded to Calcutta, where he was reunited with his wife, promoted to the rank of full general on 3rd March 1843 and in May became Commander-in-Chief, India. The next seven years of his life were to be the most significant and the most testing, most particularly since he was in his sixties when they began.

He was up against formidable enemies in the legendary Mahrattas and the equally proud and ferocious Sikhs, and he had to deal with the labyrinthine machinations of the avaricious East India Company, who made the Hong Kong Taipans look like novices when it came to the intoxicating mix of military conquest and fabulously profitable trade. And then there were the duplicitous governments back in England.

When Sir Hugh first arrived in India, the First Afghan War had just ended in disaster and the credibility of the Company, as it was known, in the Punjab and western India was looking shaky. The authority of the British East India Company had to be reaffirmed. Trouble was brewing in Gwalior, the Mahratta state, in the west of the Punjab, where the Maharajah had died in February 1843.

Lord Ellenborough, the newly appointed Governor General in India in succession to Lord Auckland, ordered Gough to come up to Cawnpore while he was in Agra assembling an army to observe developments in Gwalior. In October Gough had developed a plan where he divided his army of twenty thousand men into two, the right wing commanded by himself and the left by General Sir John Grey. The forces of Gwalior were estimated at about twenty two thousand with three hundred guns. Its extraordinary fortress towered above the city like a watchful eagle.

It was Christmas Day and Ellenborough was so confident of peace breaking out that he was dining with Lady Gough, her daughter, and Dolores, Mrs Harry Smith, the Spanish wife of the Adjutant-General of India General Sir Harry Smith. Therein lies a tale. Also in their company was Lady Grant, whose husband later recalled what had happened to them during the battle

> The ladies present had a still more exciting experience. Their presence, mounted as they were on elephants, and so towering above the low roofs of the village, early attracted the notice of the enemy, and they came almost at once under fire. Towards the close of the day, their elephants, frightened by the explosion of a powder magazine, ran away with them, and their ignorance of the fortunes of the battle added to the anxiety of their position. Major Grant was the first to reassure them with tidings of victory and he conducted them back to Sir Hugh's camp. The excitement of the day was not yet over for no sooner had they gained a much needed rest in a tent on the ground held by the enemy at the beginning of the day than (just as tea was being prepared) they were suddenly seized by British soldiers and carried out. Immediately afterwards a mine exploded, and the tent was blown to pieces. Lord Ellenborough later presented each of

the ladies with a commemorative medal, similar in design to that prepared for the troops.

Frances Gough was to wear her combat medal with pride for the rest of her life.

On 29 December 1843 Sir Hugh, in true Nelsonian style, planned to attack the enemy immediately. This urgency may also have been brought about by the fact that trouble was brewing not far away in the Sikh Empire at their capital in Lahore, and the East India Company was wary of the possibility of an alliance.

Gough now commanded an army which included the 16th Lancers and two British battalions of the 39th and 40th of Foot plus four Indian cavalry regiments and six infantry battalions, a total of 1,350 cavalry, 4,800 infantry plus 350 gunners and horse artillery, the developing weapon of choice in British India. The guns could be fired, then moved at high speed to fire from another position, which was extraordinarily effective against lines of infantry.

But the Mahratta artillery was equally effective, with larger guns and disciplined troops. During the British offensive over open ground, the regiments suffered, in particular the 39th taking 214 casualties and the 40th 162. The total, including the Indian sepoy regiments, was about 800. In another clash of arms, Gough's second column under Grey, also took a number of casualties, the 3rd Regiment of Foot 72 and the 50th, 42. But the British alongside their sepoy regiments prevailed.

Two days later, the Rani of Gwalior signed the surrender agreement whereby the Gwalior army was reduced to a maximum of 10,000 infantry, 6,000 cavalry and 32 artillery pieces plus 10,000 local troops to be commanded by British officers. Another jewel had been added to the British Crown in India.

In July 1844, Lord Ellenborough was replaced as Governor General of India by the distinguished Peninsular War veteran Sir Henry Hardinge. This was an unfortunate setback for Sir Hugh, since Hardinge was a soldier, a close contemporary of his in the army ranking just below him on the Army List, and with important connections, an acquaintance of the Duke of Wellington and Prime

Minister Sir Robert Peel. He was probably the last person the old general would have wanted looking over his shoulder every step of the way as he planned and executed a major campaign.

The new Governor General arrived in India late in the year and took up his role in Calcutta on 1 November. His priority had to be the growing unrest in the Sikh Empire that bordered the lands of India controlled by the East India Company in the north-west. One of his first decisions was to send Major George Broadfoot as British Agent to the North West Frontier, one of the most prestigious posts for an aspiring officer in the army of the East India Company, based in Lahore, to observe and report on the growing political crisis there, where the various Sikh military *Khalsa* factions were competing for control of their lands.

Nobody could have been better qualified. Broadfoot had already spent seven years in India as a young officer and was rewarded for his services by being posted to the North West Frontier, that testing ground of young British army officers. He had been placed in command of the escort for the families of the Pashtun Shah Sujah and Zaman Shah from Delhi to Kabul and managed to negotiate the perilous journey across the Punjab to Kabul before joining Sir Robert Sale's force from Kabul to Jalalabad in October 1841. He had been mentioned in dispatches for his gallantry in the desperate actions of that campaign against the Afghans between Kabul and Gandamak.

At Jalalabad, by default, he became garrison engineer and restored the defences of the town by using Gurkhas as his workforce. During the ensuing siege, Broadfoot and his friend Captain Henry Havelock prevented the surrender of the city when Sir Robert Sale was considering it. After the relief of Jalalabad he had also been part of General Pollock's attack on Afghanistan, fighting in numerous actions for which he was made a Companion of the Order of the Bath.

The Sikhs were, and are, a proud and remarkable race of people whose religion and culture grew up sandwiched between the northern Indian Muslim culture of the Moghuls and the ancient Hindu culture which prevailed in most of the rest of the enormous sub-continent. Their lands were on the borders of those controlled by the East India Company and the North West Frontier. The Sikh Empire had been ruled by Maharajah Ranjit Singh, who had died in 1839. He had been friendly and cooperative with the East India Company and had built up the *Khalsa* clans. When he died, a degree of instability ensued.

Hardinge, at the behest of Sir Hugh, agreed to strengthen the British presence on the Sikh border at Ferozepur barracks with a division of 7,000 troops being based there. There were also troops stationed at Ambala and Meerut in the border areas.

On 10 December 1845, Sikh troops crossed the Sutlej River, the official border between the Sikh Empire and lands under the control of the EIC. General Gough at the head of his army of 10,000 men began the march up from Ambala towards the Sutlej, a distance of about 140 miles through difficult country, which they completed in just seven days. They were accompanied by Governor General Hardinge, which clearly would not make Sir Hugh's life any easier. Few generals commanding an army would have welcomed another general looking over their shoulder. Gough's army was advancing towards Ferozepur on 18 December when after another hard day's march his troops stopped to rest at a place called Mudki, only 18 miles from Ferozepur.

The Sikhs, lying in wait, made a surprise attack and opened fire with artillery. At the same time, the front of the column was attacked by irregular Sikh cavalry who were driven off before the British Light Dragoons counter-charged and in turn were halted by determined Sikh infantry.

Reconnaissance units reported that the main Sikh army was just three miles away and Gough, though it was late in the day, decided to advance. Critics say that Gough could have rested for the night. But he, in his white battle coat, making him visible to his men as well as to the enemy, decided in a full-frontal infantry attack, with cold steel if necessary. His idea was to shock the enemy. Many battles in history have been won with a violent impetus, but some called it Gough's 'Tipperary Rush', referring to his Irish background and his love of Irish infantry tactics.

He ordered the advance despite the fact that some of the infantry battalions, British or Indian, were incomplete due to the difficulty of the march towards the Sutlej.

One wide line was formed and encouraged by their officers the infantry of the 9th of Foot, the 31st, the 50th and the 80th moved steadily forward as the light faded, smoke and dust making visibility more difficult. The Sikh infantry, fighting fiercely as they retreated, used rocky outcrops and clumps of forest as cover from where they could direct their fire. In the ensuing darkness a number from both sides were killed by friendly fire, some in desperate hand-to-hand fighting, the British wielding their bayonets and the Sikhs their deadly *kirpans*. It was a chaotic scene and the soldiers later called it 'Midnight Mudki' since by the end of hostilities darkness had completely fallen.

Gough, accompanied by Hardinge, only left the field at 2 o'clock in the morning. He had lost a number of senior officers, including two generals who were killed, Major General Sir John McCaskill and Major General Sir Robert Sale, 'Fighting Bob', who had fought heroically during the disastrous First Afghan War and whose wife Florentia, Lady Sale, had travelled the world from Mauritius to Burma with her husband. She wrote a fascinating first-hand account of her experiences during the Afghan campaign entitled *Journal of the Disasters in Afghanistan*.

After two days burying the dead and tending to the wounded, Gough's army now prepared to fight again. Hardly had the army recovered than they moved forward to the village of Ferozeshah, which the Sikh forces led by Rajah Lal Singh had made into a stronghold in the previous few days. Gough wanted to attack on the morning of 21 December, but Hardinge counselled him to await the arrival of General Littler with his division before moving. Gough, as always, believed in taking the offensive, but after some harsh words were spoken, Hardinge in his political capacity as Governor General of India and therefore the supreme power, overruled the Commander in Chief. The fact that Hardinge was a Lieutenant General, lower on the Army List than Lieutenant General Gough, made the moment even more galling. As a result of this disagreement, Hardinge was to write to the Prime Minister on 30 December that Gough should be removed as Commander in Chief, without his knowledge, which was a dishonourable betrayal of such an effective commander.

So, instead of going into the attack first thing in the morning, Gough had to endure the frustration, as did his troops, of waiting to start their advance against the well-prepared Sikhs until late in the afternoon. As he knew from Mudki, it was hardly an ideal time to start an engagement. In the space of three days Gough's men were again to go into a battle in the growing darkness giving them no advantage over a fierce and determined enemy on the defence.

As the different units of the army of the East India Company moved forward, they took a number of casualties from the Sikh artillery. The Bengal infantry suffered badly, as did the 62nd of Foot, who lost half their number. Major George Broadfoot, the specialist officer that Hardinge had sent as Agent to the North West Frontier, was wounded in both thighs and unhorsed. He remounted and was shot dead through the heart. He was later buried at Ferozepur next to his former commanding officer, Sir Robert Sale. Hardinge wrote:

> It is now with great pain that I have to record the irreparable loss I have sustained, and more especially the East India Company's service, in the death of Major Broadfoot of the Madras army, my political agent. He was thrown from his horse by a shot, and I failed in prevailing upon him to leave the field. He remounted, and shortly afterwards received a mortal wound. He was brave as he was able in every branch of the political and military service.

As the Sikh irregular cavalry looked to take advantage, they were driven back in a counter-charge by the 3rd Light Dragoons. Though, as at Mudki, the Sikh infantry fought bravely, they were finally pushed back in the darkness and for some reason Lal Singh did not utilise his cavalry. The fighting went on intermittently through the night, before the Sikhs finally withdrew after further attacks by the British infantry. The fighting had been so finely balanced as darkness fell that Hardinge, aware that defeat was on the cards, sent orders to his aides back at Mudki that his state papers be burned and to put Napoleon's sword, given to him by the Duke of Wellington after Waterloo, into the hands of his ADC. This hardly denoted faith in the Commander in Chief.

As Gough's exhausted men took some rest, a stroke of good fortune occurred. Another Sikh force led by Tej Singh suddenly appeared on the horizon but, mistaking the movement of cavalry and horse artillery units as a flanking manoeuvre, declined to engage. A staff officer, a Captain Lumley who apparently was suffering from sunstroke and temporary insanity, had mistakenly given the order for the units to move, which resulted in Gough's army not being attacked when they were most vulnerable at the end of the day, which would have been disastrous. Lumley was allowed to resign his commission rather than face a court-martial. It was a fortunate occurrence, actually a fluke, which probably averted disaster. Napoleon was right, luck can play a large part in a general's reputation, not just with a victory but with an encounter avoided.

During the next few weeks, after Christmas and New Year had been celebrated by the exhausted army of the East India Company, General Sir Harry Smith at the head of a division was sent by Gough to secure the return route of the army by relieving the strategic town of Ludhiana, where British barracks had been burnt down by a Sikh army of more than 10,000 troops led by Ranjodh Singh. On 21 January at Baddowal, the rear of Smith's stretched out column was attacked by marauding Sikh cavalry who captured the baggage train carried by slow-moving mules, bullocks and elephants. The British retaliated by destroying the Baddowal Fort, burning to death everyone inside.

Smith's exhausted column was now reinforced by two Gurkha battalions sent up from Delhi and seven days later he prepared to attack Ranjodh's army at Aliwal on the Sutlej River. The positioning of the Sikh forces was dangerous, they had their backs to the river and in the event of retreat they had nowhere to go.

The battle started with an artillery duel, then Smith ordered half of his infantry brigades to capture the village of Aliwal. This they achieved and then attacked the Sikh centre with enfilade fire along their lines. When the Sikh cavalry sought to attack the British left, the 16th Lancers leading a cavalry brigade drove them off and then attacked the Sikh infantry squares. In the centre the Sikh infantry took cover in a dry riverbed but were driven out by a Bengal infantry regiment and by relentless fire from the Bengal Horse Artillery.

Unlike in the previous two battles of Mudki and Ferozeshah, where the Sikhs had held the line valiantly, this time they broke and fled, abandoning their guns and baggage. They suffered about 2,000 casualties and lost more than 60 guns. It was a victory for Smith but not without loss. While Smith claimed it to be 'one of the most glorious battles ever fought in India' one should not forget that the 16th Lancers lost 144 officers and men from a total of 300 who fought.

Gough's army had now won two hard-fought victories and a complete rout of the Sikhs at Aiwal. Their morale was high but so was that of the *Khalsa* Sikhs who had strengthened their position at Sobraon with reinforcements. An experienced leader had arrived named Sham Singh Attariwal, though Tej Singh and Lal Singh remained in overall command.

Once again, the Sikh defences mistakenly had their back to the River Sutlej. The disadvantage of a defence with its back to a river is obvious. The only link with the western bank was a single pontoon bridge over the swiftly flowing river. Gough, always wanting to take the fight to the enemy, was keen to go into action as soon as Smith's triumphant division returned from Aliwal. But the heavy artillery train was delaying them and, once again, Hardinge put his political foot down and persuaded the Gough to wait for the heavy artillery to arrive. Gough must have been exasperated by these constant adjustments to his tactics though, in this case, Hardinge might have been right, since the Sikh artillery had always caused great difficulty for the army of the East India Company. The idea of attacking without delay has its merits: the enemy has less time to prepare, and the morale of the attacking units denotes a confidence that can carry the day. Delay, on the other hand, denotes uncertainty and lack of confidence.

Gough moved forward on 10 February on a morning when there was a heavy fog covering the battlefield. As soon as visibility improved, the British guns opened fire and the Sikhs responded in kind. This went on for two hours before Gough was advised that his heavy artillery was running short on ammunition. On hearing this, he reputedly commented, 'Thank God! Then I'll be at them with the bayonet.'

At Gough's command, two divisions under Sir Harry Smith and Major General Sir Walter Gilbert attacked the Sikh left, while Major General Robert Henry Dick's division attacked the weaker Sikh right, where the defences were on soft sand and were lower and weaker than the rest of the line. Nevertheless, Dick's division was driven back by Sikh counter-attacks, after initially gaining footholds within the Sikh lines, and Dick himself was killed.

As the British fell back, some frenzied Sikh soldiers attacked British wounded left in the ditch in front of the entrenchments, enraging the onlooking British soldiers. The British, Gurkhas and Bengal regiments renewed their attacks along the entire front of the entrenchment and broke through at several points. On the vulnerable Sikh right, engineers blew a breach in the fortifications and British cavalry and horse artillery pushed through to engage the Sikhs in the centre of their position.

By this time, Tej Singh had left the battlefield and his army began to retreat. It is alleged in many Sikh accounts that he deliberately weakened the pontoon bridge, casting loose the boat at its centre, or that he ordered his own artillery on the west bank to fire on the bridge on the pretext of preventing British pursuit. British accounts claim that the bridge simply broke under the weight of the numbers of soldiers trying to retreat across it, having been weakened by the swollen river. Whichever account is correct, the bridge broke, trapping nearly 20,000 of the Sikh *Khalsa* Army on the east bank. None of the trapped Sikh soldiers attempted to surrender and many detachments, including the one led by Sham

Singh, fought to the death. Some Sikhs rushed forward to attack the British sword in hand; others tried to ford or swim the river. British horse artillery lined the bank of the river and continued to fire into the crowds in the water. By the time the firing ceased, the Sikhs had lost between 8,000 and 10,000 men and the British had captured 67 guns. The destruction of the bridge did not delay Gough at all, if this had indeed been Tej Singh's plan, and the first British units began to cross the river on the evening of the battle.

By 13 February, Gough's army was only 30 miles from Lahore, the capital, with no Sikh army to deter them. They camped at the town of Kussoor and were joined there the next day by further units of the army and by the Governor General. On 15 February Gulab Singh, the ruler of Jammu, nominated by the Durbar of the Punjab arrived to make terms with the victors. The Sikhs ceded the valuable agricultural lands between the Beas and Sutlej Rivers to the EIC, allowed a British Resident at Lahore with subordinates in other principal cities from where these Residents and Agents would indirectly govern the Punjab through Sikh *Sardars*.

In addition, the Sikhs were compelled to pay an indemnity of £1.2 million which, not surprisingly, they could not find, so Gulab Singh himself acquired Kashmir from the Punjab by paying £750,000 to the East India Company, more than half of the debt owed. They surrendered the 25 guns they had captured at Sobraon and agreed to reduce their armed forces to a limit of 12,000 cavalry and 25 infantry battalions. At one o'clock in the morning of 16 February 1846 the Treaty was agreed.

On the afternoon of the 18th, the young child Maharajah Dhulip Singh arrived and was cordially welcomed by the Governor General. Sir Hugh described him as 'a very interesting boy who showed great nerve,' and Hardinge addressed him politely, saying he hoped this would lead to friendship between the two nations. Two days later, the army was outside the walls of Lahore.

On 8 March the Treaty was signed and the next day at a Durbar in the Governor General's state tent it was solemnly ratified. It was at this moment that a small tin box wrapped in an old cloth was taken out of the grasp of the nine-year-old boy Maharajah and passed hand to hand to the Governor General. When opened, it contained the fabulous Koh-i-Noor diamond. It is now part of the Imperial State Crown of the British monarch. General Gough was elevated to the peerage as Baron Gough of Chinkiang in China and of Maharajpore and the Sutlej in the East Indies on 7 April 1846. Governor General Sir Henry Hardinge was also raised to the peerage.

The war had only lasted just under three months, hardly a war, more of a series of violent engagements in a campaign of aggression and defence. General Lord Gough had been much criticised by his fellow officers, including Hardinge, who had written letters to London without his knowledge, and by the Press both in India and England. Their main criticism was that Gough had taken unnecessary and excessive casualties and had been profligate with his men in his determination to attack at any opportunity. This was factually incorrect.

His casualties had been only 8% of his forces at Mudki and 15% in the fierce fighting at Ferozeshah and Sobraon. Compare this with the losses of the Duke of Wellington at Assaye in 1803 of 81%, and there is simply no case to answer. General Gough always fiercely cared for his men.

Admittedly, these losses only relate to British regiments and clearly the regiments from Bengal, who made up the larger part of the army, took greater casualties. But it is important to remember that the native Indian regiments were not keen to fight the fearsome Sikhs at all because of their warlike reputation, and because the Sikhs were natives of India and their defeat would be the last of the opposition to the all-conquering East India Company.

'I never ask a soldier to expose himself where I do not personally lead. This my army knows and, I firmly believe, estimates,' Gough said. He was loved and admired by his officers and men and believed it was his duty to lead and encourage to victory by enduring exactly what they endured. His tactics were little different from those used by Wellington in the Peninsular War, and it is hard to find alternatives to these traditional ways of waging war.

In any event, the story was not over. Though the Sikhs had been defeated in four successive closely fought battles along the Sutlej River, the Sikh army had by no means been destroyed and the East India Company, in the guise of the British army, had not penetrated into the Punjab itself, larger than Great Britain and Ireland put together, rising from the arid plains of Northern India into the foothills of the Himalayas and the North West Frontier. After two years, the inevitable second conflict broke out, which Gough had always predicted. It was to last nearly a year longer than the first campaign.

On 12 January 1848 yet another new Governor General arrived in Calcutta. He was the 35-year-old politician James Broun-Ramsay, 10th Earl of Dalhousie. One of the first things he did was to write to Lord Gough in Simla to say that as the son of a former Commander in Chief in India who had also served in the Peninsular War under the Duke of Wellington, he would do all in his powers to support the army. This respectful letter was well received by Gough, who was old enough to have been Dalhousie's father. All was peaceful during those early weeks, then, on 19 April 1848 an event occurred which triggered the start of the 2nd Sikh War.

Patrick Vans Agnew of the elite Indian Civil Service and Lieutenant William Anderson of the Bombay European regiment, having been sent to take charge of Multan in the Sikh Empire from Diwan Mulraj Chopra, were wounded in a murderous attack and the following morning murdered there, Within a short time Sikh troops joined in open rebellion.

Lord Dalhousie agreed with the newly ennobled Lord Gough that the British East India Company's military forces were not adequately equipped with transport and supplies, or otherwise prepared to take the field immediately. This was largely due to the cut-backs that Hardinge had instigated after the first conflict and which Gough had opposed. It was foolhardy of Hardinge, a former military man, to have put these changes into effect when he was aware of future trouble in the Punjab.

Dalhousie and Gough realised the potential for the spread of the rebellion, and the necessity not merely for the subjugation of Multan, but also for the entire Punjab. Dalhousie made a chilling announcement: 'Unwarned by precedent, uninfluenced by example, the Sikh nation has called for war; and on my words, sirs, war they shall have and with a vengeance.'

Dalhousie and Gough decided not to make any moves before the army was ready for operations towards the end of 1848. On 12 May Gough informed the Governor General that he would not undertake the invasion of Punjab with a force of less than 24,000 men and 78 guns, plus reinforcements from Sindh Province if needed. Dalhousie agreed and advised him they should not move until October when the heat of summer had passed.

The first person to take action against the conspirators in Multan was the Assistant Resident, Herbert Edwardes, formerly of the 1st Bengal European Regiment, who had served in Gough's personal staff at Mudki where he was wounded, and at Sobraon. Completely on his own initiative he raised a body of Pathan Irregulars, added some Sikh volunteers and on 18 June at Kineyree routed a rebel force led by Dewan Mulraj, the Governor of Multan. With further reinforcements this remarkable young man, still in his twenties and now at the head of an army of 18,000 troops, defeated the rebels again on 1 July at Suddoosam, driving Dewan Mulraj back to the fortress in Multan where, surrounded by the Bombay army led by General William Whish, he surrendered on 22 January 1849 after negotiations led by Edwardes himself, who spoke Hindustani and Urdu fluently.

Gough observed all these actions at Multan and feared that this would lead to further outbreaks of hostility all across the Punjab. This is exactly what happened. In September the leader of the Sikhs, Shere Singh, having originally supported Edwardes, now changed sides at the head of a force of more than 3,000 cavalry and 900 infantry, which took the 2nd Sikh War beyond Multan. Shere Singh now marched north trying to join his father, Chattar Singh, in Hazara, but hesitated at the prospect of opposition from hostile tribes led by British officers. So he fortified crossings on the Chenab River, west of the Sutlej.

In the darkness of the morning of 22 November Gough and his army moved towards the river crossing at Ramnagar. The Sikhs were positioned on both sides of the Chenab, which at this place was really just a stream. The riverbed after the monsoon was full of soft mud. The 3rd Light Dragoons accompanied by the 8th Bengal Light Cavalry drove some Sikh cavalry back from their positions on the near bank but came under fire from Sikh artillery. A horse artillery unit, trying to respond, lost a 6-pounder in the mud. The brigade commander, Sir Colin Campbell, ordered infantry to retrieve the gun but Gough sensibly overruled him.

Sher Singh now ordered his cavalry to attack the hesitating British on their flank, but under the command of Lieutenant Colonel William Havelock, the 14th Light Dragoons charged again, driving the enemy back down the riverbed while being fired on by artillery. Brigadier General Charles Cureton, brigade commander of the cavalry, seeing the problem, at once rode into the riverbed and ordered his men to withdraw. Within minutes he was shot dead. Gough, too, attempted to warn Havelock, but it was too late, and the Colonel was killed soon after. British casualties, including Cureton, who had fought alongside Gough at Talavera, were 26 killed or missing and 59 wounded.

In sum the engagement was indecisive and cost the lives of two fine officers. Once again Gough was blamed for foolhardiness when, in fact, he had been observing the encounter from a distance and had given the commanders permission to operate on their own assessments. They had both made a fatal mistake riding directly into accurate Sikh fire. The fact is that Gough had intended this action to only be a reconnaissance with Cureton in charge, but due to the Sikh aggression and the British over-reaction, matters quickly deteriorated. The Sikhs had been dislodged from the riverbank and Gough's large army was relatively intact as it made the river crossing. Further contacts at nearby Sadelupour, when General Thackwell commanding the cavalry failed to take advantage of his position, were of no consequence to either side, though Gough commented, 'I placed the ball at Thackwell's feet, and he would not kick it.'

Chillianwalla was predominantly an infantry fight. Once again, the Army of the Punjab was advancing against a defensive

Sikh army commanded by Sher Singh. Dalhousie and Gough were concerned that Sher Singh would be joined by his father, Chattar Singh, who had just captured Attock in the north of the Punjab and would now be free to join him near the Jhelum River to form a large Sikh army.

It was decided that Sher Sing should be attacked as soon as possible. As Gough's army began to pitch camp on relatively flat ground and aware that the Sikh army was nearby, a battery of Sikh artillery advanced and opened fire on the British and Bengalis. They were forced to retire before Gough's artillery opened fire in turn. Then the whole of the Sikh artillery came into action and it became clear that the Sikhs had advanced from their fortified positions and were ready to fight. Cancelling the order to pitch camp, Gough formed up his regiments and prepared for battle.

He drew up his infantry in two divisions of two brigades each. On the left, Brigadier Campbell's division of Brigadier Hoggan's and Brigadier Pennycuick's brigades and on the right, General Gilbert's division of Brigadier Mountain's and Brigadier Godby's brigades. Brigadier Pennycuick's brigade provided the infantry reserve. Brigadier White's cavalry brigade was posted on the left flank with Brigadier Pope's cavalry brigade on the right.

Dense scrub made movement and observation difficult and, as always in battles on the Indian plains, the marching of troops and horses and the firing of artillery and infantry weapons created heavy clouds of dust and powder smoke, which added to the confusion. The Sikh army had its back to thick jungle and beyond were the Himalayas towering in the distance.

As the infantry formed up the artillery continued to batter the Sikh positions, and after an hour the infantry began to advance. In Campbell's division on the left, Hoggan's brigade pushed into the Sikh infantry line and drove them back, but in Pennycuick's brigade things did not go as well. They drifted away to the right, struggling to keep order in the dense scrub, and the 24th of Foot, which happened to contain a number of inexperienced young soldiers, moved too far ahead of the two accompanying Bengal Infantry battalions and overran the Sikh guns, capturing them.

The Sikh infantry at once counter-attacked, driving the whole brigade back to its start position and inflicting many casualties. In the fierce fighting Brigadier Pennycuick's son, the 17-year-old Ensign, Alexander Pennycuick, died defending his father's body, and Lieutenant Colonel Brookes, the commanding officer of the 24th was killed. The regiment suffered 518 casualties in all, including 14 officers and 241 men killed. Walt Whitman in his book of poems entitled *Leaves of Grass*, published in 1855, wrote: 'For the son is brought with the father/In the foremost rank of the fierce assault they fell.' Pennycuick's brigade then moved up and managed to check the Sikh pursuit.

Hoggan's brigade, under General Campbell's leadership, met with more success. They pushed through the strip of jungle behind the Sikh lines supported by artillery fire, coming out on the far side into a strong force of Sikh infantry, cavalry and guns. The 61st of Foot charged the body of cavalry and drove them away, before wheeling and attacking the Sikh infantry. The 46th Bengal Light Infantry drove back more Sikh cavalry and the whole brigade advanced along the length of the Sikh positions, capturing 13 guns before linking up with Gilbert's Division.

On the left flank, White's cavalry brigade found themselves confronted by a large force of Sikh cavalry when Captain Unett of the 3rd King's Own Light Dragoons led his squadron, all mounted on greys, into the charge, galloping through the broken jungle. His light dragoons then charged back, dispersing any threat to the left flank. By the end of the day only 48 officers and men were still in the saddle out of 106 who had started.

On the right flank, the ageing Brigadier Pope who could not even mount his horse without assistance and had never commanded a brigade before in battle, directed his men, the 9th Lancers, the 1st and 6th Bengal Light Cavalry and the 14th King's Light Dragoons, to advance at the trot. As they entered the Sikh lines, they in turn were attacked by Sikh cavalry and driven into a full retreat before two guns of the horse artillery opened fire, forcing an enemy retreat. Brigadier Pope was mortally wounded, as was Lieutenant Cureton, of the 14th King's Light Dragoons, the son of Brigadier

Cureton, who had been killed at Ramnagar. The failure of the cavalry exposed Godby's Bengal infantry before the 70th moved back to stabilise their position. It was hand-to-hand fighting with many casualties on either side.

One of the lighter stories that comes out of the battle was recalled by Field Marshal Sir Frederick Haines, a young officer in the 21st of Foot at the time:

> This evening, two of the 9th Lancers were sent in by Sher Singh with a letter. They had strayed beyond our Videttes [mounted lookouts] unarmed. Some horsemen surrounded them, and one of our men, making some resistance, was slightly cut in the arm. They were taken before Sher Singh, who immediately ordered for punishment the man who had struck an unarmed man. They were well treated for two days and then taken round the camp by Sher Singh, shown whatever they wished to see, given a champagne breakfast and this night sent in to us, Sher Singh boastfully declaring the two men had been captured by one Sikh.

The chaotic battle ended in darkness when both armies withdrew to their original positions. Gough's army had sustained casualties of something in the region of 2,500, with 1,000 British officers and men either killed or wounded and the Sikhs more than twice that number. In the next few days heavy rains prevented either side renewing the conflict. Once again, the battle had started late in the day and ended up with the two sides fighting in darkness in a jungle, particularly disadvantageous for the attacking army, giving the defending Sikhs an advantage.

One interesting outcome of the battle was the slur cast on the competence and courage of the British light cavalry, which continued to reverberate right into the Crimean War five years later, and it may have been an element in the disastrous but heroic Charge of the Light Brigade. Captain Nolan, who played a key role in the events, had served in India with the 15th Hussars during the Sikh Wars, and was shocked and ashamed by poor old Pope's handling of the light cavalry brigade at Chillianwalla. Maybe at Balaclava he was trying to make amends.

The other and most important outcome of the battle was that it energised those, totally unfairly, criticising Lord Gough for his tactics. Not only Hardinge, who should have known better, but also his successor, the smooth politician Lord Dalhousie, criticised him behind his back and even persuaded the ageing Duke of Wellington, himself no stranger to huge losses of his own troops, to have him replaced by Sir Charles Napier, who took ship for Calcutta a few days later.

These two Governor Generals had done nothing but impede and stall the progress of Gough's two campaigns, which encouraged much criticism of him in the press both in India and London. Gough was not fully aware of the degree to which the back-stabbing had continued and won his final and best victory before his replacement had arrived. Hugh Gough that brave and honourable servant of his country was to have the last laugh.

The weather finally cleared, and Gough resolved not to attack the Sikhs until General Whish had joined him with his division from Multan, even though Sher Singh tried to lure him once again into a premature battle. The army of Chattar Singh soon joined up with Sher's army, bringing 1,500 Afghan cavalry commanded by the son of Dost Mohammed, the Amir of Afghanistan, who had so humiliatingly defeated the British in the First Afghan War. By the end of January, looking for supplies, they were compelled to march east to Gujerat near the Chenab River.

In response, Gough sent Lieutenant William Hodson with a force of light cavalry to Wazirabad on the far side of the Chenab to watch for any Sikh incursions across the river. This young officer was later famous during the Indian Rebellion as Hodson of Hodson's Horse, who captured the Mughal King of Delhi. On 15 February 1849, Gough also moved towards the Chenab, to follow the Sikh army and wait for Whish's Multan division. He ordered Whish to send more troops to support Hodson.

During the next few days Gough was joined by Whish's division, Dundas's Bombay brigade and Markham's Bengal brigade, bringing his forces to 24,000 with 96 guns. In front of him was a Sikh army numbering 60,000 with 59 guns drawn up south of Gujerat. The Sikh infantry in the centre along with their artillery were positioned between the dry Dwara River and the fully flowing Katela River. On their right and left were the cavalry and in front of them various small dwellings which they had fortified.

The British, Bengal and Bombay troops assembled for the battle soon after dawn on 21 February and the seventy-year-old Gough rode down the line in his familiar white 'Fighting Coat', cheered on vigorously by his men. They loved him and admired him for his constancy, caring and courage. Like all great generals he would always do what his men would do, and his dogged determination to achieve victory was infectious.

He was now to lead a fully prepared army in a fight of his choosing, which is what he had wanted to do since the beginning of the Sikh Wars. Gough planned to launch his main attack along the side of the Dwara riverbed, while the cavalry brigades held the Sikh left and centre. His infantry brigades on the right would be Hervey's, Pennycuick's and Mountain's brigades, with Markham's brigade in support. To the left of Hervey's would be the heavy guns on the bank of the Dwara. On the left bank of the Dwara were Carnegy's, McLeod's and Dundas's brigades, with Hoggan's in support. White's cavalry brigade would cover the left flank.

At a signal the Army of the Punjab advanced two miles towards the Sikh positions, then paused as the Sikh guns opened fire before Gough ordered his gun batteries forward, with a covering of skirmishers, and an artillery duel began with only one possible result, since the Bengal and Bombay gunners outnumbered the Sikh guns nearly two to one. The firing continued for more than two hours before the Sikh guns faded. The decisive point came when the two Bengal horse artillery batteries managed to direct enfilade fire along the enemy guns, which destroyed them. As this happened the cavalry units on Gough's right began to prepare to attack the Sikh left.

The main infantry attack now began as Pennycuick's and Mountain's brigades moved forward towards the centre of the

Sikh lines, still under heavy fire from the surviving guns. The village of Bara Kalra now became a focus point when the 2nd Bengal Fusiliers, part of Gilbert's division, after fierce fighting managed to push the Sikh infantry back. The Sikhs counter-attacked, pushing the Bengal Fusiliers back out of the village and were met with close range grape-shot fire from the Bengal Horse Artillery.

At the same time, Lieutenant Colonel Hervey's brigade, led by the 10th of Foot and the 8th Bengal Infantry, attacked the nearby village of Chota Kalra. Again, they were met with fierce resistance and, while the 52nd Bengal Infantry defended their right flank, Brigadier Markham's brigade advanced with supporting fire from Bengal Horse Artillery, and Hervey's brigade took the village.

Once the left bank of the Dawa riverbed had been cleared, Major General Sir Colin Campbell's division was able to advance unopposed and directed enfilade artillery fire right across the Sikh positions. A further Sikh cavalry attack was stopped by batteries of the Bengal Horse Artillery, which was followed up by a charge of the Sindh Horse and 9th Lancers driving the enemy from the field.

By now most of the Sikh forces were in full retreat and, unlike in previous battles of the two wars, did not stand and fight. They had finally been roundly defeated by the aged Gough, who was still unaware that he had already been replaced as Commander in Chief of the Army in India. General Napier had not yet arrived from England.

Gough's cavalry now pursued the fleeing enemy for 12 miles towards the Jhelum River, and guards were positioned on the Chenab River allowing Sikh soldiers across only if they surrendered their weapons. British and Indian casualties were relatively light, 96 killed and 750 wounded. A large number of casualties occurred at the taking of Bara Kalra, where the 2nd Bengal Infantry suffered severely. The Sikh army probably lost more than 2,000 killed, wounded or captured. General Gilbert, with a force of infantry, cavalry and artillery, continued the pursuit the next day, marching fifty miles to the north in three days before reaching Rawalpindi on 14 March and taking the surrender of Sher Singh and Lal Singh. Five days later he crossed the Indus at Attock, driving Dost

Mohammed's Afghans back into Afghanistan and on 21 March he marched into Peshawar.

The war was over, the Punjab became part of British India and as a result, many good Sikh soldiers, upholding their proud military history, joined the army of the East India Company, which became ultimately the Indian Army, fighting on the British side during subsequent wars including both world wars in the 20th century.

In the ensuing months, the Earl of Dalhousie was advanced to Marquess and Lord Gough was created Viscount Gough of Goojerat in the Punjab and of the City of Limerick in June of 1849. He retired from active service later that year after more than sixty years as a serving officer. He had started all those decades before as an unknown young Georgian Ensign and ended his remarkably varied career as a Victorian general of distinction. He was promoted to full general five years later and was proud to be made Colonel of his old regiment, the 87th of Foot, the Royal Irish Fusiliers as well as Colonel of the Royal Horse Guards, the Blues. Those regiments could have chosen no finer soldier. He was promoted to Field Marshal on 9 November 1862 and died in his bed at St Helen's House, his home near Dublin, on 2 March 1869 at the age of ninety.

Immediately, proposals for a monument to this distinguished hero were put forward, and a fine equestrian statue of him by J. H. Foley the Irish sculptor who had created the statue of Prince Albert on the Albert Memorial and, more fittingly, a figure of Caractacus, which Gough would have much admired, was placed with great ceremony in Dublin's Phoenix Park in 1880.

Referring to the statue, General Sir John Michel said:

> Keep it, Irishmen, as an everlasting memento of your glory. Treasure it as a sacred deposit. Glory in it as a statue of one who was an honour to your country, one whose whole life, whether civil of military, was one continued career of kindness, honour, honesty of purpose, nobility of heart, combined with the purest loyalty and the most enthusiastic patriotism. He was loved and honoured by his countrymen.

> He was par excellence our Irish chevalier, sans peur at sans reproche, and to wind up all, he was heart and soul an Irishman.

Unsurprisingly, not all Irishmen agreed with these words. After being repeatedly vandalised in the 1940s and 1950s, the statue was finally rescued and moved to Chillingham Castle in Northumberland in 1990. The inscription reads:

> In honour of Field Marshal Hugh Viscount Gough, K.P., G.C.B., G.C.S.I., an illustrious Irishman, whose achievements in the Peninsular War, in China, and in India, have added lustre to the military glory of his country, which he faithfully served for seventy-five years. This statue (cast from cannon taken by troops under his command and granted by Parliament for the purpose) is erected by friends and comrades.

Hugh Gough was a soldier's soldier, modest, straightforward, honest and decisive. His career shows he is one of those few generals in history whose destiny was not decided by politicians. He was given duties to carry out and he surely did that without questioning those orders.

As a general he was victorious in two very difficult campaigns in the Far East encountering extreme weather conditions in unfamiliar terrains against unknown opposition. He always completed what was asked of him in the best way he knew

EPILOGUE

General George S. Patton was acutely aware of his own destiny. At times he considered himself a Roman legionary or a medieval crusader, even a Napoleonic general. Though these thoughts were fantasy, they did in fact have a kernel of truth: that commanders in different ages display similar characteristics, characteristics not always suited to peace. Perhaps his death, so soon after hostilities had ended in a road accident tells us something. Maybe peace would not have suited such a man of war. The chaos and violence of human conflict, which appears to be man's inevitable fate, pushes certain men to the fore where they seem to thrive, sometimes perpetrating deeds which in times of peace are unacceptable.

No general would be remembered if there were no conflicts. That is the nub. 'Ability is nothing without opportunity,' said Napoleon. Generals who have not fought in great battles are quickly forgotten. But there are always conflicts:

> War was always here. Before man was, war waited for him. The ultimate trade awaiting its ultimate practitioner.
>
> Cormac McCarthy, *Blood Meridian*, 1985

So, what differentiates these generals is that they, by chance, were thrown into the cauldron of human conflict where every decision they made was written in the blood of their own men as well as their opponents. In these violent episodes they took their chances and made their sacrifices by virtue of their own belief in themselves, imprinting their genius on the men they commanded. It is a rare quality which we can only admire and fear in equal parts, as these men of action go about their dangerous business.

Dr Johnson was right in his ruminations about Socrates and King Charles XII.

INDEX

Abdul Rezak Pasha 218
Abercromby, General Ralph 242
Abram Petrovich Hannibal 211
Abydos 46
Achilles 98
Acropolis 131-132
Adela, daughter of William the Conqueror 86
Adhemar, bishop of Le Puy 81-84
Adige, river 152
Adriatic 17, 19-20, 55, 59, 69-70, 74, 87, 114-115, 124, 126
Aegina 118
Aeschylus 131
Agra 255
Ahlden, schloss 186
Airolo 235
Aix-la-Chapelle 204
Albani, Cardinal Alessandro 162
Albano 52
Alberada of Buonalbergo 67
Aleppo 83, 87
Aleppo, emir Riwan of 81
Alexander I, Czar 238
Alexander Nevsky Monastery 237
Alexander the Great 8, 13-14, 64, 79, 133, 166, 178, 181
Alexander, Field Marshal 241
Alexandretta 80
Alexis, son of Peter the Great 180
Aliwal 261-261
Almaraz 244
Almondar, king of Arabs 43
Alsace 149, 204, 206, 234
Altdorf 90, 236
Alte Veste 100-101
Alt-Ranstadt, Schloss 165, 175
Amalasontha
Amalfi 73-74
Ambala 258
Ammatas 46
Amoy 250, 253
Amalasontha 48
Anastasius, Emperor 41, 45
Anatolia 37, 42, 69-70, 76, 79, 84-85, 124, 144
Ancona 52-53
Andermatt 236
Anderson, Lieutenant William 266
Anglo-Dutch War 120
Anglo-Irish 9, 241
Anna Comnena 65, 69-70, 74, 76
Anne, Queen of England 148-149, 153, 157
Anthing, Colonel 210
Antioch 43, 55-56, 66, 78-79, 81-88
Antiochus 12, 37, 67
Antiochus III 37
Antoine Heinsius, Grand Pensionary of the United Dutch Provinces 149, 153
Antonina 44-45, 63
Apamea 56
Apulia 27, 59, 62, 67-69, 72-74, 86-88
Arabia 42
Arcanania 126
Areopagus 131
Argenson 200
Argos 129
Ariminum, Rimini 17
Arminius 184
Arta 71
Assaye, battle of 265
Assisi 59
Athalaric 48
Athens 118, 125, 130-132, 185
Attica 132
Attock 269, 274
Auckland, Lord, Governor General of India 247, 255
Augsburg, Peace of 97
Augustus Frederik II, the Strong, King of Poland, Elector of Saxony 161, 167, 168, 169-175, 184, 189
Augustus Frederik III 161, 186, 190, 193
Augustus Rutowski 189
Austerlitz, battle of 209
Azov, Sea of 221
Bad Windsheim 102
Baddowal 261
Baden, Margrave Louis of 141-142, 149-150, 153
Badoer, Pietro 114
Baetis, river 24
Baghdad 60, 88
Baldwin 76, 83, 85
Baltic Sea 167, 179
Bamberg 99
Baoshan 252
Bar, Confederation of 217
Bara Kalra 274
Barbaro, Luca, Antonio 117, 119, 121
Barbary corsairs 114
Bari 69, 73-74, 87
Barozzi, Andrea 121
Barrosa, battle of 244-245
Basilica of San Vitale 39
Basta, Giorgio, General 90
Batavian Republic 242
Battaglia, Girolamo 117
Batthyany, Grafin Eleonore 162
Bavaria 93-95, 97, 99-100, 107, 146-149, 194, 207
Bavaria, Max Emmanuel, Elector of 143, 148
Beas, river 264
Belgrade 143, 159-160, 186, 188
Bellotto, Barnardo, painter 163

Bender, Moldavia 180
Bengal Horse Artillery 262, 273-274
Berbice 242
Berg, General Major Maxim 215
Berwick, Duke of 190-192
Bessarabia 227, 232
Bethlehem 84
Bethlen, Gabriel, Prince of Transylvania 92
Bezborodko, Prince 228
Biron, duc de 192, 200
Black Forest 149
Blankett, John, Commodore 242
Blenheim, battle of 149, 151-152, 154, 156-157, 165
Blois, count Stephen of 76, 78, 82, 86
Bohemia 89-92, 94-95, 97, 99-100, 104-107, 194-195
Bohemond II, son of Bohemond I 87
Boii, tribe 20
Bologna 90
Bonaparte, Joseph 244
Borner, General 146
Bosnia 94, 144-145
Boufflers, Marshal 155, 157, 184, 186
Bourbon, Mary of, Princess of Carignano 139
Bragadin, Andrea 122
Brandeis 95
Brandenburg 94, 105, 107, 186, 213-214
Breitenfeld, battle of 99
Brenta, river 113
Breslau 106
Brest-Litovsk 217
Breuner, Colonel 108
Broadfoot, Major George 257, 260
Broglie, duc de 195
Brookes, Lieutenant Colonel 270
Brandenburg 94
Brunswick, Christian of 93-94
Brunswick, Duke of 126, 185
Brussels 138, 143, 200
Bubna, Johann 105
Buda, Hungary 142, 145
Bug, river 228
Bulgaria 41, 208
Bulla 47
Bundner Oberland 236
Bunker Hill 242
Bunzelwitz 215
Burgundy, Duke of 154
Burma 259
Butler, Colonel Walter 108-109
Butrinto 70
Buzes 55-56
Byzantine Empire 41-42, 48, 63, 68-69, 73, 87-88
Carlberg, Lieutenant 181
Cadiz 28, 244
Calabria 63, 67, 69, 72, 74
Calcinato 152
Calcutta 254, 257, 266, 272
Callinicum 43
Caloprino 113
Calvinists 105
Cameroon 211
Campania 37, 53
Campbell, Brigadier Sir Colin 268-270, 274
Campo Formio, Treaty of 230
Candia (Crete), War of 116
Cannae 14, 18, 20, 22, 27-29, 31, 33, 38, 66
Canosa di Puglia 66
Canton 248-249, 253
Canusium 22, 27, 66
Cape Colony 242
Cape Town 242, 251
Caractacus 275
Carlyle, Thomas 207
Carnavalet, Hotel 183
Carnegy, Brigadier 273
Carnot 234
Carpi 146
Carthage 13-16, 22, 25, 29-30, 35-38, 46-47, 49
Cassano d'Adda, battle of 232
Castel Tornese 130
Castello 120, 135
Castro, War of 114
Catalonia 153
Catherine II the Great, Czarina 210, 217, 219, 221-222, 224, 229-230
Catholic League 93-94
Catinat, Marshal 143, 146
Cato 13, 31, 37-38
Cawnpore 255
Cecile, younger sister of Constance 86
Cenaze Hasan Pasha, grand vizier 224
Cephalonia 72, 126
Cesenatico 115
Charles Bonaventure de Longueval, count of Bucquoy 92
Charles II, King of England 145, 170, 185
Charles III, King of Spain 153
Charles V, Emperor 138, 141
Charles VI, Emperor 137, 157-159, 161
Charles X, King of Sweden 166
Charles XI, King of Sweden 166, 169
Chartres Cathedral 86
Chateauroux, Duchesse de 197
Chattar Singh 267, 272
Cheb 108
Chenab, river 267, 272, 274
Chernyshev, Major General Zakhar 214
Chiari 146
Chillianwalla, battle of 240-241, 268, 272
Chillingham Castle 276
China 241, 247, 249-253, 265, 276
Chios 116
Chota Kalra 274
Christian IV, King of Denmark 93
Christina Everhardina of Brandenburg-Bayreuth, Electress of Saxony 186

Chuenpi 248
Chur 236-237
Church of the Holy Sepulchre, Jerusalem 83
Churchill, Sarah, Duchess of Marlborough 157
Chusan 248, 251, 254
Civitavecchia 52
Clausewitz 150
Clermont, Comte de 200
Clermont, France 66, 72-73
Coalition, First, Second 209-210, 230
Coblenz 154
Coigny, Marshal 196
Coldstream Guards 244
Commercy, general Prince Charles of Lorraine 146, 148
Comnena, Anna, daughter of Alexius, historian 65, 69-70, 74
Comnenus, Alexius I, Byzantine Emperor 79
Comnenus, John, nephew of Alexius 74
Conde 139, 193
Constantinian 58
Constantinople 40-42, 44-45, 47-48, 50, 52, 55-57, 60, 62-63, 66, 69, 71, 76-78, 82, 84, 87, 115, 119, 136, 211
Conti, Prince Louis Armand 139-140, 142, 200
Copenhagen 168
Corfu 72, 126, 128
Cork 243
Cornaro, Girolamo 134
Corone 126-127
Correr, museo, Teodoro 112, 123
Cortona 18
Cortone 63
Cossacks 178, 213, 215, 220, 222-223, 226-228, 232
Council of Forty 119
Courland, Duke of
Craig, Major General Sir James 242
Cremona 123, 147
Crimean War 271
Cromwell, Oliver 93, 241
Crostolo 148
Crusaders, Crusades 60, 65, 73, 76-83, 86-87, 113, 115
Ctesiphon 56-57
Cumberland, Duke of 198, 203
Cureton, Brigadier General Charles, Lieutenant, son of Charles 268, 270-271
Cyclades, islands 118
Cyprien, Bishop of Antioch 84
Cyprus 81-82
D'Asfeld, Marquis 192
D'Aubusson, Marquis 121
D'Este, Prince Almerigo 120
Daimbert, Archbishop of Pisa, papal legate 84
Dalhousie, James Broun-Ramsay, 10th Earl of 266-267, 269, 272, 275
Dalmatia 48
Damascus 80, 90
Damat Ali Pasha, Grand Vizier 159
Danishmend 84-85
Danube, river 43, 145, 149-150, 159-160, 163, 188, 207, 224
Danzig 174
Dao Guang, Chinese Emperor 249, 251-253
Dara 42-44, 56
Dardanelles 116, 118-119, 124
De Beaufort, Duc 121
De Belle-Isle, Duc 190, 194-195
De Caderousse, Duke 121
De Chateau Thierry, Duke 121
De Croy, Charles Eugene 169-170
De la Feuillade, Duke 121, 152
De Meilham, Senac 198
De Noailles, Duc 121-122, 191-192, 196-197
De Ribas, Jose, Admiral 226
De Seytres, Hippolyte 195
De Valliere, Joseph Florent 196
De Witte, Hans 98
Debrezin 126
Decimus 46
Demerara 242
Denain, battle of 158
Denmark 93-96, 108, 167-168, 180-181
Derzhavin, Gavrila 237
Dettingen, battle of 196
Devereux, Captain 109
Dhulip Singh, Maharajah 264
Diabolis 87
Dick, Major General Robert Henry 263
Diwan Mulraj Chopra 266
Dnieper, river 179, 221, 223
Dniester, river 228
Dolores, Lady 255
Donaustauf 207
Donauworth 150
Donkin, Colonel 243
Dorpat 170
Dorylaeum 78, 83
Dost Mohammed, Amir of Afghanistan 272
Douai 157
Doyle, Colonel Charles 243
Dragomestre 126
Drake, Colonel, Irish soldier of fortune 156
Dresden 60, 184, 193, 213
Ducker, Carl Gustav, General 180
Dumouriez, General 217
Duna, river 171
Dunamunde 172
Dundas, Brigadier 272-273
Dutch Republic, United Provinces of Holland 145, 151
Dutch United East India Company 242
Dwara, river 273
East India Company 242, 247, 254, 256-258, 260-262, 264-266, 275
Ebro, river 15, 25

Ecclefechan 207
Edessa 56, 83-85
Edwardes, Herbert 267
Elbe, river 94, 99
Elizabeth I 89
Elizabeth the Great, Czarina of Russia, daughter of Peter the Great 211
Ellenborough, Lord, Governor General of India 255-256
Elliot, Charles, British Superintendent 248-250
Elmas Mehmed Pasha 144
Elphinstone, Rear Admiral Sir George 242
Epirus 13, 69-70, 74
Erizzo, Francesco 123
Esseqibo 242
Ettlingen 191
Euphrates, river 43-44, 56, 84
Euripus, river 133
Famagusta 242
Favart, Charles-Simon 201
Favart, Justine 201
Faventia, battle of 58
Ferdinand II, Archduke 91, 93, 98, 108, 110
Ferdinand III, Emperor 107
Fersen, Ivan, General 228
Feuillade, Louis de la 121, 152
First Afghan War 254, 259, 272
Flanders, Count Robert of 76, 78, 80, 83-84
Fleming, Count 169
Focsani 223-224
Foley, J.H., sculptor 275
Fontainebleau, Palais de 202
Fontenoy, battle of 183, 198-199, 205
Formosa 250
Foscolo, Leonardo 117
France 66, 68, 73, 82, 86, 107, 110, 133, 137, 139, 142, 146-148, 151, 153, 155, 157-158, 161, 171-172, 183, 185, 188 190, 192-194, 196-198, 200, 202-203, 206, 208-209, 211, 213, 217-218, 230, 232-234, 241, 245
Franconia 90
Frankfurt 140
Fraustad 175
Frederick IV, King of Denmark and Norway 167
Frederick V, King of Palatinate
Frederic Augustus, Count von Cosel 189
Frederick the Great 8, 161, 194, 196, 207, 213-214
Frederick William I, King of Prussia 189
Friedberg Forest 215
Friuli 120, 123
Fulcher of Chartres 81
Gabriel, lord of Mitelene 84
Gadebusch, battle of
Gaius Flaminius, consul 18
Gallas, General 106, 108
Gamba, Antonio 208, 235
Gandamak, battle of 257
Gargano, mount 68
Gelimer 46-47
Genoa 59, 233-234
George I, King of England 102, 110
George II, King of England 160, 193, 197-198
Geraldine, Major 109
Germania, town 41
Germanus 55
Germany 89, 93-100, 104-107, 126-127, 143, 149, 158, 191, 194
Gibamund 46
Gibraltar 244
Gilbert, Major General Sir Walter 263
Giray, Quaplan, leader of Tatars
Giustinian, marcantonio, doge 133
Glarus 236
Golden Fleece, Order of 142
Golnau 215
Gordon, John, Lieutenant Colonel 108-109
Goths 48-49, 51-55, 58-59, 62
Grabousa, islands 122
Gradisca 91
Graham, Lieutenant General, later Lord Lynedoch 244-245
Great Northern War 167, 184, 187, 204, 212
Greder, regiment 188
Greece 41, 67, 69, 74, 124-125, 130, 132, 134, 136, 145, 185
Gregory VII, Pope 71
Grey, General Sir John 235, 255-256
Grimaldi, Bartolomeo 123
Grodno 175-176
Guiscard, Robert, Count of Apulia and Calabria 66-67, 69-73, 87-88
Gujerat 272
Gulab Singh, ruler of Jammu 264
Gumushtekin, emir of Siwa 84-85
Gurkhas 257, 263
Gustavus Adolphus, king of Sweden 8, 98-100, 104-105, 108, 110, 176, 181, 185
Gwalior, Rani of 255-256
Hadrian, Roman Emperor 14, 30
Haines, Field Marshal Sir Frederick 271
Halil Pasha, Grand Vizier 159-160
Halle 94, 102-103
Hamburg 95
Hamilcar, father of Hannibal 14, 24, 27
Hangzhou 252
Hannibal Barca 14
Hanno the Great 14-15, 28
Hanover, Elector of 126
Hapsburgs 90, 96, 141-142, 145-146, 153, 164, 194, 204

Hardinge, General Sir Henry, Governor General of India 256, 258-260, 262, 264-266, 272
Hasan Pasha 222-224
Hasdrubal Gisco 25
Hasdrubal the Fair, son-in-law of Hamilcar 14
Hastings, battle of 67
Hauteville, Tancred de 67
Hauteville, Richard de 69
Hauteville, Roger de, King of Sicily 73
Havelock, Captain Henry 257, 268
Hazam Ali, Ottoman commander, Grand Admiral 116
Heilbronn League 105
Heinrich Holk 102-103, 105
Helden Platz 137
Henry I, king of England 86
Henry IV, emperor of Germany 71
Hervey, Lieutenant Colonel 273-274
Hesse-Cassel, Prince of 187
Hesse-Darmstadt, Georg of 105
Hildiger 52-53
Hindustani 267
Hippo 47
Hispania 14-17, 23-25, 27-30
Hodson, Lieutenant William 272
Hofkriegsrat, Imperial War Council 146, 148, 161, 163, 231, 233, 235
Hoggan, Brigadier 269-270, 273
Holstein 94
Holstein, Duke of 172
Holstein-Gottorp, Hedwig Leonora of, Queen of Sweden 96
Holy League 127, 142, 145
Holy Roman Empire 89, 96, 143, 224, 237
Hong Kong 247, 249, 253-254
Hugh of Vermandois 73, 76, 82
Hungary 90, 107, 126, 142, 145, 159-160, 163, 194
Hypatius 45
Ibera, battle of 23
Iliturgi, battle of 23, 29
Illyria 20, 45, 71
India 203, 207, 241-243, 247, 249, 254-262, 264-266, 271-272, 274-276
Indus, river 274
Ingria 167, 169
Islam 48, 65, 81, 141
Ismael Pasha
Istria 91, 113
Ivanovna, Anna, Duchess of Courland 189
Izmail 224, 226-227
Jalalabad 257
James III, the Old Pretender 197
Jefferson, Thomas 229
Jerusalem 48, 57, 65-66, 83-84, 237
Jesuits 93, 97
Jhelum, river 269, 274
Jiulong, river 250
Johanna Tugendreich von Loeben 188
John of Cappadocia 45
John the Armenian 47, 54
John the Bloodthirsty 52, 54, 59, 62
Johnson, Dr Samuel 8, 166, 182, 278
Joseph I, Emperor 137, 157
Joseph II, Emperor 224, 233
Joubert, General Barthelemy 233
Jourdan, Marshal 245
Judaism 48, 65
Julius Caesar 8, 36, 41, 71, 111
Junker 241
Justin I, Emperor 41
Justinian, the Great, Emperor, Flavius Petrus Sabbatius 39-42, 44-45, 47-48, 50, 53-55, 57-58, 62-64, 79
Jutland 95
Kabul 257
Kalamata 127
Kara Mustapha, Grand Vizier 141
Karababa 133
Karel of Zierotin 91
Karlowitz, Treaty of 45
Katela, river 273
Kazakhstan 220
Keogh, Ensign Edward 244
Kepler, Johannes 90
Kerbogha, atabeg of Mosul 81-82
Kherson 221
Ki Ying, Manchu negotiator 253
Kielapha 127-128
Kiev 175
Kinburnska 221
Kinsky, Wilhelm, Count 267
Klissow, battle of 172
Knyphausen, Dodo, General 103
Koca Yusuf Pasha, Grand Vizier 228
Koh-i-Noor diamond 264
Kolberg 215
Konchanskoye 228-229
Koniecpolski, Herman Stanisla 96
Koprulu, Ahmed, Grand Vizier 122
Kosciuszko, Tadeusz 228-229
Kozludzha, battle of 218
Kracow 172-173
Kray, General Paul 233
Kucuk Kaynarca, Treaty of 219
Kufstein Dragoons 142
Kulansu 254
Kunersdorf, battle of 213
Kutuzov, General 209, 226-227, 239
Lahore 256-257, 264
Lal Singh, Raja 259-260, 262, 274
Laufeldt 203, 205
Lecourbe, General 235
Lecouvreur, Adrienne 189
Legnago 123, 146

Leine, schloss 185
Leipzig 99, 102, 104, 165, 175
Lemberg, Lvov 174
Leopold I, Emperor 137, 140-141, 145
Lepanto, battle of 128-129
Leslie, Walter, Major 109
Levenhaupt, General 177-179
Liangjiang Province 252
Ligonier, General 201, 203
Lille 155, 183-184, 186
Limerick 198, 241, 275
Lisbon 178, 243-244
Lithuania, Grand Duke of 170-171
Littler, General 259
Livonia 167, 169
Livy, Titus Livius 21, 25, 27, 33, 36
Lorraine, Duke of 141-142
Louis XIV, King of France 121, 139, 145-147, 152, 155, 158, 170, 185, 187-188, 200, 202
Louis XVIII, King of France 231
Louis, the Dauphin 202
Louvois, Marquis de 138-139, 190
Lubeck 95-96
Lublin 173
Lucius Caecilius Metellus 22
Lucius Postumius Albinus 20
Ludwig I of Bavaria 207
Lumley, Captain 261
Luneburg 131-132
Lutzen 10, 104
Maastricht 203-204
Macdonald, General Jacques 232
Macedon, Kingdom of 14, 25
Macedonia 59, 71
Maciejowice, battle of 228
Mackenzie, Lieutenant General Randoll 243
Madagascar 205
Madras Army 247, 260
Magdeburg 94, 99-100
Mago 18, 24-26, 28, 33
Mainz 98, 143, 192
Maison du Roi, French regiment 156
Malatitze 177
Malplaquet, battle of 10, 156-157, 187, 202
Malta 17, 122, 125, 127, 230
Manchu 2532-253
Maniots 126-127
Mantua 146-148, 233
Manukov, Fedosey 210
Maqsud, descendant of Genghis Khan 226
Marathon, battle of 131
Marcello, Lorenzo 119
Marcus Atilius Regulus 20, 34
Maria Theresa, Empress 160, 163, 194, 237
Markham, Brigadier 272-274
Marlborough, John Churchill, Duke of 148-158, 164-165, 183-184, 186-187, 190, 193, 200, 204
Marmora, Sea of 119
Marsin, Marshal 149-150, 152
Massena, Marshal 224, 236
Masterson, Sergeant Patrick 244
Matthews, Admiral 193
Matthias, Archduke, Emperor 90, 92, 108
Maxentius, Emperor 51
Maximian, Bishop 39
Maximilian, Elector of Bavaria 93-95, 97-98, 100-101, 107, 127, 134
Mazarin, Cardinal 137-138
Mazeppa, Ivan 178-179
Mazzini, Olympia 137
McCaskill, Major General Sir John 259
McLeod, Brigadier 273
Mecklenburg 94-95
Mediterranean Sea 13, 16, 22, 31, 36, 68, 79-80, 112, 114-116
Mehmet Pasha 129
Melbourne, Lord 250
Menshikov, Prince 211
Mesopotamia 42, 56-57
Methoni 114
Mezzogiorno, southern Italy 68-69
Michel, General Sir John
Michelsohnen, Ivan, General
Mies 108
Milan 53-54, 146, 153, 194, 232, 234
Milvian Bridge 51-52
Mindon 42-43
Minerva, temple of 131
Ming Dynasty 252
Minsk 176
Mithoni 128, 136
Mithradates, King of Pontus 84
Mocenigo brothers, Alvise, Tommaso, Lazzaro 115-119, 135
Modena, San Carlo Collegio 113
Modon 114
Mohacs, battle of 142
Moldavia 159, 180, 219, 223
Monemvasia 130, 134
Mongols 60
Mons 155, 157, 187
Montbrun, Marquis de 121
Monte Baldo 146
Monte Cassino 60
Montespan, Madame de 138
Montgomery, General 7-8, 207, 241
Moore, Lieutenant General Sir John 243
Moravia 90-92
Morea, Peloponnese 124-126, 128, 130, 134, 136, 160
Moreau, General Jean Victor 232-233
Moritzburg, castle of 184
Morner, Major General 172
Moscow 177, 182, 187, 196, 210, 212, 217, 219-220, 226

Moselle, river 149
Mount Etna 55
Mount Papua 47
Mouseion Hill 131
Mucellium, battle of 58
Mudki 258-262, 265, 267
Muizenberg 242
Mulhausen 95
Multan 267
Mundus 45, 48-49
Munich 98, 100
Munster 110, 150
Mysore 247
Nanjing 252-253
Napier, General Sir Charles 272, 274
Naples 49-50, 58, 148, 194
Napoleon 8-9, 12, 112, 177, 183, 187, 208-209, 226, 230, 234, 237, 261, 277
Narva, battle of 169-170, 176, 212
Nauplia 129, 136
Naxos 117
Negroponte (Euboea) 116, 130, 132-134, 136
Nerbudda Incident 250-251
Netherlands 138, 148, 155, 160-161, 164, 167, 194, 196, 200, 203-204
Nicaea 76-78, 80, 85
Nicene Creed 76
Niederulm, castle 192
Niemann, Henry, Captain 109
Ningbo 251-253
Nini, Morosini's cat 112
Nisibis 42, 56-57
Nolan, Captain 271
Normandie, regiment de 198
Normandy, Duke Robert Curthose of 83
Normans 66, 68, 70-73, 76, 78, 241
Norsemen 68, 133
North West Frontier 257, 260, 266
Northumberland 276
Novi Ligure, battle of 233-234
Novikov, Stepan 222
Nummers, General 217
Nuremberg 90, 100-101
Nushirvan, King of Persia 55-58
Oates, Captain James 244
Ochakov 221-223, 226
Oder, river 107
Odessa 224
Ogilvie, General 175
Opium War 247, 253
Orange, Prince of 156
Oriol, regiment 222
Orleans, duc d'
Ormonde, Duke of 138, 152
Orontes, river 79
Orthez 245
Orvieto 54
Orzinuovi 123
Osimo 54, 59
Osman Pasha 223
Osnabruck 110
Ostrogoths 40, 48-50, 57, 62
Otranto 59
Otranto, straits of
Otto II, Holy Roman Emperor 113
Otto Wilhelm 131, 185, 197
Ottomans 97, 115-117, 119, 123-125, 127-128, 130, 132-134, 140-142, 144-145, 159, 180, 185, 204, 209, 218-219, 221-226, 228
Oudenarde, battle of 154
Oxenstierna, Axel, Count, Swedish chancellor 101, 105
Padua 90, 120
Pakistan 240
Palais Royal 138
Palamidi 129
Palatinate 91, 154, 166
Palermo 49
Palladio 135
Palmerston, Lord 249-250
Panin, count Nikita 219
Panixer Pass 236
Papal States 122, 127
Pappenheim, Gottfried, Marshal 100, 102-104
Parker, Admiral Sir William 251, 253
Paros 117
Parthenon 131-132
Paschal III, Pope 86
Pashtun Shah Sujah 257
Passarowitz, Treaty of 160
Passau 140-141
Patkul, Johann Reinhold 169, 171, 174
Patras 129
Patton, General George S 8
Paul I, Czar 210, 229-230, 237-238
Pavia 200
Pearl, river
Peel, Sir Robert, British Prime Minister 257
Peking 249, 253
Peloponnese 46, 119, 124, 145, 159-160
Pelops, King 124
Pennycuick, Brigadier John 240, 269-270, 273
Perrault, Charles 184
Persarmenia, Georgia 42
Persia 40, 42-43, 48, 55-56
Peschiera 123, 146
Peshawar 275
Peter I, the Great, Czar 145, 169, 182, 187, 198, 211, 212
Peter III, Czar 217, 219
Peter the Hermit 81
Petrovaradin, fortress of 159
Pharis 47
Philip II, King of Spain 141
Philip V, King of Spain 146, 148, 155
Philip, Duke of Anjou 145-146
Philip, King of France 73, 86
Philippsburg 161, 191-192
Philus 22
Piazzetta 135
Piccolomini, Ottavio, General 106, 108
Piedmont 143, 153
Pilsen 107-108
Piper, Carl, Count 165-166, 168, 172-173, 179
Piraeus, (Porto Leone) 130, 132-133

Pirzin 223
Pitt, William, the Younger 234
Placentium, Piacenza 17
Plutarch 211
Pnyx Hill 131
Po, river 16-17, 152
Podolia 217
Polish-Lithuanian Commonwealth 228
Pollock, General 257
Poltava 174, 178, 180, 212
Pomerania 96, 98, 176, 180, 215
Pompadour, Marquise de 200
Pondicherry 205
Poniatowski, Stanislaus, King of Poland 217
Poros 133
Port Tolon 129
Porta Asinaria, Rome 50
Portugal 129
Portus 60
Potemkin, Prince Grigory 222-224, 227-228
Pottinger, Henry, British Superintendent 249, 251
Pozen 174
Pragel Pass 236
Pragmatic Sanction 160, 194
Prague 90-92, 100, 104, 110, 185, 194-195
Preobrazhensky, Life Guard regiment 227
Pressburg 146, 194
Preveza 126
Prince Regent 245
Priuli, Laura 113
Procopius of Caesarea 42, 44-45
Puerto Rico 242
Pugachev, rebellion, Yemelvan 219, 221
Puglia 20, 27, 66-67
Punic Faith 15, 35
Punic Wars 13-15, 22-23, 28, 35, 38
Punitz 175
Punjab 240-241, 254, 257, 264, 266-269, 273, 275
Pushkin, Alexander 212
Pyhajoggi 169
Pylos, Old Navarino 128
Pyrenees 16, 27, 247
Pyrrhus 8, 13
Qiantang, river 251
Qobad, King of Persia 43-44
Quadrilateral, the 146
Quedlinburg, Abbey of 186
Quintus Curtius 167, 211
Quintus Fabius, dictator 19, 30
Rabb, Theodore 89
Radziejowski, Cardinal 171-172
Rain am Lech 99
Rakoczi, Prince Fransis 148
Ramillies, battle of 152-153, 156, 165
Ranjit Singh, Maharajah 258
Ranjodh Singh 261
Rastadt, Treaty of 158
Ravenna 39-41, 51-55, 59
Rawalpindi 274
Recamier, Madame 183
Regensburg 97-98, 100
Rehnskiöld, Major General 169
Restitution, Edict of 97, 104-105, 107
Rethymno, Cretan port 115
Reuss, river 236
Rhone, river 16
Richard of Salerno 84-85
Richard the Lionheart 85
Riga 167, 169, 171
Rimini 52-53, 115
Rimsky-Korsakov, General 234-236
Romania 223
Rome 13-16, 18-24, 26-27, 29-31, 36-38, 40-41, 48-54, 57-63, 68, 71, 73, 83, 86, 174
Roucoux 201, 205
Rousseau, Jean Baptiste 162
Rudolf II, Holy Roman Emperor 90
Russia 93, 145, 161, 167-168, 170, 172, 174-177, 180, 195, 198 209-211, 213-214, 217-218, 221, 227-228, 230, 237
Sacred Road 130
Sadelupour 268
Saguntum 14-16, 33, 35
Salamanca 245
Salamis 213
Sale, Lady Florentia 259
Sale, Major General Sir Robert, 'Fighting Bob' 257, 259
Salerno 69, 84-85, 87
Salm, Prince 157
Salona 49, 59, 130
Saltykov, General 213
Samoylov, General 226
San Marco Argentano 67
San Marco piazza 112
San Nicolo, church 135
San Sophia 41, 45
Santa Marina, church in Venice 113
Santa Maura 128
Santi Giovanni e Paolo, Basilica dei 136
Santiago de Compostela 93
Santo Stephano, chiesa di 136
Sapienza 126
Sarajevo 145
Saratov 219-220
Sars, Wood 156
Sava, river 143, 159
Savannah, Georgia 218
Savoy, Victor Amadeus, Duke of 140, 142-143, 146, 152
Saxe-Coburg, Prince Josias 223-224
Saxe-Lauenburg, Franz Albrecht, Duke of 106
Saxe-Weimar, Bernard of 102-103, 108
Saxony, Elector of 161, 170, 175, 184, 193
Saxony, Maria Josepha of 202
Scheldt, river 198
Schlick, Count 106
Schlisselburg, grenadier regiment 222

Schlosshof, Palais 163
Schweidnitz 106, 215
Scipio, Gnaeus Publius, the Bald, uncle of Scipio 17
Scipio, Publius Cornelius, father of Scipio 16
Sefer Pasha 128
Seine, river 68
Sejm, Polish council 172, 217
Seldjuk 76
Seleucid Empire 37, 79, 88
Seleucus I, Nichator 79
Semyonovsky Life Guard Regiment 212
Seneca 37
Senigallia 115
Serrurier, General Jean-Mathieu-Philibert 232
Seven Years War 203
Seville 28, 30, 245
Shanghai 248, 252,-253
Shannon, Bugler Paddy 245
Shere Singh 267
Sheremetev, General 177
Shovell, Admiral Sir Cloudesley 153
Sicily 15, 17, 30-31, 34, 38, 46, 49, 55, 68-69, 73-74
Siebenbrunn 160
Sikelgaita, Lombard wife of Guiscard 69, 72
Sikh Wars 271, 273
Sikhs 254, 257-260, 262-265, 267-269, 271-272, 274
Silesia 94, 100, 106, 175-176, 194, 213, 215
Silesian War, 3rd 213
Silva Litana, battle of 20
Simla 266
Sindh Province 267
Singapore 254
Sisauranum 57
Sittas, General 42, 44
Smerdionzce 218
Smith, General Sir Harry, Adjutant-General of India 255, 261-263
Smolensk 176, 217
Smyrna 132
Sobieska Maria Karolina, Duchess of Bouillon 189
Sobieski, James 176
Sobieski, King John III of Poland 141
Sobraon 262, 264-265, 267
Socrates 8, 278
Sophia Dorothea 185
South Africa 241
Spain 14, 24, 34, 37-38, 141-143, 145-146, 148, 153, 157, 170, 190, 194, 243, 245-246
Sparta 125
Spinalonga 122
St Andrew, Order of 222
St Gotthard Pass 208
St Margaret Gate, Cremona 147
St Mark 121-122, 130, 135
St Peter 80
St Polen 194
Starhemberg, Graf Guido, General 146
Steinau 107, 171, 173
Stenbock, Magnus, governor of Kracow 169, 173
Stephens, Frances Maria 243
Stockholm 166-167, 181
Stotzas 49
Stralsund 95, 180-181
Strasbourg 190, 206
Strazoldo, General, Count 126
Stuart, Prince Charles Edward, the Young Pretender 197
Suda, Cretan port 115, 122
Sudan 211
Suddoosam 267
Sulechow, battle of 213
Suleiman the Magnificent 142
Sura 55
Susa 153
Sutlej, river 258-259, 261-262, 264-267
Suvorov, Vasili 210
Suzdal, regiment 216-217
Sweden 9, 98-99, 107, 110, 165-172, 174, 176, 180-181, 184-185, 197, 210, 212
Switzerland 208, 229, 233-236
Syria 43, 55-56, 67, 79-80, 84
Table Bay 242
Talavera, battle of 243-244, 246, 268
Tallard, Marshal 149-150
Talleyrand 230
Tancred, nephew of Bohemond 68, 74, 76-77, 79-81, 83, 85-87
Taranto 66
Tatikios 77, 79, 81-82
Taurus Mountains 61, 79
Tavanes, Count of 121
Taverne 235-236
Tej Singh 261-264
Temeswar, Banat of 160
Thackwell, General 268
Thebes 132-133
Theiss, river 144
Theodatus, King of Ostrogoths 48-50
Theodora, Empress 39-40, 44-45, 47, 53, 55, 63
Theodoric 48
Theodosius 30, 44, 46
Thermopylae 130
Thirty Years' War 89, 91, 96, 99, 110, 132
Thrace 41, 59, 74
Thuringia 94
Thurn, Count Jindrich Matthias 91, 105
Tiber, river 51-52, 60
Tiberius Sempronius Longus, consul 17
Ticinus, river 17
Timisoara, fortress of 159
Tipperary 258
Tivoli 59
Tolstoy 203, 239
Tongres 201
Tonning 168
Totila, King of the Goths 58-62
Toulouse 245
Toulouse, count Raymond of 76, 83

Tournai 155, 187, 199
Townshend, Charles 155
Trajan 30, 41
Trasimene, lake 18, 21, 34
Trautmansdorff, Maximilian von 106
Trcka, Adam, Lieutenant Field Marshal, brother-in-law of Wallenstein 105-106, 109
Trebbia 18, 21, 232-234
Trinidad 242
Troy 98, 116
Tsaritsyn 219-220
Tserclaes, Johann, Count of Tilly 93
Turenne, Marshal 8, 158, 185, 190, 193, 202
Turin, Treaty of 143
Turks 70, 76, 78-80, 82, 85, 90, 94, 118, 122, 126-131, 134, 140-141, 159-160, 188, 205, 219, 221-226, 238
Turtukaya 219
Tuscany 58, 125, 127
Tyniec, fortress 217
Ukraine 174, 178, 180
Ulm 149, 194
Ulrika Eleonora, the Elder, Queen of Sweden 166
Unett, Captain 270
University of Altdorf 90
University of Olomouc 90
Urban II, Pope 72, 82
Urbino 52, 54
Urnerloch, tunnel 236
Utrecht 158
Valier, Andrea, historian 115, 123
Valliere, Madame de la 196
Vandals 46-48, 57, 60
Varangian Guard 70, 133
Vauban, Marshal 210
Vauvenargues, Marquis de 195
Vellingk, General 169-170
Vendome, Marshal 148, 152
Verona 58, 146, 152, 231
Vespasian 41
Via Egnatia 71, 87
Victoria, Queen 223, 247
Vienna 92-95, 98-99, 106-108, 123, 137, 141, 143-146, 148, 157-158, 160-162, 191, 194, 213, 231, 233-235
Villars, Claude Hector, Marshal of France 137, 142, 155-158, 187, 190, 192-193
Villeroi, Marshal de 146-147, 152
Vilnius 172, 211, 228
Vistula, river 176, 228-229
Viszthum, Count 171
Vitoria, battle of 7, 245
Volga, river 219-220
Voltaire 165-166, 182-184, 189, 192, 195, 198, 211
von Arnim, Hans Georg 100, 106
von Degenfeld, Hannibal 127
von der Schulenburg, General Johann 184
von Eggenberg, Prince Hans Ulrich 107
von Harrach, Count Karl 92
von Hotze, General Friedrich 234-235
von Ilow, Christian, General 109
von Konigsmarck, Auroral 184
von Konigsmark, Count Otto William 128
von Lacy, Count 214
von Lowendahl, Ulrich 198, 204
von Mansfeld, Ernst 92-94
von Nachod, Georg 92
von Platen, General 215
von Reck, Ivan, Major General 222
von Seydlitz, General 214
von Steinau, General Adam 171
Wade, Field Marshal 197
Walhalla Memorial 207
Warsaw 172, 174-175, 217, 228-229
Washington, George 218
Wawel, castle 218
Wazirabad 272
Wehrmacht 93, 221
Wellesley, Lieutenant General Sir Arthur/Duke of Wellington 7, 12, 207, 240-241, 243-245, 253-254, 256, 261, 265-266, 272
Westphalia, Treaty of 185
Whampoa 248
Whish, General William 267, 272
White Eagle, Order of the, Poland 188, 238
White Mountain, battle of 92
White, Brigadier 269
Whitman, Walt 270
Wild Geese, Irish regiments 156, 198
William the Carpenter 181
William the Conqueror 67, 86
Witigis, King of the Ostrogoths 50-52, 54-55
Wittelsbach, House of 166
Worskla, river 179
Wratislaw, Count Johann 149, 153, 157
Wurttemberg 94-95
Wutgenau, Johann 192
Yaghi Syan, governor of Antioch 80
Yang Fang, General 248
Yangtze, river 252
Yi Jing, cousin of the Emperor 251
Zabergan 63
Zagan 99
Zama 10, 12, 32, 37-38
Zaman Shah 257
Zarnata 127
Zealand 168, 172
Zenta 144, 160
Zhenjiang, battle of 252-253
Zhukov, General 8, 209
Zoroastrianism 55
Zurich, battle of 235-236